Korea 2013: Politics, Economy and Society

Korea 2013: Politics, Economy and Society

Volume 7

Korea Yearbook

Edited by

Rüdiger Frank
James E. Hoare
Patrick Köllner
Susan Pares

Associate Editors

Stephen Epstein and Moon Chung-in

BRILL

LEIDEN • BOSTON
2013

ISSN 1875-0273
ISBN 978-90-04-26113-6 (paperback)
ISBN 978-90-04-26297-3 (e-book)

This book is printed on acid-free paper.

CONTENTS

PREFACE

On behalf of the editors of *Korea: Politics, Economy and Society*, I warmly welcome readers to the 2013 edition of the yearbook. This year's volume is a special one for the editors as it will bring the yearbook series, which started seven years ago, to an end. In fact, the yearbook series has an even longer pedigree. Its precursor, a German-language yearbook on Korea, was published between 1996 and 2006 by the Hamburg-based Institute of Asian Affairs. In 2007, the editor of the German yearbook on Korean politics, economy and society, Patrick Köllner, then teamed up with Rüdiger Frank, professor of East Asian Economy and Society at the University of Vienna and a leading expert on contemporary North Korea, and with James E. Hoare and Susan Pares, two former British diplomats and enthusiastic contributors to Korean (and East Asian) studies in the United Kingdom, to publish an international, English-language version of the yearbook. The four editors had successfully worked together on a few occasions prior to the launch of the Korea yearbook series. Yet they did not foresee that working together on the new publication would become the great and extremely gratifying experience that it has been over the past seven years.

The editors of *Korea: Politics, Economy and Society* have tried to give the publication a distinctive character by combining regular, concise overviews of domestic affairs in South and North Korea, inter-Korean relations, and the foreign relations of the two Koreas, with peer-reviewed articles addressing political, economic and social developments in either part of the Korean peninsula or examining aspects of inter-Korean relations. It might be noted that the editors, collectively or individually, did not always agree with particular viewpoints and assessments put forward by contributing authors—but they were always united in their belief in the need for a pluralistic approach to contemporary Korean affairs and studies. Hopefully, the yearbook series has paid testimony to this belief. Various senior scholars based in Asia, Europe, Oceania, and the United States have contributed to the yearbook, as have many young scholars from all over the world. The editors take especial pride in having been able to present plenty of fresh and original research from young scholars, often based on their doctoral dissertations. Some of the best articles in the yearbook were awarded special prizes, courtesy of the Academy of Korean Studies, which has provided crucial financial backing to the yearbook series during the past few years.

As all good things have to come to an end at some point, it might well be best to stop when things are still working fine. When James Hoare and Susan Pares announced in 2011 that, for reasons of age, they would soon like to retire as editors, the two other editors knew that it would be impossible to adequately replace them. Both Jim's and Susan's input into and dedication to the yearbook series have been tremendous. From the beginning, Jim contributed the regular overview articles on foreign relations of the two Koreas to the yearbook and, for the first few years, the overview articles on inter-Korean relations as well. His manifold connections were instrumental in securing a number of illuminating papers written by scholars and former officials. Susan did a truly outstanding job in terms of language editing and general editing. Even contributions by native speakers gained when she applied her skills to the texts. During the past few years, Susan also carefully assembled the yearbook's regular chronologies detailing recent developments on the Korean peninsula. It has been a real privilege to work together with such fine colleagues. As lead editor of the yearbook, I would also like to salute Rüdiger, who has played an indispensable role in making the yearbook series a great success. He provided not only regular coverage on North Korean affairs but, despite his many other obligations, always proved reliable and indeed inspired, helping in so many ways to bring the yearbook forward.

Over the past seven years, the editors have benefited immensely from various people's support. Sabine Burghart did a great job in recent years covering inter-Korean relations for the overview section of the yearbook. The yearbook's associate editors over the years, first professors Charles Armstrong at Columbia University and Park Sunghoon at Korea University and, later on, Stephen Epstein at Victoria University of Wellington and Chung-in Moon at Yonsei University, helped to make the yearbook a truly international undertaking. The editors are also very grateful to a number of colleagues who reviewed submitted papers. Closer to home, particular thanks go to Siegrid Woelk, who gallantly served for six years as the yearbook's editorial manager. At the GIGA German Institute of Global and Area Studies, special thanks are also due to Kerstin Labusga, who efficiently took charge of formatting this year's manuscript, and last, but certainly not least, to Axel Kapteina for providing wonderful archival assistance and for making sure that manuscripts reached the publisher in time and in good order. Keith Pratt, professor emeritus at Durham University, kindly provided the map of the Korean peninsula for the yearbook. Frank Shulman did a great service by referencing the yearbook. In Leiden, Brill editors Albert Hoffstadt and Patricia Radder enthusiastically embraced the idea of a Korea yearbook series from the beginning and provided unstinting support throughout, for which the editors are very grateful.

Patrick Köllner

Dunedin, June 2013

LIST OF REFEREED ARTICLES PUBLISHED SINCE 2007

South Korea

1 *Politics and foreign relations*

Online Grassroots Journalism and Participatory Democracy in South Korea (Ronda Hauben), 2007: 61–82

Fission, Fusion, Reform and Failure in South Korean Politics: Roh Moo-Hyun's Administration (Youngmi Kim), 2008: 73–94

Assassination, Abduction and Normalisation: Historical Mythologies and Misrepresentation in Post-war South Korea-Japan Relations (John Swenson-Wright), 2008: 95–124

The Disparity Between South Korea's Engagement and Security Policies Towards North Korea: The Realist-Liberal Pendulum (Alon Levkowitz), 2008: 125–147

The South Korean Left's 'Northern Question' (Joonbum Bae), 2009: 87–115

Conflict Management in Urban Planning: The Restoration of the Ch'ŏnggyech'ŏn River in Seoul (Annette J. Erpenstein), 2010: 85–112

The Role of Think Tanks in the South Korean Discourse on East Asia (Thomas Kern and Alexander Ruser), 2010: 113–134

Nation Branding in South Korea: A Modern Continuation of the Developmental State? (Alena Schmuck), 2011: 91–117

From 'Cold Friendship' to Strategic Partnership: The Transformation of South Korea's Political Relations with India (Niclas D. Weimar), 2011: 119–145

The Concept of Middle Power and the Case of the ROK: A Review (Dong-min Shin), 2012: 131–151

2 *Economy*

The Lone Star Scandal: Was it Corruption? (James C. Schopf), 2007: 83–111

Emergence of China and the Economy of South Korea (Joon-Kyung Kim and Chung H. Lee), 2007: 139–163

Changing Perceptions of Inward Foreign Direct Investment in Post-Crisis Korea (1998–2006) (Judith Cherry), 2007: 113–137

Dynamics of Korean Industrial Relations: Challenges for Foreign Invested Companies in the Metal Sector (Peter Kloepping), 2009: 143–175

Cheju Island as a Medical Tourism Hub in Northeast Asia (Jürgen Mühl), 2009: 177–204

South Korea's Economic Policy Response to the Global Financial Crisis (Werner Pascha), 2010: 135–164

'Green Growth': South Korea's Panacea? (David Shim), 2010: 165–187

South Korea's Economic Relations with India: Trends, Patterns and Prospects (Durgesh K. Rai), 2010: 189–215

Shopping Abroad the Korean Way: A Study in Resource Acquisition (Stefania Paladini), 2011: 147–174

KORUS, KOREU and Beyond: South Korea's Free Trade Drive (Patrick Flamm and Patrick Köllner), 2012: 97–108

3 *Society*

New Ancestral Shrines in South Korea (Heonik Kwon), 2007: 193–214

The Political Economy of Patriotism: the Case of *Hanbando* (Mark Morris), 2007: 215–234

Korean Modernism, Modern Korean Cityscapes, and Mass Housing Development: Charting the Rise of *Ap'at'ŭ tanji* since the 1960s (Valérie Gelézeau), 2007: 165–191

Higher Education Reform in South Korea: Success Tempered by Challenges (Peter Mayer), 2008: 149–170

The New Korean Cinema Looks Back to Kwangju: *The Old Garden* and *May 18* (Mark Morris), 2008: 171–198

Scapegoat, Beggar and President for the Economy: The Image of Lee Myung-bak as Seen through Political Cartoons in *Chosun Ilbo* and *Hankyoreh* (Katharina Polley), 2009: 205–225

The Korean Comfort Women Movement and the Formation of a Public Sphere in East Asia (Thomas Kern and Sang-hui Nam), 2009: 227–255

North Korea

1 *Politics and foreign relations*

Negotiating with North Korea: Lessons Learned and Forgotten (Robert Carlin), 2007: 235–251

A Brief History of the Sino-Korean Border from the 18th to the 20th Century (Larisa Zabrovskaya), 2007: 283–297

The US–DPRK 1994 Agreed Framework and the US Army's Return to North Korea (C. Kenneth Quinones), 2008: 199–229

The International Community and the North Korean Nuclear Programme (Sebastian Harnisch and David J. Roesch), 2011: 333–360

North Korea after Kim Jong Il: The Kim Jong Un Era and its Challenges (Rüdiger Frank), 2012: 109–129

2 *Economy*

Benchmarks of Economic Reform in North Korea (Patrick McEachern), 2008: 231–249

Beyond Lips and Teeth: The Economics of the China–North Korea Relationship (Tim Beal), 2011: 303–331

Special Economic Zones, Trade and Economic Reform: The Case of Rason Special City (Bernhard J. Seliger), 2012: 209–237

3 *Society*

Perilous Journeys: The Plight of North Koreans in China (Peter Beck, Gail Kim and Donald Macintyre), 2007: 253–281

Statistical Explorations in Terra Incognita: How Reliable are North Korean Survey Data? (Daniel Schwekendiek), 2009: 277–300

Migration Experiences of North Korean Refugees: Survey Evidence from China (Yoonok Chang, Stephan Haggard and Marcus Noland), 2009: 301–328

A Meta-Analysis of North Koreans Migrating to China and South Korea (Daniel Schwekendiek), 2010: 247–270

From the 'Soviet Era' to the 'Russian Renaissance': Evolution of the Narrative about Russia and Russians in the North Korean Cultural Discourse (Tatiana Gabroussenko), 2011: 275–302

A New Deal: Graphic Novel Representations of Food Issues in Post-famine North Korea (Martin Petersen), 2012: 181–208

The two Koreas: connections and comparisons

CHRONOLOGY OF EVENTS IN THE KOREAN PENINSULA 2012

SOUTH KOREA

09–11.01.12	President Lee Myung-bak visits China to mark 20th anniversary of Sino–ROK diplomatic relations, discusses situation on Korean peninsula following death of Kim Jong Il with President Hu Jintao.
15–17.01.12	Prime Minister Kim Hwang-sik visits Oman and the United Arab Emirates (UAE) to secure agreement on stable oil supplies for ROK.
04–11.02.12	President Lee visits Turkey, Saudi Arabia, Qatar and the UAE to secure oil supplies.
27.02.–30.04.12	US and ROK armed forces conduct annual Key Resolve/Foal Eagle military exercises.
11.03.12	President Lee expresses ROK support for Japan in *Asahi Shimbun* article commemorating 1st anniversary of Fukushima disaster.
15.03.12	Korea–US Free Trade Agreement (FTA) enters into effect.
25, 26.03.12	President Lee meets President Obama in Seoul in run-up to 2nd Nuclear Security Summit (NSS), and President Hu Jintao in sidelines of summit.
26–27.03.12	2nd NSS held in Seoul. Emphasis on preventing nuclear terrorism.
27.03.2012	Japanese government approves 3 new high-school textbooks claiming Takeshima/Tokto as Japanese territory, eliciting protests from ROK government.
06.04.12	Japan's 2012 diplomatic blue book reaffirms Japanese territorial claims over disputed islands. ROK reacts with protests.
11.04.12	Saenuri Party led by Park Geun-hye wins in ROK general elections.
19.04.12	Inch'ŏn District Court issues 30-year prison sentence and fine of 20 million won on captain of Chinese fish-

	ing vessel responsible for clash on 12.12.11 with 2 ROK coastguard vessels and death of a ROK coastguard. China rejects ROK's 'unilateral application' of law on Exclusive Economic Zones.
25.04–03.05.12	Issue of safety of imported US beef raised again in ROK after US dairy cow found to have bovine spongiform encephalopathy.
30.04.12	9 Chinese fishermen detained in Yellow Sea after clashing with ROK coastguards; 4 of latter injured. 2 Chinese arrested, 02.05.12.
02.05.12	ROK and China launch FTA talks.
13–14.05.12	5th trilateral summit of leaders of China, ROK and Japan held in Beijing. Agreement to begin official negotiations on trilateral FTA.
14.05.12	President Lee visits Myanmar, meets President Thein Sein and Aung San Suu Kyi.
18.05.12	ROK successfully launches 3rd multi-purpose satellite, Arirang-3.
24.05.12	ROK Supreme Court rules that Japanese companies are responsible for compensating Korean citizens conscripted for labour during Japanese colonial period, overturning decisions of lower courts on recovery of damages.
06.06.12	Inch'ŏn port signs memorandum of understanding on co-operation with Shenyang, China.
14.06.12	US Secretary of State Clinton and US Defence Secretary Panetta host 2+2 dialogue with their ROK opposite numbers.
16.06.12	US deploys Army Tactical Missile System missiles and Multiple Launch Rocket System artillery to US Forces Korea to increase firepower in ROK.
17–25.06.12	President Lee attends 7th G20 leaders' summit in Mexico, 18–19.06.12, and UN Conference on Sustainable Development (R+20) in Rio de Janeiro, 20–21.06.12; visits Chile, 21–23.06.12, and Colombia, 23–25.06.12.
29.06.12	ROK postpones signing of General Security of Military Information agreement with Japan on sharing military intelligence and exchanging military goods and services. Lack of public consultation given as reason.
20.07.12	ROK activist Kim Young-hwan returns to ROK after 114 days in detention in China, alleges he was tortured.

31.07.12	Japan's 2012 defence white paper reiterates Japanese claims to Toktc/Takeshima. Immediate hostile reaction from ROK.
10.08.12	President Lee visits Tokto.
14.08.12	Psy's Gangnam Style video ranked first on YouTube's 'Most Viewed Videos' monthly chart. Video reaches one billion views on YouTube, 21.12.12, first video to do so.
20–31.08.12	ROK and US conduct annual joint military exercise Ulchi Freedom Guardian.
23.08.12	ROK admits to importing Iranian crude oil during July despite stating it would not do so.
03.09.12	ROK and Japan announce they have temporarily suspended military exchange programme.
07–14.09.12	President Lee visits Russia, 08–09.09.12, to attend 20th Asia–Pacific Economic Co-operation (APEC) summit in Vladivostok; Greenland, 09–10.09.12; Norway, 10–12.09.12; and Kazakhstan, 13.09.12.
10.09.12	2 ROK firms, POSCO and the Hyundai Group, hold ground-breaking ceremony for distribution centre in Hunchun city, China.
11.09.12	ROK and Japan reported to be seeking increased budgets for 2013 to deal with their respective claims to sovereignty over Tokto/Takeshima.
14.09.12	Office of prime minister of ROK relocates from Seoul to Sejong city.
19–21.09.12	President Karimov of Uzbekistan visits ROK, 2 countries agree to promote joint construction and development projects in Uzbekistan.
23.09.12	Prime Minister Noda of Japan reported as reiterating that matter of compensation for Korean 'comfort women' was closed.
27.09.12	ROK hosts Proliferation Security Initiative exercise in waters off Pusan.
07.10.12	Following 2 years of negotiations, ROK announces new missile agreement with US to extend range of ROK ballistic missiles from 300 km to 800 km and increase payload weight for unmanned aerial vehicles from 500 kg to 2.5 tons.
08–10.10.12	President Thein Sein of Myanmar visits ROK, meets President Lee.
16.10.12	ROK coastguard officer kills a Chinese fisherman when coastguards board Chinese fishing vessel charged with

	illegal fishing. ROK detains 2 Chinese vessels and 24 surviving fishermen. ROK expresses 'regret' over shooting of Chinese fisherman, 18.10.12.
19.10.12	ROK secures non-permanent seat on United Nations Security Council (UNSC) for second time. 2-year term starts January 2013.
20.10.12	UN Green Climate Fund votes to establish its secretariat in Seoul.
26–27.10.12	US Assistant Secretary of State Kurt Campbell visits ROK to discuss DPRK, economic issues and regional co-operation.
07.11.12	President Lee visits Indonesia and Thailand.
18–20.11.12	President Lee attends 21st ASEAN summit, 15th ASEAN+3 summit and 7th East Asian Summit meeting in Phnom Penh.
20.11.12	Trade ministers of ROK, China and Japan meet in sidelines of ASEAN+3 summit to open officially talks towards 3-way free trade pact.
20–22.11.12	President Lee visits UAE, discusses future strategies for co-operation with president of UAE.
29.11.12	ROK cancels planned launch of Naro-1 space rocket because of technical abnormalities.
03–05.12.12	President Zardari of Pakistan visits ROK, meets President Lee.
13.12.12	Korean Cultural Centre opens in New Delhi, first in South Asia.
19.12.12	Park Geun-hye wins presidential election for Saenuri party.
21.12.12	ROK releases defence white paper, repeats claims to Tokto/Takeshima. Japanese protests are rebutted by ROK. DPRK media dismiss white paper, 27, 28.12.12.

NORTH KOREA

01.01.12 Joint new year editorial from *Rodong Sinmun*, *Chosŏn Inmingun* and *Ch'ŏngnyŏn Chŏnwi*.

11.01.12 DPRK reportedly test-fires 3 short-range ballistic missiles over East Sea.

16.01.12 Associated Press opens full-time news bureau in DPRK.

01–03.02.12 Naguib Sawiris, chairman and CEO of Orascom Telecom, visits DPRK.

08.02.12 10 North Koreans arrested in Shenyang, China. To be deported back to DPRK along with 21 others arrested in other regions.

16.03.12 DPRK announces intention of launching earth observation satellite between 12.04.12 and 16.04.12 to commemorate Kim Il Sung's 100th birthday.

03.04.12 Japan extends sanctions against DPRK for further year.

04–06.04.12 Chinese People's Liberation Army delegation visits DPRK.

05.04.12 Dedication of Hŭich'ŏn hydroelectric power station in Chagang province.

11.04.12 Delegates' conference of Korean Workers' Party (KWP) names Kim Jong Un 1st secretary of KWP. Kim becomes standing member of the KWP Central Committee Political Bureau and of presidium of politburo. Kim Jong Il is proclaimed KWP's 'eternal secretary-general'.

13.04.12 DPRK attempts unsuccessfully to launch satellite, announces failure of launch.

13.04.12 5th session of 12th Supreme People's Assembly (SPA) held in Pyongyang. Kim Jong Un elected 1st chairman of National Defence Commission (NDC).

15.04.12 Military parade in Pyongyang to mark Kim Il Sung's centenary, displays new long-range missile and missile transport vehicle. Kim Jong Un makes 1st public speech.

25.04.12 Chinese Vice-Foreign Minister Cui Tiankai warns DPRK that a nuclear test would violate China's national interest.

08.05.12	DPRK seizes 3 Chinese fishing boats and detains 28 Chinese fishermen. Releases fishermen, 21.05.12.
08–11.05.12	DPRK military delegation headed by Ri Yong Ho, chief of general staff of Korean People's Army (KPA), visits Laos.
10–17.05.12	Kim Yong Nam, president of the presidium of the SPA, leads DPRK delegation to Singapore and Indonesia, to discuss economic partnership.
15.05.12	US House of Representatives passes bill to extend DPRK Human Rights Act until 2017.
25.05–23.06.12	DPRK reports dry weather and consequent drought in most areas of the country since April.
30.05.12	Revised DPRK constitution states the country is a 'nuclear-armed state'. ROK and US reject such a status. China expresses its support for Korean denuclearisation, 01.06.12.
31.05–02.06.12	Russian Vice-Minister of Finance Storchak reported to have visited DPRK, to have signed bilateral agreement that cancelled 90 percent of DPRK's Soviet-era debt of US$11 billion, while proposing investing remaining 10 percent in joint educational, medical and energy projects in DPRK.
19.06.12	US announces it will extend economic sanctions against DPRK for further year.
27.06.12	Russian–DPRK joint exchange plan for 2013–14 signed in Moscow.
06.07.12	Russia–DPRK inter-governmental treaty on order in Russian–DPRK border areas signed in Moscow.
10–17.07.12	DPRK Foreign Minister Pak Ui Chun attends 19th ASEAN Regional Forum in Phnom Penh. Meets Chinese Foreign Minister Yang Jiechi, 11.07.12.
15.07.12	Vice-Marshal Ri Yong Ho dismissed from all his posts on grounds of illness. Replaced by Vice-Marshal Hyon Yong Chol.
18.07.12	Kim Jong Un awarded title of marshal of DPRK.
9.07–06.08.12	DPRK reports heavy rains and flooding, including typhoon Khanun, between late June and end July have caused loss of life and damage to farmland and property
24–28.07.12	DPRK and Chinese ministers of public security meet in China.

25.07.12	DPRK media identify Ri Sol Ju as Kim Jong Un's wife.
07–03.08.12	Wang Jiarui, head of International Department of Chinese Communist Party's Central Committee, visits DPRK, meets Kim Jong Un.
04.08.12	Following on-site inspections, UN World Food Programme says it will send 336 tons of emergency food aid to DPRK in wake of flooding, following request from DPRK for assistance.
04–10.08.12	Kim Yong Nam visits Vietnam and Laos.
09–10.08.12	DPRK and Japanese Red Cross officials meet in Beijing to discuss possible retrieval of remains of Japanese who died in northern part of Korean peninsula during World War II. 1st such talks in 10 years.
13–18.08.12	Jang Song Thaek, vice-chairman of NDC, leads delegation on visit to China for talks on economic and trade matters, including development of 2 special economic zones of Rasŏn and Hwanggŭmp'yŏng and Wihwa.
15, 22.08.12	DPRK reports further heavy rains in most areas of country.
16.08.12	UN Central Emergency Response Fund allocates over US$1 million in emergency relief to DPRK following flood damage.
26.08–01.09.12	23-member group from US Pacific Council on International Policy visits DPRK at invitation of DPRK government.
28–29.08.12	Typhoon Bolaven strikes DPRK, causes deaths and injuries and destroys crops and houses.
28.08–04.09.12	Kim Yong Nam attends 16th summit of NAM countries in Tehran. Meets President Ahmadinejad, 01.09.12, and UN Secretary-General Ban Ki-moon.
29–31.08.12	DPRK and Japan hold working-level inter-governmental talks in Beijing, 1st for 4 years.
13.09.12	DPRK media state 300 people killed and 600 injured or missing in recent heavy rains and typhoon.
17.09.12	Russia and DPRK sign debt adjustment agreement in Moscow.
25.09.12	SPA holds 2nd meeting, announces extension of compulsory schooling from 11 years to 12.
27.09.12	DPRK test-fires short-range missile into Yellow Sea.

30.10–05.11.12	8th meeting of DPRK–Syria joint economic committee held in Pyongyang agrees to increase co-operation on trading and exchange of technologies.
15–16.11.12	Japan and DPRK meet in Ulan Batar to discuss long-standing issues, agree to hold future discussions.
16.11.12	DPRK celebrates its 1st Mother's Day. Greetings cards issued.
17–24.11.12	Delegation led by Choe Thae Bok, chairman of SPA, visits Mongolia.
27.11.12	DPRK and Mongolia sign agreement in Pyongyang on co-operation between their countries' respective security organs.
01.12.12	DPRK announces window of 10–22.12.12 for launch of satellite.
02.12.12	Japan postpones talks scheduled for 5–6.12.12 with DPRK on improving relations.
11.12.12	Kenneth Bae (Bae Jun Ho), Korean-American tour operator, reported held in DPRK after entering country on 03.11.12 with tour party of 5. One tour member found carrying computer hard disk that apparently contained sensitive information. DPRK confirms his detention, 21.12.12, for unspecified offence.
12.12.12	DPRK successfully launches Kwangmyongsong–3 satellite using Unha–3 rocket over Yellow Sea.
17.12.12	US announces it will implement tougher sanctions against DPRK.

INTER-KOREAN RELATIONS AND SIX PARTY TALKS

03–07.01.12	Kurt Campbell, US assistant secretary of state for East Asian and Pacific affairs, visits China, ROK and Japan to discuss developments in DPRK following death of Kim Jong Il. Visits ROK, 04.01.12.
09–11.01.12	Lim Sung-nam, ROK special representative for Korean peninsula peace and security affairs, visits China, meets Wu Dawei, China's special representative for Korean peninsula affairs.
12–13.01.12	Shinsuke Sugiyama, director-general for Asian and Oceanian affairs and Japanese envoy to the Six Party Talks, visits ROK, meets Lim Sung-nam.
17.01.12	Lim Sung-nam and Sugiyama meet Kurt Campbell and Glyn Davies, US special representative for DPRK policy, in Washington, agree to hold door open for talks with DPRK.
31.01–03.02.12	Glyn Davies and Clifford Hart, US special envoy for Six Party Talks, visit Russia, meet Vice-Foreign Minister Igor Morgulov and Grigory Logvinov, ambassador-at-large for Six Party Talks, to discuss bilateral and security issues.
09.02.12	Lim Sung-nam and Igor Morgulov meet, agree to promote resumption of Six Party Talks.
12.02.12	Social media campaign in ROK to prevent forced repatriation of 30 North Koreans arrested in China in 02.12.
21–24.02.12	ROK campaign to assist DPRK refugees in Chinese detention. Foreign Ministry announces it will seek support from UN Human Rights Council, 21.02.12. President Lee urges China to follow international norms, 22.02.12. DPRK Red Cross denies presence of any DPRK refugees in China, 25. 02.12.
23–24.02.12	3rd round of US–DPRK talks in Beijing on resumption of Six Party Talks. Delegates led by Kim Kye Gwan, 1st vice-foreign minister of DPRK, and Glyn Davies.
29.02.12	In two parallel announcements, DPRK agrees to moratorium on nuclear tests, missile launches and uranium enrichment programme (UEP) activity, and allows International Atomic Energy Agency (IAEA) inspectors

	to monitor suspension of UEP; US agrees to take forward a donation of nutritional assistance.
07–09.03.12	Ri Yong Ho, DPRK vice-foreign minister and envoy to nuclear disarmament negotiations, and Lim Sung-nam attend academic forum on security at Syracuse University, US. The two do not appear to have met.
16.03.12	DPRK invites IAEA inspectors to return to DPRK.
22.03.12	UN Human Rights Council passes resolution condemning DPRK treatment of repatriated DPRK defectors and political prisoners, extends term of its special rapporteur on DPRK human rights by further year.
13.04.12	US announces it will cancel deal with DPRK to provide food aid.
16.04.12	UNSC issues presidential statement condemning attempted launch of DPRK satellite on 13.04.12, demands DPRK comply with earlier UNSC resolutions 1718 (2006) and 1874 (2009), abandon nuclear weapons and nuclear programmes, and conduct no further launches. China supports statement. UNSC issues further sanctions against DPRK. Statement rejected by DPRK, 17.04.12.
16.04.12	DPRK withdraws offer to accept IAEA inspections at its nuclear facilities in response to US withdrawal of offer of food aid.
28.04.12	DPRK defectors active in ROK send 10 balloons with anti-DPRK leaflets across Demilitarised Zone (DMZ) into DPRK.
28.04–09.05.12	GPS signal jamming observed on air flights and ships coming to or leaving ROK. Total of 609 domestic flights operated by 10 ROK airlines and 48 flights operated by 22 foreign airlines reported affected, together with 175 vessels and 1 US military aircraft. ROK Communications Commission directly accuses DPRK of responsibility, 04.05.12. Jamming ceases, 14.05.12. DPRK denies responsibility, 18.05.12.
02.05.12	UN expands sanctions against DPRK after failed rocket launch, but China agrees to only 3 firms being targeted.
03.05.12	All permanent members of UNSC urge DPRK to 'refrain from further actions which may cause grave secu-

rity concerns in the region, including any nuclear tests'. DPRK rejects UNSC joint statement, 06.05.12.

04.05.12 ROK's Eximbank reminds DPRK's Choson Trade Bank that 1st repayment instalment of US$5.83 million food loans, agreed in 2000, falls due on 07.06.12. DPRK misses deadline of 15.07.12. ROK issues 3rd notice to DPRK, 27.09.12; and 4th notice, 07.12.12.

30.05.12 Seoul Central District Prosecutor's Office reports 2 men under arrest on suspicion of supplying GPS jamming technology to DPRK.

31.05.12 ROK *JoongAng Daily* reports arrest of Lee Gyeong-ae, DPRK spy who entered ROK in 2011 posing as defector.

12.06.12 UNSC extends term of panel of experts overseeing sanctions on DPRK for further year.

25–27.06.12 Grigory Logvinov visits ROK, meets Lim Sung-nam and Cho Hyun-dong, director-general of DPRK nuclear affairs and ROK deputy envoy to Six Party Talks, to discuss resumption of Six Party Talks.

05.07.12 Roh So-hui, pro-DPRK activist who illegally entered DPRK from China on 24.03.12, seized on return to ROK across Military Demarcation Line at P'anmunjŏm. DPRK protests at his arrest, 06.07.12. Roh charged with pro-enemy activities under National Security Law (NSL), 09.08.12.

23–26.07.12 DPRK resumes dispatch of balloons carrying propaganda leaflets across border.

03.08.12 Hyundai Asan delegation visits Mt Kŭmgang resort to mark 9th anniversary of suicide of former Hyundai Group chairman, Chung Mong-hun. Confirms, 06.08.12, that DPRK has taken over Hyundai facilities at resort, but says they are 'fairly well maintained'.

17.08.12 ROK branch of World Vision relief organisation visits Kaesŏng to discuss aid to DPRK in wake of flood damage. Agrees to provide 500 tons of flour, 26.08.12. Flour finally dispatched, 21.09.12.

24.08.12 ROK Korea NGO Council for Co-operation with North Korea meets members of DPRK National Reconciliation Council in Kaesŏng, agrees to send aid to DPRK. Eventually makes 2 deliveries of flour.

27.08.12	ROK urges DPRK to give notice before discharging water from Hwanggang dam on Imjin river, as happened several times without warning from 17.08.12.
03–12.09.12	After exchange of messages, DPRK rejects aid offered by ROK as flood damage alleviation: flour, noodles and medicine. Seeks rice, cement and heavy construction equipment.
07.09.12	Seoul Central District Prosecutor's Office seeks arrest of DPRK spy named as Kim, who arrived in ROK, 06.12, as refugee. Confessed to being agent of DPRK Ministry of State Security.
12.09.12	DPRK defector couple who had spent 4 years in ROK from 2008 return to DPRK. (Story only reported in DPRK media on 08.11.12.)
27–28.09.12	Northeast Asia Co-operation Dialogue, forum for informal dialogue among all countries involved in Six Party Talks, meets in Dalian, China. DPRK attends.
01.10.12	ROK reveals it has 614 sets of remains of DPRK soldiers killed in the Korean War that have been retrieved in ROK since 2000, but which DPRK has so far refused to accept.
02, 06.10.12	ROK reports 2 incidents of defection by KPA soldiers across DMZ. Earlier defection on 17.08.12 also reported.
17.10.12	Japanese, ROK and US officials involved in Six Party Talks meet in Tokyo, confirm they would co-operate in addressing DPRK's nuclear activities through the talks.
22.10.12	KPA issues direct threat to shell Imjingak pavilion at DMZ if activists proceeded with plan to launch propaganda balloons into DPRK from there.
26.10.12	ROK *Hankyoreh* newspaper reports 3 ROK students questioned by police after 'retweeting' DPRK website Urimizokkiri. Such activity prohibited under NSL.
29.10.12	ROK activists launch propaganda balloons from Imjingak pavilion in DMZ towards DPRK.
05.11.12	DPRK warns United Nations General Assembly (UNGA) that war could break out at any time on Korean peninsula, asserts DPRK is nuclear state and Six Party Talks have become 'almost a dead body'.
19.11.12	Hyundai Asan officials visit Mt Kŭmgang resort to mark 14th anniversary of opening of joint inter-Korean

project. ROK calls on DPRK to stop organising tours for foreigners while excluding ROK visitors, urges inter-governmental talks.

27.11.12 3rd Committee of UNGA adopts resolution by consensus on DPRK violations of human rights. DRPK delegation rejects resolution.

01.12.12 DPRK Committee for Peaceful Reunification of Korea publishes 7-point 'open questionnaire' for Park Geunhye, calling on her to clarify her stance towards DPRK.

05.12.12 ROK opens 2nd resettlement centre for DPRK defectors at Hwach'ŏn.

05.12.12 Seoul Central District Court sentences DPRK spy to 4 years' imprisonment for spying on defectors for DPRK.

08.12.12 DPRK states it will make positive efforts to open way for South Koreans to visit Mt Kŭmgang resort, accuses ROK of blocking tour programme.

12.12.12 UNSC meets to condemn DPRK satellite launch of 12.12.12 and to discuss appropriate measures.

12.12.12 Seoul Central District Court sentences former DPRK spy to 5 years' imprisonment. Woman arrived as refugee via Thailand a year before.

20.12.12 DPRK reports ROK Saenuri party candidate elected in ROK presidential election on 19.12.12.

24.12.12 UNSC decision in response to DPRK rocket launch delayed because of Chinese resistance to tougher sanctions against DPRK.

Chronologies prepared by Susan Pares from the following sources: Cankor (Canada–Korea Electronic Information Service), *Comparative Connections*, *DPRK Business Monthly*, Korea Focus, Korea.net, *Korea: People and Culture*, North Korea Newsletter (Yonhap).

SOUTH KOREA IN 2012: DOMESTIC POLITICS, THE ECONOMY AND SOCIAL ISSUES

Patrick Köllner

1 INTRODUCTION

2012 was a 'super election year' in the Republic of Korea (ROK—South Korea). Every twenty years the election for the National Assembly (NA), the country's unicameral parliament, which runs on a four-year cycle, and the country's presidential election—ROK state presidents get elected for a non-renewable five-year term—take place in the same year.[1] This was the case in 2012. While the two electoral races proved quite tight, in the end South Korea's conservatives managed to triumph both in the parliamentary election of April 2012 and the presidential election eight months later. South Korea's new president, 60-year old Park Geun-hye, who assumed office in February 2013, thus also possesses a majority in parliament, which should make governing easier than would have been the case otherwise—although, given the adversarial character of party politics in the ROK, some degree of parliamentary gridlock is likely to occur nonetheless. Despite earlier indications that political change was in the air, the majority of South Korean voters opted eventually for greater continuity, but only after the ruling Saenuri Party had undergone some face-lifting and had distanced itself from the increasingly unpopular incumbent president, Lee Myung-bak. Lee not only became a 'lame duck' in the process but also faced a slate of corruption scandals involving close associates and relatives.

---

[1] In spring 2013, discussions about the introduction of a four-year term for the president, who would then be able to seek one further term of office, got under way. Parliamentary elections could be held concurrently with presidential ones under such a system. Earlier attempts to make relevant constitutional amendments, which require the approval of two-thirds of lawmakers and fifty percent of voters, failed—former President Roh Moo-hyun tried to effect such change (too) late during his term in office. Yet, constitutional change might be in the offing this time. In principle, all major political parties support the relevant changes, and there is also popular support.

Cronyism had in fact characterised at least some high-profile personnel decisions taken by Lee during his five years in power. In this regard, the former Chief Executive Officer and mayor of Seoul operated very much like an 'old-style' politician. On a broader level it can be noted that more than twenty-five years after the country's transition to democracy, graft and corruption still remain deeply ingrained in South Korea's political culture. The question, though, is against what benchmarks politics in South Korea should be measured. While in absolute terms, the integrity and ethical behaviour displayed by many political actors in South Korea leave much to be desired, the case can be made that in relative terms, overall levels of corruption have declined compared to the pre-democracy era and certainly pale in comparison to the situation in, say, nearby China (or North Korea for that matter). Moreover, the personal stakes of getting involved in politics have become much smaller over time. While sympathy for the North, real or perceived, might still get you into jail under the provisions of the National Security Law, political actors are overall fairly free to voice their standpoints, opinions and grievances. Protests are possible in a way that they were not in the past. Different lifestyles and orientations now get increasingly tolerated (unless you are a conscientious objector). As noted in earlier overview articles, South Korean politics are often not pretty to behold, but democracy has nonetheless become firmly embedded over the past nearly three decades.

How might Lee Myung-bak's term in office be evaluated? The picture is arguably an ambivalent one. Against the background of former President Roh Moo-hyun's tumultuous and politically divisive five years at the helm of the South Korean state, Lee was elected on the basis of his promise to focus on economic growth and prosperity and his image as a 'can-do' politician. While Lee's administration failed to substantially boost the country's growth rate, per-capita income and standings in global economic terms as envisioned in his '747' campaign slogan, the ROK emerged quite fast and relatively unscathed out of the global financial and economic crisis of 2008/2009. Though the ROK economy certainly benefitted in this regard from sailing in the tailwind of the still buoyant Chinese economy, effective crisis management also played a role in realising this positive outcome. Per-capita income has risen somewhat over the past few years, bringing material living standards in the ROK (measured in purchasing power parity-terms) ever closer to the OECD average. The ROK now ranks alongside New Zealand and not that far behind Japan or Great Britain in terms of per-capita income.[2] On the other hand, income inequality further widened during Lee's term in office; among other things, wage differences between regular and non-regular employees are vast, and the median wage gap between male and female employees is the highest among OECD member states. Old-age poverty has become a serious issue, with nearly 50 percent of senior citizens living in relative poverty, i.e. on less than half of the median income, the highest proportion among OECD countries.[3] Addressing the ever more pressing issues of inequality and poverty has arguably not figured prominently on the agenda of the Lee administration. Moreover, high-quality affordable childcare, which might also help to raise the ROK's low female labour participation and fertility rates, remains as elusive as ever.

With respect to South Korea's international linkages and global profile, the Lee administration, however, showed a great deal of dynamism, inter alia, by seeing free trade agreements with the European Union (EU) and, more controversially, with the United States (US) through, by pursuing an active (but not always uncontroversial) 'resources diplomacy', by increasing development co-operation funds and by actively contributing to peace-keeping operations around the globe, by hosting a number of high-profile conferences—including in 2012 the Second Nuclear Security Summit in Seoul—and by playing an active role in the G20 process as well as by promoting trilateral co-operation between the ROK, Japan and China. In passing it might also be mentioned that both the United Nations (UN) and the World Bank are now led by ethnic Koreans. In sum, the Lee Myung-bak administration's quest for 'middle-power status' and global recognition achieved some visible results. In 2012, the ROK also prevailed against competition from Germany, Mexico, Namibia and Switzerland when it was decided that the secretariat of the UN-linked Green Climate Fund, which provides support to developing countries to limit or reduce their greenhouse gas emissions and to adapt to the impacts of climate change, would be based in Songdo city near Incheon (Inch'ŏn)

---

[2] See OECD, 'National Accounts at a Glance 2013', 31 January 2013. Online: www.oecd-ilibrary.org/economics/national-accounts-at-a-glance_22200444 (accessed 16 May 2013).

[3] Older workers tend to leave companies by age 55 and only 20 percent of senior citizens in the ROK receive pensions. See OECD, *OECD Economic Surveys: Korea*, Overview, April 2012, pp.17–19. Online: www.oecd.org/eco/50191444.pdf (accessed 14 May 2013).

International Airport. In fact, promoting green, low-carbon growth both at home (which also entails increased reliance on nuclear energy) as well as abroad might constitute one of the more lasting legacies of Lee Myung-bak's years in the Blue House. While Lee was a very welcome visitor to both Washington and Beijing (amongst other capitals), his image at home suffered from the beginning, blemished by a string of scandals and a perceived aloofness to the needs and views of the 'common people'. Lee's conservative Christianity and the way he allegedly favoured Christians in terms of high-level posts and other situations also came under attack. There was also much criticism concerning some key political projects of the Lee administration, most prominently the four-rivers restoration project (2009–11), which sought to dredge, dam and beautify four major rivers, while also creating jobs in construction and beyond, at a cost of around US$20 billion.[4] One of Lee's last acts in office also caused a political row. He pardoned 55 people, including a number of politicians and businessmen close to him, who had been convicted of bribery.[5]

While the national elections in the ROK sparked particular interest in 2012, some other developments and events also merit mentioning. The South Korean economy lost some steam as demand for manufactured goods from the ROK cooled in the EU, which was struggling with a major sovereign debt crisis, but subsequently also in China. The ROK's export-reliant economy only grew by 2 percent, the lowest growth since the crisis year of 2009. The Bank of Korea responded to the more gloomy economic climate by cutting the base rate twice, a much expected move in view of similar steps taken in other developed economies and continuing low inflation in the ROK itself. In 2012, South Korea's population passed the 50 million-mark. The country today ranks 26th in the world in terms of population but is only one of seven countries with a per capita income of over US$20,000 and a population of over 50 million. In July 2012, the ROK's new second political centre, Sejong city, was officially opened. By 2015, a sub-

---

[4] See, e.g. International River Foundation, 'South Korea's Four Major Rivers Project', Brisbane, 20 September 2012. Online: www.riverfoundation.org.au/articles/Four_Major_Rivers (accessed 16 May 2013). The South Korean Board of Audit and Inspection pointed out some flaws in the project in a report released in early 2013. See AFP, 'Audit slams S. Korea's $20 bn river project', 18 January 2013. Online: www.terradaily.com/reports/Audit_slams_S_Koreas_20_bn_river_project_999.html (accessed 16 May 2013).

[5] See 'Pardon me', *The Economist*, 2 February 2013. Online: www.economist.com (accessed 13 May 2013).

stantial part of the national administration will have moved from Seoul some 120 km further south. Large numbers of civil servants can be expected to engage in commuting on a weekly basis. The port city of Yeosu (Yŏsu) on the ROK's south coast hosted the three-month 2012 Expo, in which more than 100 countries and nine international organisations presented exhibits under the theme of 'Living Coast and Ocean'. In the summer of 2012, South Korean athletes impressed during the Olympic Games in London. The ROK national team did very well in a number of disciplines and South Korea became fifth in the final medals standing. The South Korean of the year, however, was undoubtedly the K-pop artist Psy, whose smash-hit 'Gangnam Style' became a worldwide phenomenon (see section 5 below).

2 THE 2012 NATIONAL ASSEMBLY ELECTION AND ITS AFTERMATH

The parliamentary election of 11 April 2012 had been widely expected to lead to a change of majority in the National Assembly. After all, the ruling Saenuri Party (New Frontier Party, NFP, known until December 2011 as Hannara-dang or Grand National Party, GNP) had already lost the mayoral election in the capital Seoul in late October 2011.[6] Moreover, President Lee, who hailed from the ruling party, was widely unpopular und continued to be dogged by a slew of scandals. A number of close associates of the president, including the then head of the Korea Communications Commission, Choi See-joong, who was widely seen as Lee's political mentor, and even the president's elder brother, Lee Sang-deuk, a policymaker of the ruling party, were felled in the first half of 2012 by corruption and bribery charges. The older Lee was arrested in July on suspicion of having taken bribes from the heads of two failing savings banks to help their institutions avoid scrutiny. Already in February, the speaker of the NA, Park Hee-tee of the NFP, had also stood down amid allegations of bribery in connection with his 2008 election to the chairmanship of the GNP. He was subsequently formally indicted, together with another of President Lee's close associates, Kim Hyo-jae, who was charged with assisting in this

6 See 'South Korea in 2011', *Korea 2012: Politics, Economy and Society*, pp. 27–28, for details.

'cash for votes' affair.[7] Shortly before the NA election, a new scandal erupted when a whistle-blower leaked information concerning over 2,600 files assembled by journalists of the Korean Broadcasting System (KBS), pointing at illegal surveillance activities by a government 'ethics team'. The surveillance activities had allegedly been carried out between 2008 and 2010 and among others had targeted journalists, opposition politicians, and critics of the president. The scandal, however, proved unwelcome news to both the incumbent government and the opposition, as a substantial number of the surveillance activities had apparently been ordered when former President Roh Moo-hyun, who later committed suicide in 2009, had still been in power.[8]

The chances for the opposition of emerging victorious from the 2012 parliamentary elections were further boosted when the main opposition party, the centre-left Democratic United Party (DUP), managed to co-ordinate candidacies in 69 marginal single-seat constituencies with the smaller, left-wing Unified Progressive Party (UPP). While the DUP entertains strong links with the more moderate Federation of Korean Trade Unions (FKTU), the UPP is informally linked to the more radical Korean Confederation of Trade Unions (KCTU). Both opposition parties took shape only in late 2011 out of two merger moves on the left of South Korea's political spectrum.[9] On the basis of primary elections in the 69 constituencies, the two parties announced in March 2012 a joint list of candidates, comprising 57 candidates from the DUP and 12 from the UPP. In spite of its name the DUP is hardly a united party: factional fault lines exist between the former followers of South Korea's two progressive presidents, Kim Dae-jung (1998–2003) and his successor Roh Moo-hyun (2003–08). The latter faction seemed to have the upper hand in 2012, as suggested by the fact that Han Myeong-sook, a confidante to the late Roh Moo-hyun who also served as South Korea's (so far only female) prime minister from April 2006 to March 2007 became DUP party leader in January. Han emerged victorious from a party leadership contest which involved not only some 127,000 party members and

---

[7] See Economist Intelligence Unit (EIU), *Country Report South Korea*, February 2012, p. 12, and July 2012, p. 24. Online: http://www.eiu.com/public (accessed 29 April 2013).

[8] See 'Snooping dogs Lee', *The Economist*, 7 April 2012. Online: www.economist.com (accessed 13 May 2013).

[9] See 'South Korea in 2011', *Korea 2012: Politics, Economy and Society*, pp. 29–30, for details.

21,000 party conference delegates but also 643,000 non-party members who had registered to participate in the vote (80 percent of the non-party members voted by mobile phone).[10]

Han resigned three months later, a few days after the NA election, which saw the DUP and the UPP gaining a substantial number of seats but failing to overturn the NFP majority in the parliament. While the DUP went up 38 seats from 89 before to 137 after the election, even in conjunction with the 13 seats gained by its putative coalition partner, the UPP,[11] the two opposition parties remained 11 seats short of a majority. The NFP, on the other hand, lost 24 of the 176 seats held before the election, but the remaining 152 sufficed to retain the upper hand in the 300-seat National Assembly. NFP candidates succeeded in more than half (127) of the country's 246 local single-seat constituencies, doing, as expected, particularly well in the eastern half of the country, where it could claim all constituency seats in Gangwon (Kangwŏn) and North Gyeongsang (Kyŏngsang) provinces as well as in Daegu (Taegu) and in Ulsan. It also won the majority of seats in Incheon, in South Gyeongsang and North Chungcheong (Ch'ungch'ŏng) provinces and in Busan (Pusan). The NFP also was the most popular party overall, gaining 42.8 percent (or more than 9.1 million votes) under the proportional representation section of the mixed electoral system, which accounts for 54 seats in parliament. The DUP here was a distant second with 36.5 percent of the popular vote (less than 7.8 million votes). As the DUP was successful in its local bastions in the southwest (North and South Cheolla (Ch'ŏlla) provinces plus the city of Kwangju), the main battlegrounds proved again to be the capital and the surrounding Gyeonggi (Kyŏnggi) province. In both areas, the DUP managed to win a majority of seats but even then not enough to

[10]See 'Former P.M. Han takes DUP helm', *Korea Herald*, 15 January 2012. Online: www.koreaherald.com/view.php?ud=20120115000280 (accessed 17 May 2013). See also EIU, *Country Report South Korea*, February 2012, pp. 1–14. Online: http://www.eiu.com/public (accessed 29 April 2013).

[11] A few months after the election, an internal investigation by the UPP found that the party's proportional representation list for the election had been rigged. One of the lawmakers allegedly involved in the rigging process, Lee Seok-ki, subsequently made for further negative publicity when he suggested that South Korea's national anthem should be replaced by the folk song 'Arirang'. While 'Arirang' gained entry in 2012 into the UNESCO World Heritage List, it is also considered as North Korea's unofficial national anthem. A radical faction within the UPP is known for its sympathies for the North. To redeem itself in the public eye, the party subsequently voiced concern over the 'grave' human rights situation and dynastic leadership succession in the North. See EIU, *Country Report South Korea*, June 2012, pp. 10–11, and July 2012, p. 25. Online: http://www.eiu.com/public (accessed 29 April 2013).

unlock the NFP's overall majority in the NA. The remainder of seats went to a smaller conservative party, the Chungcheong-based Liberty Forward Party (securing five seats, down from 15 before the election) and to a few independent candidates.[12]

How did the NFP manage to escape from the jaws of defeat? And viewed from the other side, how did the opposition manage to lose the election that was theirs to win? Arguably, the NFP's biggest asset was party leader Park Geun-hye, who had assumed the party's helm only in late 2011. Subsequently, she saw through not only a change in the party's name but, more importantly, also changes in the party's platform, thus moving the party further to the centre. Furthermore, she effectively purged the party of a number of supporters of President Lee Myung-bak by denying them candidacies.[13] In consequence, Park managed to distance the NFP effectively from the incumbent president and managed to turn the election from a more 'retrospective' to a more 'prospective' one.[14] As *The Economist* noted, 'Ms Park blunted the DUP's strategy of framing the election as a chance to judge the current government, while she beat the opposition on its own ideological turf. She promised greater welfare provision and less emphasis on economic growth above all else.'[15]

The campaign itself saw only few substantive exchanges between the government and the opposition. A low turnout of 54.3 percent signalled the limited excitement generated by the election. The opposition, which ran a poor and uninspired campaign, was not able to mask its manifold internal divisions. The DUP also turned some voters away by its flip-flopping on the issue of the recently ratified US–South Korea Free Trade Agreement, which it first vowed to repeal once in government, only to withdraw that pledge thereafter. The NFP, while far from shining, looked all the better in direct comparison and in the light of the intra-party 'reforms' that had taken place since Park Geun-hye had taken the party's lead. The daughter of South Korea's former dictator, who served as president between 1962 until his

[12] For a good overview of the election results see the Wikipedia entry on the 2012 National Assembly election at http://en.wikipedia.org/wiki/South_Korean_legislative_election,_2012 (accessed 17 May 2013).

[13] For details see EIU, *Country Report South Korea*, March 2012, pp. 12–13, and April 2012, p. 11. Online: http://www.eiu.com/public (accessed 29 April 2013).

[14] Yul Sohn and Won-Taek Kang, 'South Korea in 2012: An Election Year under Rebalancing Challenges', in: *Asian Survey* 53 (2013)/1, pp. 198–205, here p. 200.

[15] 'Progressives set back', *The Economist*, 14 April 2012. Online: www.economist.com (accessed 13 May 2013).

assassination in 1979, emerged as the clear winner from the parliamentary election. On the opposition side, Moon Jae-in from the DUP, who managed to win a seat in the NFP's stronghold of Busan, increased his chances of winning his party's nomination to run for the presidency later in the year. Overall, the close outcome of the April parliamentary elections showed that South Korea's voters were almost evenly divided between the left and the right of the political spectrum, making for an exciting presidential race later in the year.[16]

Convening the new 19th National Assembly took longer than scheduled as the NFP and the DUP began a row over the distribution of chairmanships of the parliament's 18 standing committees. Whether the revised National Assembly Act (also known at the National Assembly Advancement Act), passed in May 2012 with the aim of reducing confrontations between the government and the opposition, will really help to defuse tensions and provide for more orderly parliamentary operations inside the NA remains to be seen. The gridlock and paralyses which have often characterised the work of South Korea's parliament will not easily be solved by institutional engineering, as these phenomena reflect the basic adversarial character of legislative politics in the ROK.

One other institution that could be relied upon to function properly was once again the South Korean Constitutional Court. In August 2012, the court ruled in a unanimous decision that a five-year old legal provision which had required Internet users to reveal their real names when posting on Internet forums was unconstitutional. The court said that the law in question, which had been introduced after a number of public figures had committed suicide after false rumours had been spread about them online, amounted to prior censorship. The law also 'violated citizens' privacy, was technically difficult to enforce and was ineffective at stopping online criticism', the court said.[17] Only a few days before the court's decision, the ROK's other highest-level

[16] For discussions of the outcome of the 2012 NA election see, for example, EIU, *Country Report South Korea*, May 2012, pp. 1–12, and June 2012, p. 23. Online: http://www.eiu.com/public (accessed 29 April 2013). See also Norbert Eschborn, 'Korea-Wahl 2012: Verlieren heißt gewinnen und umgekehrt' [Korea election 2012: Losing means winning and vice versa], Seoul: Konrad Adenauer Foundation, 12 April 2012; and Christoph Pohlmann, '(Noch) kein Politikwechsel in Südkorea' [(Still) no political change in South Korea], Seoul: Friedrich Ebert Foundation, April 2012.

[17] Evan Ramstad, 'South Korea Court Knocks Down Online Real-Name Rule', *Wall Street Journal* (Asia edition), 24 August 2012. Online: http://online.wsj.com/article/SB10000872396390444082904577606794167615620.html (accessed 17 May 2013).

court, the Supreme Court, had recommended raising the penalties for people spreading false information online or on social media such as Twitter during election campaign periods. Adequately regulating the Internet will continue to prove challenges for policymakers in South Korea and beyond.

3 THE 2012 PRESIDENTIAL ELECTION

History has not been kind to South Korea's presidents. Not a single ROK president spending a full term or more in the Blue House has left the office gracefully or with an untarnished reputation: South Korea's first president Syngman Rhee was exiled, Park Chung-hee got shot, both Chun Doo-hwan and Roh Tae-woo were later sentenced to death (only to be pardoned in the name of national reconciliation), Kim Young-sam, Roh Moo-hyun and Lee Myung-bak had their reputations sullied by corruption charges against family members, while Kim Dae-jung saw his legacy tainted when it emerged that the landmark summit with the North Korean leader Kim Jong Il in 2000 had been made possible by the provision of large sums of money.[18] Still, there is no dearth of contenders for the country's political top job. In the NFP, four candidates other than the frontrunner Park Geun-hye initially threw their hat into the ring. They were former party chairman Chung Moon-joon from the Hyundai dynasty, Kim Moon-soo, the governor of Gyeonggi province, South Korea's most populous province, Yim Tae-hee, a former chief of staff of President Lee Myung-bak, and Ahn Sang-soo, a former mayor of Incheon. All these candidates lacked however public support; in an opinion poll conducted in May 2012 none of them could garner more than 2.5 percent. Another candidate, Lee Jae-oh, a confidante of President Lee, emerged in June. By July, however, it was clear that Park Geun-hye would be the party's official candidate in the December election. The two last other remaining candidates, Chung Mong-joon and Lee Jae-oh, withdrew their candidacies after the NFP had decided not to go for an open primary system to determine its presidential candidate.[19] In late September, Park apologised for several aspects of her father's rule in South Korea, including

[18] See also Andrew Salmon, 'Presidential candidates: are you mad?', *Korea Times*, 16 October 2012, p. 8.

[19] See EIU, *Country Report South Korea*, June 2012, p. 10, and July 2012, p. 23. Online: http://www.eiu.com/public (accessed 29 April 2013).

the 1961 military coup that had brought him to power, the 1972 Yushin Constitution, which had allowed him to stay in power indefinitely, and the so-called Inhyukdang incident of 1975, which had resulted in the execution of eight people accused of spying. Park walked a tightrope with the apology, trying to distance herself from the dark side of her father's rule while attempting not to alienate voters who continued to hold Park in high esteem for spearheading the country's economic development push.[20]

On the opposition side, the DUP's official candidate was officially announced some two months later. After having won all 13 regional primaries, the 59-year old Moon Jae-in, a former human rights lawyer and close associate of Roh Moo-hyun, whom he had also served as presidential chief of staff, became the party's official standard bearer. (Moon had received 56.5 percent of all votes cast; the second placed, former Gyeonggi governor Sohn Hak-kyu, gained 22.2 percent, and the third and fourth placed, Kim Doo-kwan and Chung Se-kyun, 14.3 and 7 percent respectively.) The presidential election subsequently became a three-person race when Ahn Cheol-soo, a 50-year old doctor turned successful anti-virus software developer, philanthropist and Seoul National University professor, declared his long-awaited bid for the presidency on 19 September.[21] Ahn had shaken South Korea's political system in 2011 when he emerged as a possible candidate for mayor of Seoul. In the end, Ahn did not compete in that election but threw his support behind the eventual winner of that contest, Park Won-soon, who was not affiliated to any political party. Park's win signalled the electorate's unease with established party politics in the ROK.[22] The question now became whether the two progressive candidates, Moon and Ahn, would compete until the very end or whether one of them would stand down to avoid splitting the liberal camp.

---

[20] 'Park apologizes for suffering caused by late father's rule', *Korea Times*, 24 September 2012. Online: http://koreatimes.co.kr/www/news/nation/2012/09/116_120695.html (accessed 24 September 2012); and EIU, *Country Report South Korea*, October 2012, p. 22. Online: www.eiu.com/public (accessed 29 April 2013).

[21] KBS World Radio, 19 September 2012, as cited in Amnesty International, Korea Koordinationsgruppe, *Korea Konzertriert*, 83rd edition, September/October 2012, p. 7; and EIU, *Country Report South Korea*, October 2012, p. 20. Online: http://eiu.com/public (accessed 29 April 2013).

[22] See 'South Korea in 2011', *Korea 2012: Politics, Economy and Society*, p. 28 for details. For profiles of Ahn and Moon see 'Moonrise and the kingmaker', *The Economist*, 13 August 2012. Online: www.economist.com (accessed 13 May 2013); and EIU, *Country Report South Korea*, November 2012, pp. 21–24. Online: www.eiu.com/public (accessed 29 April 2013).

Polls saw Ahn and Moon fairly close together in terms of popular support. In substantive terms, all three candidates agreed on many things, including the need for creating jobs and expanding social welfare at home and, internationally, on the need for reconciliation-cum-co-operation in Northeast Asia and re-engagement with North Korea. With respect to the latter, Park vowed to engage in 'trustpolitik' towards the North if elected, aiming at striking a balance between the hardline approach adopted by President Lee and the 'sunshine policy' pursued by his two predecessors in the Blue House.[23]

The buzzword of the election campaign became 'economic democratization', a rather fuzzy term indicating 'a process of leveling out the playing field so that all players, big and small, have an equal chance of success in the economic and financial markets'.[24] Although details were mostly unclear, economic democratisation was supposed to entail putting the screws on South Korea's mighty business conglomerates, the *chaebol*, ensuring fair competition and offering support in terms of funds and regulations for smaller enterprises.[25] While there were differences between the three presidential hopefuls—with, for example, Moon vowing to spend more on social welfare than Park, Ahn being perhaps the most outspoken among the three when it came to reigning in the *chaebol*, and Park pledging to shorten compulsory military service by three months to 18 months—all three candidates went straight for the median voter, promising to fight against rising inequality amidst (moderate) economic growth. It was clear that the 'gung-ho' approach to economic growth that had Lee Myung-bak brought to power in 2008 was no longer in tune with the mood of the electorate. Park Geun-hye continued to move her party to the left, positioning the NFP more squarely in the centre. In late November, shortly before the official nomination deadline closed, the final showdown for the presidential election was set when Ahn announced that he would withdraw from the race. Before that decision there had been

---

[23] See Choi He-suk, 'Park, Ahn call for Asia cooperation', *Korea Herald*, 17 October 2012, p. 3; 'Park's progress', *The Economist*, 11 May 2013. Online: www.economist.com (accessed 13 May 2013); and EIU, *Country Report South Korea*, December 2012, p. 20. Online: http://eiu.com/public (accessed 29 April 2013). On 'trustpolitik' see also the overview article on 'Relations between the two Koreas in 2012', Section 4, in this volume.

[24] Kim Ji-hyun, 'Chaebol bashing tops election agenda', *Korea Herald*, 17 October 2012, p. 11.

[25] See EIU, *Country Report South Korea*, January 2013, pp. 30–31. Online: http://eiu.com/public (accessed 29 April 2013).

talks between the Ahn and the DUP camps with the aim of uniting both camps. It soon became clear. however, that the DUP was not willing to play second fiddle to Ahn by not presenting a candidate of its own (as it had done in the 2011 mayoral election in Seoul). Ahn, on the other hand, was not willing to just serve as prime minister in a possible Moon Jae-in administration. As polls continued to indicate that a presidential election involving both Ahn and Moon would result in a victory by Park, and thus a repeat of the opposition's 1987 trauma, when a split opposition had helped Roh Tae-woo to become president, Ahn finally threw in the towel.[26] Being just 50 years old at the time of the 2012 presidential election, Ahn might have yet another chance to go for the country's political top job. (In a parliamentary by-election in April 2013, Ahn gained a seat in the NA.)

The presidential election on 19 December generated much excitement as signalled by a turnout rate of 75.8 percent, the highest since 1997. The outcome was fairly close, with Park winning 51.55 percent of the vote and Moon winning 48.02 percent, according to the National Election Commission. Still, more than a million votes separated Park (15.8 million votes) and Moon (14.7 million votes) in the end. Four independent candidates received respectively less than 0.2 percent of the vote. Moon managed to capture a majority of votes in the capital Seoul and in the two Cheolla provinces, Ms Park did better elsewhere including in the particularly embattled metropolitan areas around Seoul. While regional cleavages again played a substantial role in the presidential election, generational fault lines were at least equally visible: voters over the age of 50 overwhelmingly supported Park, while younger voters favoured Moon. With her win in the presidential election, Ms Park has effectively emerged from the long shadows of her father. Her middle-ground platform served her well in the presidential election, while the DUP's Moon did not manage to attract all supporters of Ahn Cheol-soo—and perhaps also did not manage sufficiently to erase the voters' memory of the presidency, in a number of ways ill fated, of his former boss Roh Moo-hyun.

In a country where only half of women work and men account for nearly 85 percent of legislators, South Koreans finally elected their first female president. In February 2013, Ms Park returned to the Blue

---

[26] See 'Ahn bows out', *The Economist*, 23 November 2012. Online: www.economist.com (accessed 13 May 2013), and EIU, *Country Report South Korea*, December 2012, p. 21. Online: www.eiu.com/public (accessed 29 April 2013).

House, where she had lived for 18 years until her father's death in 1979. (After her mother's death in an assassination attempt on Park in 1974, Ms Park had also served as first lady.) Perhaps unavoidably, Park has been compared to Britain's Margaret Thatcher and Germany's Angela Merkel, who unlike Ms Park, however, were (or are) married and represented quite different political styles. And unlike both Thatcher and Merkel, Park is a second-generation political leader, thus following in the footsteps of other past Asian heads of government (and sometimes of state) such as Benazir Bhutto (Pakistan), Indira Gandhi (India), Megawati Sukarnoputri (Indonesia), Chandrika Bandaranaike Kumaratunga (Sri Lanka), and the current Bangladeshi Prime Minister, Sheikh Hasina.[27] Markets reacted positively to Ms Park's election, who in terms of foreign policy offers mostly continuity. While President Park can be expected to affirm the importance of the security alliance with the US, the importance of good relations with China, and more free trade at the bilateral and regional level, both socio-economic challenges at home and the regime in the North will very much put her to test during her term in office.

4 The South Korean economy in 2012

South Korea's heavy reliance on trade—exports account for around 50 percent of the country's economic output—makes the country vulnerable to slowdowns in the global economy. The limits to export-led growth were plain to see in 2012 when the debt crisis in the EU and the precarious economic situation in the US not only reduced demand for South Korean goods in those two regions but also contributed to a slow-down of the Chinese economy, the ROK's main trading partner, which in turn had negative consequences for South Korean exports. Exports declined early in 2012 on a year-on-year basis and the ROK experienced its first trade deficit in two years. In the second half of the year exports picked up some steam but overall did not grow much

[27] Nobert Eschborn, 'Park Geun-hye erreicht ihr Lebensziel' [Park Geun-hye reaches her goal in life), *Länderbericht Korea*, Seoul: Konrad Adenauer Foundation, 20 December 2012. See also Justin McCurry, 'South Korea elects first female president', *Guardian Weekly*, 4 January 2013, p. 11; 'A homecoming', *The Economist*, 19 December 2012. Online: www.economist.com (accessed 13 May 2013); and EIU, *Country Report South Korea*, January 2013, p. 22. Online: http://www.eiu.com/public (accessed 29 April 2013).

compared to 2011, while imports declined slightly. Domestic consumption and facility investment also remained weak, all resulting in a—by past South Korean standards—rather moderate GDP growth rate of 2 percent (see Table 1). This marked the lowest gain since 2009,

Table 1 ROK basic economic data

	2008	2009	2010	2011	2012
Nominal GDP (trillion won)	1,026	1,065	1,173	1,235	1,272
Nominal GDP (billion US$)	931	834	1,015	1,114	1,130
Real GDP growth (%)	2.3	0.3	6.3	3.7	2.0
GDP per capita (US$ at PPP)	26,658	26,886	28,693	30,180[a]	31,197[a]
Exports (billion US$)	434.7	358.2	461.4	551.8	552.6[a]
Imports (billion US$)	429.5	320.3	421.4	520.1	514.3[a]
Trade balance (billion US$)	5.2	37.9	40.1	31.7	38.3[a]
Balance of payments (current account, billion US$)	3.2	32.8	29.4	26.1	43.1[a]
Debt stock (billion US$)	405.0[a]	417.5[a]	430.3[a]	444.5[a]	426.6[a]
International reserves (billion US$, end of year)	201.2	270.0	291.6	306.4	327.0
Consumer prices (%)	4.1	2.7	3.1	4.2	1.4
Producer prices (%)	8.5	-0.2	3.8	6.7	0.7
Unemployment rate (%)	3.2	3.7	3.7	3.4	3.2

Notes: Data actual unless noted. [a] Economist Intelligence Unit estimate.
Source: EIU, *Country Report South Korea*, May 2013, p. 9.

when the country was most severely affected by the global financial crisis.[28] While industrial heavyweight Samsung Electronics posted another record operating profit in 2012 (29.5 trillion won, around 20.8 billion Euros/US$27.5 billion),[29] many other South Korean companies struggled. Amidst lower inflation rates than in previous years and rate cuts in other major economies, the Bank of Korea (BOK)'s monetary

[28] Yonhap, 26 March and 25 May 2013, in BBC Monitoring Global Newsline Asia Pacific, 27 March and 25 May 2013.

[29] *Maeil*, 2 April 2013, cited in *Deutsche Bank South Korea Newsletter*, April 2013, p. 2. The market capitalisation of Samsung Electronics on South Korea's main bourse reached 208 trillion won (US$183.3 billion) at end of 2011, which is similar to the GDP levels of New Zealand, Peru or Romania. The same report also noted that between 2002 and 2011, the sales of South Korea's top 10 *chaebol* combined rose from 53.4 percent to 76 percent of GDP. See Kim Yon-se, 'Top 10 conglomerates' sales equal 76% percent of GDP', *Korea Herald*, 27 August 2012. Online: www.koreaherald.com/common_prog/newsprint.php?ud=20120827000963&dt=2 (accessed 27 August 2012).

policy became more accommodative in 2012. The bank cut the base rate for the first time since 2009 in July, and then again in October, bringing it down to 2.75 percent.[30]

While officials from the BOK as well as policymakers tend to downplay the risks that South Korea's rising household (or consumer) debt entails for the country's financial stability and overall economic health, some economists are far less sanguine. When business conglomerates were forced to deleverage their debt levels after the 1997–98 Asian financial crisis, banks in South Korea began to focus more on consumers to sustain asset growth. Non-bank institutions such as mutual savings banks, targeting poorer borrowers, also grew substantially, helped by looser regulation. Lured by easy money, which helped to fund the housing boom in the mid-2000s, many South Koreans took out credits to finance consumption, to pay for their children's university education or, in many cases, to invest in apartments. In 2011, the debt load of South Korean households rose to 164 percent of disposable income. The ROK's total household debt now amounts to something like one quadrillion won (more than US$900 billion), equalling nearly an entire year's gross domestic product. While officials like to point out that the collective value of personal financial assets still comes close to double the household debt burden, worried economists note that 70 percent to 80 percent of Korea's privately-owned assets is in real estate. And many of the privately owned apartments and houses are now worth much less than they were at the height of the speculation bubble a few years ago, thus trapping millions of South Koreans in negative equity. Demand for new housing has remained sluggish since 2008, putting pressure on the construction industry, which is unable to recoup trillions of won invested in developing estate. Nearly 84,000 completed apartments remained unsold by February 2012. In Seoul, apartment prices fell by over 8 percent in 2011 and 2012. The debt repayment burden faced by many Koreans alone explains why domestic consumption has remained lacklustre over the past few years. Domestic demand can only be expected to pick up substantially again when not only economic growth accelerates but also trickles to down to individual households.[31]

---

[30] See EIU, *Country Report South Korea*, July 2012, p. 35, and October 2012, p. 30. Online: www.eiu.com/public (accessed 29 April 2013).

[31] See Simon Mundy and Laeticia Ock, 'S Korea consumer debt nears crisis levels', *Financial Times*, 22 September 2012, p .4; Simon Mundy and Song Jung-a, 'South Korea's rate cut has Gangnam's estate agents yearning for a new tune', *Finan-*

Figures released by the BOK in 2012 indicated that the total stock of foreign direct investment (as opposed to gross inflows) had virtually stagnated in 2011; the overall stock inched up from US$134.2 billion at the end of 2010 to US$135.7 billion at the end of 2011. Another report released earlier in the year said that in 2010 exports by foreign-invested companies stood at US$62.6 billion or 11.6 percent of South Korea's exports in that year.[32] Relative to the size of the economy, on-the-ground engagement by foreign enterprises has remained fairly low compared to other OECD member states or indeed other Asian foreign direct investment destinations. Complex regulations and what is at best ambivalent public sentiment towards foreign ownership account for some of this phenomenon. Some potential foreign investors might also have been deterred by militant unionism in the ROK, though this has arguably declined in recent years. Unionisation has also gone down. The 580,000-strong KCTU and the more moderate 700,000-strong FKTU today account for barely 5 percent of the national workforce. And, as noted by the Economist Intelligence Unit, in South Korea where at least one quarter of the workforce lacks security and earns over 40 percent less than regular workers, '[p]ublic sympathy for trade unions is waning: many see bank or car workers as pampered labour aristocracies.'[33] Labour market dualism is prevalent in South Korea. The question is whether it will be overcome again or whether it will become even more deeply entrenched. The OECD, for one, argued in its most recent economic survey of ROK that the government should do more to address labour market dualism. According to the organisation, a 'comprehensive approach is required to break down dualism, including reduced employment protection for regular workers, improved social insurance coverage for non-regular workers and expanded training for non-regular workers.'[34] It remains to be seen, though, whether the current and future governments are willing and able to face up to this challenge.

---

cial Times, 10 May 2013, p. 2; Kim Tong-hyung, ' "Day of reckoning" may come soon', *Korea Times*, 15 October 2012, p. 9; and EIU, *Country Report South Korea*, April 2013, p. 26, and May 2013, p. 23. Online: http://www.eiu.com/public (accessed 29 April 2013).

[32] EIU, *Country Report South Korea*, September 2012, p. 25. Online: www.eiu.com/public (accessed 29 April 2013; and Yonhap, 13 February 2012, in BBC Monitoring Global Newsline Asia Pacific, 13 February 2012.

[33] EIU, *Country Report South Korea*, August 2012, p. 22. Online: www.eiu.com/public (accessed 29 April 2013).

[34] OECD, *OECD Economic Surveys: Korea*, Overview, April 2012, p. 30. Online: www.oecd.org/eco/50191444.pdf (accessed 14 May 2013).

5 South Korea's music industry and the Psy phenomenon

On the back of the speedy development and spread of the Internet coupled with the digitalisation of its core product, the music industry has come to evolve into a global enterprise. For decades, North America and Europe (and later on also Japan) had been the only relevant markets, while artists with a broader appeal usually hailed from the US or the United Kingdom (UK). The past few years have, however, seen major changes in the industry. As late as 2011, customers could download music from an online music store such as market leader iTunes (Apple) only in 23 countries. By early 2013, the number of countries in which iTunes operates had increased to 119. And while the illegal downloading of music still constitutes a major challenge for the industry, it did not mean the death knell for music labels, as some had feared. Worldwide music sales have in fact stabilised since 2010 at around US$15 billion per year, of which, in 2012, US$9.4 billion were spent on physical products (CDs and records) and US$5.8 billion on legally downloaded digital files. The top 20 sales markets now take in a number of non-Western economies including South Korea. Legal downloads in countries such as India and China are still small in relation to the size of the population, but such markets have begun to matter commercially and they grow much faster than the established ones. Furthermore, artists from countries other than the US and the UK have begun to sell well. In 2012, the ten most downloaded singles included two by artists from outside the 'West', of whom one was South Korean artist Psy. His hit single 'Gangnam Style' sold 9.7 million times, putting him at number 3 in terms of (legal) global downloads in that year.[35]

Legal downloads do not necessarily mean that much of the money thus spent ends up in the pockets of artists and music labels. Business models differ. In most Western countries, customers pay around 99 cents per music track, of which 30 percent stays with the online store and 70 percent goes to artists and music labels. The music-download market operates differently in South Korea. There, music fans mostly use music streaming services run by an oligopoly of companies which charge monthly fees of around 9,000 won (US$8); for that, you get 150 files during the period. Artists and music labels collect only

---

[35] Marcus Theurer, 'Die Globalisierung der Popstars' [The globalisation of pop stars], *Frankfurter Allgemeine Zeitung*, 3 May 2013, p. 22.

around 30 won (around 3 cents) per streamed file, and slightly more for downloaded songs. That sum must then be split between performers, writers and the label itself.[36] While music downloads are hugely popular in South Korea, labels such as SM Entertainment still make more money from the sale of CDs. It has been estimated that in the ROK itself downloads and streams of 'Gangnam Style' earned Psy less than US$60,000 dollars in 2012. No surprise then perhaps that producers and their better known artists try to make as much money as possible by using the artists' popularity for appearances in advertisements, promoting new cell phones and the like.[37]

One way to make serious money as a South Korean music artist is to export your output to other countries where the rewards can be bigger. Japan has been such a market for Korean pop-music (K-pop for short) over the past ten years or so. K-pop has also become very popular in parts of Southeast Asia and elsewhere in Asia. It has also made some forays into Europe and Latin America. As part of its external cultural policy and in order to increase the country's 'soft power', the South Korean government promotes the international diffusion of K-pop in various ways. One artist who by now certainly does not need such official support is Park Jae-sang, better known under his artistic name of Psy (derived from the word 'psycho', indicating his being 'crazy about music, dancing, performance').[38] Psy released his first album in 2001 and went on to win a number of music awards in South Korea, where he came to be known as 'the bizarre singer'. He managed to attain some fame in the ROK, although he differs in terms of appearance—he is somewhat chubby and does not exactly match local ideals of beauty—and in terms of lyrics from many mainstream artists, including the carefully selected and groomed boy and girl bands which have dominated the K-pop scene in recent years. Because they allegedly contained 'obscene lyrics', public broadcasters banned some of Psy's songs, and a number of his albums were officially only available to adult customers.

---

[36] 'Top of the K-pops', *The Economist*, 18 August 2012. Online: www.economist.com (accessed 13 May 2013).

[37] See *The Economist*, 18 August 2012; and 'Cashing in on Gangnam Style', Stuff.co.nz, 6 December 2012. Online: www.stuff.co.nz/technology/digital-living/8044783/Cashing-in-on-Gangnam-Style (accessed 22 May 2013).

[38] See the detailed Wikipedia entry on Psy, from which the information given here was culled. Online: http://en.wikipedia.org/wiki/Psy (last accessed 22 May 2013).

Until 2012, Psy was only very little known outside his home country. This all changed with the online YouTube release of his 'Gangnam Style' music video in June 2012, which features the by now famous and often imitated horse-riding dance moves. The 'Gangnam Style' song title refers to the posh suburb of Seoul from which Psy hails and which he mocks in the song. The 'Gangnam Style' video not only became an instant hit in his native South Korea but took on an incredible global dynamic, registering a mind-boggling one billion views by late December 2012, making it by far the most viewed music video in history. Psy appeared in autumn 2012 in various major US TV shows and met the UN Secretary-General Ban Ki-moon, who expressed his desire to work with Psy, given the latter's 'unlimited global reach'. Psy won the MTV Europe Music Award for best video in 2012 and also four awards at the MNet Asian Music Awards in Hong Kong. He gave a number of large concerts in various parts of Asia and the US, inter alia performing live with Madonna and also, to an estimated audience of one million, in New York's Times Square on New Year's eve. Before that he participated in a charity Christmas concert in Washington attended by President Obama.[39] The South Korean Ministry of Culture, Sports and Tourism, which had earlier severely criticised some of Psy's songs and albums, now warmly embraced the artist and bestowed upon him the Okgwan Order, a 4th grade Order of Cultural Merit, for his cultural achievements. By becoming the country's globally best-known artist, in 2012, Psy became a national hero. What an incredible year for the 35-year-old singer!

[39] Psy's participation in anti-American performances in the early 2000s, for which the artist apologised in late 2012, caused some stir in the US media at the time (see Wikipedia entry).

NORTH KOREA IN 2012: DOMESTIC POLITICS, THE ECONOMY AND SOCIAL ISSUES

Rüdiger Frank

1 Introduction

This overview discusses domestic developments in the Democratic People's Republic of Korea (DPRK—North Korea) in 2012. It follows the established practice of preceding volumes of *Korea: Politics, Economy and Society* in presenting a systematic analysis of the main regular publications and events such as the New Year joint editorial and the annual session of the Supreme People's Assembly (SPA). The editorial, which is studied intensively in North Korea, provides insights into the strategic planning of the leadership, even though these are often obscured by repetitive and propagandistic phrases. The annual parliamentary session is the only regular official meeting of the top North Korean leadership that the public is informed about. Rare information on economic issues is provided, most importantly on the state budget. This is also a time for the announcement of personnel changes.

Other outstanding events of the year are examined, with a focus on the economy but also going beyond. The areas of interest common to all these analytical endeavours are leadership, ideology, and general trends of development such as a 'neoconservative' or 'neo-orthodox' trend the author has identified in North Korea in recent years.

The most pressing question is how the new leader Kim Jong Un has done in his first year in office, and what kind of outlook this offers for the future of North Korea. The author combines evidence from official statements and secondary sources with first-hand impressions gained from his two visits to the country in 2012.

2 The 2012 New Year Joint Editorial

The year 2012 started as usual with the programmatic joint editorial, published by the organs of the Party (*Rodong Sinmun*), the military (*Chosŏn Inmingun*) and the youth organisation (*Ch'ŏngnyŏn Chŏnwi*). It was titled 'Glorify this year 2012 as a year of proud victory, a year when an era of prosperity is unfolding, true to the instructions of the great General Kim Jong Il'. (The title of the 2011 editorial had been 'Bring about a decisive turn in the improvement of the people's standard of living and the building of a great, prosperous and powerful country by accelerating the development of light industry once again this year'.) Even though it was the first under the new leader, the 2012 editorial brought no big surprises. As was to be expected, the death of Kim Jong Il just three weeks before was a central theme. The general motto for dealing with this situation was 'turning sorrow into strength and courage' (*sŭlp'ŭmŭl himgwa yogiro pakkuda*).

The first points among the many legacies of Kim Jong Il as promoted in the editorial related to the economy and, as in 2010 and 2011, included the improvement of the people's standard of living. Completion of the Hŭich'ŏn power station, fish farms and fruit farms, as well as the reconstruction of the capital, received particular attention.

The question of loyalty to Kim Jong Un was the next major theme. It was presented as an indispensable part of the overall strategy towards development and maintenance of the country's independence. In this context the Korean Workers' Party (KWP) was named the 'great guide' (*widaehan hyangdoŭi tang*), charged with ensuring the 'might of ideology and unity', which is called the 'first and foremost national power'.

A major task for ideology was to integrate the newly emerging cult around the late Kim Jong Il into the existing admiration of Kim Il Sung. A few hints on how this could be done were provided by the editorial: 'Our people are all the descendants of Kim Il Sung, who inherited his ideas and cause, and the soldiers and followers of Kim Jong Il', or: 'The road to socialism which Kim Il Sung had pioneered and Kim Jong Il had led along'. The new leader's place was described in these terms, using the title that has by now become the standard way of addressing him: 'The dear respected comrade Kim Jong Un [*kyŏng'aehanŭn...tongji*] is precisely the great Kim Jong Il'.

A new ideological catchphrase contained in the editorial was 'flames of Hamnam'[1] (*hamnamŭi pulgil*), first mentioned in *Rodong Sinmun* on 26 October 2011 in reference to a visit by Kim Jong Il. As the Korea Central News Agency (KCNA) wrote on 24 January 2012: 'The flames of Hamnam represent the stout offensive spirit to carry out the tasks assigned by the party on the highest level in the shortest period, the strong spirit of national self-esteem to advance ahead of the world level of its own accord and the spirit of pioneer to open the gate to prosperity before anybody else at their native places and work sites.'

Innovation was named as the driver of economic progress in the coming year. Light industry and agriculture were identified as the year's strategic sectors: 'The food problem is a burning issue in building a thriving country'. The inclusion of agriculture marked a return to the 2010 editorial, while in the 2011 version, light industry had received preferential treatment. In a rare move for a usually quantity-focused socialist country, quality was again mentioned as a target, this time more broadly than in the year before. Import substitution and the development of local industries were once again promoted as key strategies. Among other priorities for economic policy were to 'solve the problem of power shortage', improve railway transportation, and increase steel and fertiliser production. Unlike in 2011, however, the production of consumer goods was not mentioned at all. Another explicit goal was to reach and surpass global standards.

Arts and sports were to be promoted, not least to 'frustrate the manoeuvres of the imperialists' ideological and cultural infiltration and [to] root up alien elements in the way of life.' This time, however, specific ambitious goals of the 2011 editorial such as the creation of a 'sports myth' or becoming a 'football power' were omitted.

A rare reference to the fact that Kim Jong Un was not officially made successor by his father is the line 'true to the lifetime intentions of Kim Jong Il' (*saengjŏnŭi ttŭt'*), according to which the military should support Kim Jong Un as the new supreme commander. Note that the editorial mentions intentions, not decisions or orders.

One of the most popular slogans of 2011, 'at a go' (*tansume*), was emphasised as a guide for 2012 too. While caution is due regarding the expressiveness of the results of a simple counting of terms in

---

[1] Hamnam stands for *Ham*gyŏng *Nam*do, the name of a province in the central eastern section of the DPRK.

propaganda articles, Table 1 below offers a comparative perspective on the last four editorials.

Table 1 Comparing the frequency of key terms in the joint editorials (2009–2012)

	Kim Il Sung	Kim Jong Il	Kim Jong Un	Sŏn'gun	People's life	Light industry	Agricul-ture
2009	2	8	0	33	1	1	1
2010	3	9	0	15	19	9	11
2011	10	8	0	14	19	21	4
2012	9	31	15	17	3	5	3

Source: Chŏng, Sŏng Chang (2012), *2012 Nyŏn Pukhan Sinnyŏnkongdongsasŏlgwa Chŏngch'aek Kijoŭi Pyŏnhwa* [North Korea's 2012 New Year joint editorial and policy change], Sejong Commentary No. 241, Seoul: The Sejong Institute.

A somewhat new emphasis in the editorial was the demand that Party officials should 'actively learn' from the 'militant temperament of the commanding officers of the KPA' (Korean People's Army) in their efforts to carry out the orders of Kim Jong Un. Party officials were reminded that they exist for the sake of the people and should always act according to 'the will and interests of the people' and that 'considering people's convenience' should be their 'absolute and highest priority'. In the previous year, the military had been instructed to 'absolutely trust and follow the party and the leader'. This time, a similar slogan was included but it referred only to the Party's Central Committee.

In terms of foreign policy, there were no changes compared to previous years. The editorial promoted unification along the lines of the two inter-Korean summit declarations and the need to maintain peace and security in Northeast Asia.

3 Main Events in 2012

After the new leader had taken over, the central question was over the impact of this change on actual politics. To what degree would he continue along established paths, and which modifications to the usual routine would occur?

As already seen, the year 2012 started, as was customary, with a joint editorial; a deviation from that practice would only occur one year later. On 22 January, the cabinet held one of its quarterly enlarged plenary meetings to review the past year's economic plans and to discuss economic tasks for the coming year.

The month of April promised to be an interesting one, with at least four mega-events. First, on April 11, came a KWP conference, the fourth since the party's foundation. It was followed on April 13 by the annual session of the SPA (the North Korean parliament) and a rocket launch that was seen by the West as a missile test. On 15 April, the long-announced celebrations to mark the 100th birthday of the country's late founder Kim Il Sung took place.

The main task of the Party conference was the continued formalisation of Kim Jong Un's succession; no programmatic decisions were made. The KWP statutes were amended. Resembling the declaration in 1998 of Kim Il Sung as the eternal president of the country, it was stated that 'Kim Jong Il is the eternal General Secretary of the KWP and eternal leader of the KWP and the Korean people and that the KWP is the party of Kim Il Sung and Kim Jong Il.' The 'only guiding idea of the party' was renamed Kimilsungism-Kimjongilism. The post of first secretary of the KWP was created to 'represent and lead the whole party as its head and...materialize the ideas and line of Kim Il Sung and Kim Jong Il' (KCNA, 11 April 2012). At the proposal of Kim Yong Nam (president of the presidium of the SPA), Kim Jong Un was appointed to this top post and also became chairman of the KWP's Central Military Commission and a member of the presidium of the political bureau of the KWP Central Committee. (See Section 6.1 below for further promotions.) The North Korean state media also published detailed personal information on regular and alternate politburo members, creating the impression of a more collective form of leadership.

The annual SPA session proceeded as usual, with the exception of another step towards formalising the rule of the new leader. Kim Jong Il was made the eternal chairman of the National Defence Commission (NDC). Kim Jong Un was then elevated to the newly created top post of first chairman of the NDC. Premier Choe Yong Rim reported on the work of the cabinet, and Minister of Finance Choe Kwang Jin made the budget report (see Section 7 below). On the same day, 13 April 2012, North Korea's state media announced: 'The DPRK launched its first application satellite Kwangmyongsong-3 at the Sohae Satellite Launching Station in Cholsan County, North Phyongan Province at 07:38:55 a.m. on Friday. The earth observation satellite failed to enter its preset orbit. Scientists, technicians and experts are now looking into the cause of the failure' (KCNA, 13 April 2012). Both the openness of this message and the speed of the announcement of the failure were exceptional and fuelled hopes for a more open and pragmatic leadership style of the new leader.

Again on 13 April, a new Kim Jong Il bronze statue was unveiled at the country's most prestigious, central spot, Mansudae hill in Pyongyang. In fact, it was two new statues, because the old one of Kim Il Sung had not only been moved to the side but also undergone a substantial makeover. His clothes were changed from what is often called a 'Mao suit' to a Western suit and tie, glasses were added to his face, and the previously stern look was changed into a broad smile. The adjusted iconography will be discussed in more detail in Section 4 below, but we should note that in their impact such changes go far beyond being merely cosmetic.

On 15 April, the centenary of Kim Il Sung's birth was celebrated with a huge military parade, during which a number of advanced weapons such as missiles were shown.[2] According to a South Korean newspaper, the show of 880 units of 34 kinds of arms was the largest display in such a parade in the DPRK's existence (*Korea JoongAng Daily*, 15 April 2012).[3] On this occasion, Kim Jong Un, breaking with his father's more aloof style, gave his first public speech. He emphasised the improved military capabilities of his country and declared that North Korea could no longer be blackmailed with nuclear weapons. He also said that his people would no longer have to tighten their belts, and confirmed his desire for peace, prosperity and reunification (KCNA, 15 April 2013).

Three months later, on 12 July, the Kimilsung Socialist Youth League (the country's youth organisation) held its first conference since March 2002 in the presence of Vice-Marshal Choe Ryong Hae, vice-chairman of the KWP Central Military Commission. It expressed its support of the new leader and revised its rules. In particular, the positions of 'first secretary' and 'secretary' of youth league committees at all levels were renamed 'chairman' and 'vice-chairman', obviously in reaction to the change in the top titles as adopted in April.

---

[2] The author had a chance to watch the parade for over an hour as it left Pyongyang.

[3] *Korea JoongAng Daily*, 15 April 2012. Online: http://mengnews.joinsmsn.com. (accessed 21 March 2013).

Also in July, rumours emerged in South Korea about economic reforms up north, dubbed 'June 28 measures'. When the North Korean media in early September announced the unusual[4] opening of another session of the country's parliament, expectations were therefore high. Would Kim Jong Un announce a sweeping reform plan?

The SPA session was held on 25 September. However, none of the expected decisions was publicised, except that one official who was regarded as being reformist was appointed as the new chair of the SPA's budget committee. The central decision of the parliament was to reform the universal 11-year compulsory education system as adopted in 1972 by adding one year to the curriculum. Noteworthy was the explicit pragmatic emphasis on general basic knowledge and basic knowledge of modern technologies, rather than ideology. In particular, education in computer technology and foreign languages as well as mathematics, physics, chemistry and biology was stressed.

On 22 October, a regular Cabinet meeting was held. Hopes that decisions on economic reforms would finally be made public did not materialise. The meeting merely discussed the latest figures regarding the budget and on the implementation of the education reform.

On 5 December, for the first time since 2007, a national meeting of judicial officers was convened in Pyongyang. According to KCNA, the participants expressed their resolve to 'bring about a new turn in the socialist law observance under the leadership of the dear respected Kim Jong Un and thus strictly establish a revolutionary legal order throughout society.' Whether this was just a routine event, part of the countrywide campaign of expressions of loyalty to the new leader, or the reaction to a potentially growing discontent is subject to speculation.

The last month of the year saw another rocket launch, this time more successful. On 12 December, the state news agency reported: 'Scientists and technicians of the DPRK successfully launched the second version of satellite Kwangmyongsong-3 into its orbit by carrier rocket Unha-3, true to the last instructions of leader Kim Jong Il' (KCNA, 12 December 2012). The West's reaction to what was again interpreted as a missile test was furious, leading to a chain of events that resulted in a serious deterioration in the security situation on and around the peninsula in the first half of 2013.

---

[4] This had happened only twice during the leadership of Kim Jong Il.

Kim Jong Un had thus come full circle. At the beginning of the year, along with hopes for economic and political progress, doubts were raised whether he would be able to keep his grip on power. Speculations were rampant on the way his rule would be formalised, whether he would adopt a more collective leadership style or even initiate a new economic reform drive, and what he would do to improve inter-Korean relations. By the third quarter of 2012, it became clear that despite speculations about the stability of his leadership, he had remained in power. He had formalised his succession, had given his first public speech, and was confident enough to move away from established patterns. By the end of 2012, it was clear that at least formally he was the top man in North Korea. He had done many things differently from his father, in many instances echoing the style of his grandfather, Kim Il Sung. However, while we do not know whether it was because of personal convictions or in reaction to domestic pressure, he did not deviate from the previous emphasis on military strength. Hopes for a fresh start in international relations with the new leader had vanished; North Korea was, in an unfortunate way, back to normal.

4 SUCCESSION AND THE IMAGE OF THE LEADERS

The further management of succession as it was started in late December 2011 was a major ideological challenge for North Korea in 2012. In the country's leader-centred system, legitimacy of the new leader is traditionally built by elevating his ancestors and connecting himself to these personalities as closely as possible.

Kim Jong Un, or those who provided advice to him, immediately started upgrading the hitherto subdued image of Kim Jong Il. It was decided that his body would be embalmed and displayed in the same palace where his father Kim Il Sung rests, and that statues of Kim Jong Il should be erected throughout the country. His birthday, 16 February, had been celebrated before, but it was now named 'Day of the shining star' (*Kwangmyŏngsŏng*, which is also the name of the North Korean satellite). Somewhat oddly, it was explicitly mentioned in a related announcement of the KWP politburo that portraits should show him 'with a smile on his face' (KCNA, 12 January 2012). A new medal named after Kim Jong Il was created and handed to top officials. The official name of the leader-based ideology of the country was renamed from Kimilsungism to Kimilsungism-Kimjongilsim. The elevation of Kim Jong Il to 'eternal' leadership as general secretary of the Party and chairman of the National Defence Commission in April has to be seen in the same light. On 18 January the 100th and final volume of the collection of Kim Il Sung's works was published, implying that the task of publishing the works of Kim Jong Il would now follow.

In May, it became known that the DPRK's basic law had been revised to include reference to Kim Jong Il's eternal leadership.[5] The 'Kim Il Sung constitution' now became the 'Kim Il Sung Kim Jong Il constitution'. On 6 October, KCNA reported that the police academy was renamed the 'Kim Jong-il People's Security University'. In December 2012, images of the refurbished Kŭmsusan Palace of the Sun were released, where Kim Jong Il lies in state a few floors beneath his father. Throughout 2012, Kim Jong Il was largely promoted as a patriot (*aegukka*) in North Korean propaganda.

In addition to the upgrading of the status of his late father, Kim Jong Un's image—almost non-existent, as he had only been introduced to the public in September 2010—was built up further. The propaganda machine tried to turn the youth of Kim Jong Un into something positive, emphasising his youthful spirit and the fact that his two predecessors also had accomplished important feats at a young age. One isolated move was a reported attempt to include Kim Jong Un's late mother, Ko Yong Hui, in the official pantheon as the 'mother of Pyongyang' (*Asahi Shimbun*, 27 February 2012). On 10 April, KCNA reported the cultivation of a new strain of flower, an orchid hybrid (*Cymbidium* Lillian Steward). What is remarkable is that Kim Jong Un 'saw the flower and named it Manbokia'.[6] Korean leaders traditionally are symbolised by a flower; the Manbokia could later become the Kimjongunia. By the way, it is an orchid like the Kimilsungia, but unlike the Kimjongilia, which is a begonia.

Following in the tradition of his predecessors, Kim Jong Un has started publishing his own works. Among the first instances was 'On effecting a drastic turn in land management to meet the requirements for building a thriving socialist nation', published on 27 April 2012. Documentaries have been released of Kim Jong Un's inspections trips

---

[5] See the Naenara website, http://www.naenara.com.kp/ko/great/constitution.php?1.

[6] *Manbok* in Korean means 'full stomach' or 'great happiness'.

on 26 May 2012, to boost his image as an energetic and caring leader. The last phrase of Kim Jong Un's public speech on 15 April was turned into a new song for his glorification, called 'Onwards towards the final victory'. On 18 July, Kim Jong Un awarded himself the title of marshal (*wŏnsu*) and took formal command of the armed forces. Only two days before, one of his hitherto closest confidants, army chief Ri Yong Ho, had suddenly been removed from all his posts, officially because of health issues. The move fuelled speculations about a power struggle.

In addition to such demonstrations of 'hard power', Kim Jong Un has also been fighting for the hearts of his people. The date 16 November has been designated as 'Mother's Day' in North Korea, in yet another attempt by Kim Jong Un to show his loving care for his people. A national meeting of mothers, so far the fourth in the DPRK's history, had taken place one day earlier.

4.1 *Kim Jong Un's leadership style*

This has been the subject of keen observation throughout 2012. Admittedly among the more entertaining subfields of North Korean research, it nonetheless has a number of serious implications if we consider that in a dictatorship, the person of the leader has a much bigger impact on actual politics than would be the case in a pluralist system with limited tenure and well-established checks and balances. For an understanding of North Korea, the personality of the leader matters.

In January 2012, it was noted that the birthday of Kim Jong Un, which is rumoured to be 8 January, was not celebrated as a public holiday. This suggested that the new leader would keep a low profile for a while. Comparisons were made with Kim Jong Il, who had stayed away from the public for three years after his father's death in 1994. However, starting with his first public speech at the military parade in April, Kim Jong Un has been quite active. He continued the tradition of his predecessors of travelling round the country giving on-the-spot guidance, in much publicised visits to military and civilian units. During these visits, he behaved in a very approachable manner: he laughed, smiled, and had close physical contact with his subjects. As is usual in the case of North Korea, interpretations of this behaviour diverge. Opinions range from an expression of his open personality, an attempt to mimic his grandfather Kim Il Sung, or even the reaction to a lack of public support.

Among the most remarkable public actions of Kim Jong Un were his comments during a visit to the Mangyŏngdae funfair on 9 May 2012. Mangyŏngdae is the official birthplace of Kim Il Sung and thus among the country's most sacred and symbolic areas. KCNA reported in unusual detail and openness. Kim Jong Un was quoted as criticising 'bad management of roads', 'faulty arrangements', and 'scraped-off paint'. He plucked weeds from the pavement with an 'irritated look' and then spoke 'in an excited tone'. He 'scolded' officials in a 'serious tone' and insisted that officials should regard his words as a 'serious warning' to better serve the people (KCNA, 9 May 2012). He assigned the task of renovating the funfair to the military under Choe Ryong Hae, then director of the KPA's General Political Bureau.

How can we interpret these remarks? Aside from causing somebody a heart attack— such criticism can have serious consequences for the individuals affected—Kim Jong Un sent out a number of messages. The first one is centuries old: whatever in his country is in a bad state, it is the fault of incompetent officials, not of the top leader. Discontent should thus be directed at those officials, while the only hope for a solution lies with the leader. Kim Jong Un also exhibited a kind of attention to details that is not untypical for dictators, boosting his image as an omnipotent and omnipresent figure. In combination with open threats ('serious warning'), this will instil fear into his subjects. In addition, we find here further proof for his emphasis on 'the people's lives', something that he started paying public attention to right after he entered the limelight in December 2011. This policy, known as *panem et circenses* (bread and circuses) in imperial Rome, has been followed through most of the year 2012. The fact that the army was tasked with ironing out the error at the funfair can be seen as a move to appease the military—or to show the leader's trust in Choe Ryong Hae, who is allegedly a competitor to the unfortunate Ri Yong Ho.

The next major deviation from the behaviour of his father and, in fact, even his grandfather[7] was the public introduction of a first lady. The wildest rumours started after a woman was shown next to Kim Jong Un during a North Korean TV broadcast in early July 2012. On

[7] Kim Jong Suk (1919–49), mother of Kim Jong Il, received only posthumous promotion as the 'woman commander of Mt Paektu'.

25 July, the state media confirmed that this woman, identified as 'comrade Ri Sol Ju', is Kim Jong Un's wife. Speculation then shifted to her identity and background. According to the South Korean intelligence agency NIS, she was born in 1989, graduated from Kŭmsŏng Middle School No. 2 in Pyongyang, studied vocal music in China, and had been a singer in the Ŭnhasu Orchestra until 2011. She allegedly married the North Korean leader in 2009 (Yonhap North Korea Newsletter No. 221, 2 August 2012). She does not seem to be from one of the top families, which is important information, as politics in North Korea is heavily family based. We can only conjecture whether she was chosen because of this background, or whether the entrance of a new family may lead to a distortion in the balance of power among the 'aristocracy'.

Most South Korean commentators assumed that her public introduction was part of an attempt by the new leader to appear more seasoned and experienced. Traditionally, marriage has been considered in Korea to mark something of a rite of passage. Whether this was the only or the primary reason for her sudden introduction remains unclear. Perhaps the leader just wanted to show off his attractive wife, or he wanted to make sure that the child she was carrying at that time would be regarded as legitimate. What is remarkable is that once introduced, she was an almost constant presence, accompanying Kim Jong Un on over two- thirds of his publicised visits from early July. Then she disappeared from the North Korean media in early September as suddenly as she had emerged two months before. When she came back into the spotlight at the end of October after a 50-day absence, signs of her pregnancy were hard to overlook.

The interesting things to note are the aggressive PR policy employed by Kim Jong Un, the stark contrast to the image of his father, and the volatility of events. Despite numerous 'official' anecdotes, revealing details about the truly personal life of the leader has for good reasons not been customary in North Korea. It makes him more of a worldly being, and thus vulnerable; and it limits his future options. Ri is now known as Kim Jong Un's wife to every North Korean. If he shows up with a different wife five years from now, this will raise questions. The revelation of her pregnancy means a lot in a country where the exact age of the top leaders has so far been a well-kept secret. Her style, which has quickly become a new standard among North Korean women, is distinctly Western and perhaps a notch too extravagant in a country where the frugality of the previous leader has been emphasised extensively. Whatever the situation, this and a somewhat bizarre cultural performance involving the unauthorised use of Disney characters led some commentators to hope for a market-oriented reform policy under Kim Jong Un.

Although he was certainly not speaking on behalf of the current leadership, it is interesting to note that another member of the Kim family chose to give public statements in 2012. Kim Han Sol, 17-year-old son of Kim Jong Un's eldest brother Kim Jong Nam, gave a rare interview to a Finnish TV station which was published on 16 October 2012.[8] He was a student at the United World College in Mostar (Croatia) at that time. In his interview with a former UN under-secretary, aside from a few rather paternalistic remarks he calls Kim Jong Un a dictator and talks rather openly about his parents.

5 Bread and circuses

The new leader started his rule in late 2011 with the promise of a better life for his people. Ideologically, it was thus important to show a number of achievements in 2012. Some of these projects had been started under Kim Jong Il but were nevertheless credited to Kim Jong Un, whose fortune in this regard was, somewhat superstitiously, interpreted among the population as a hopeful sign for the new era. Accomplishments in 2012 include 'hard' economic projects, such as power stations, but also 'soft', bread and circuses projects including amusement parks.

The power shortages in North Korea are one of the main structural problems of the economy. It was thus good news when KCNA reported on 21 February that after 11 years of construction, two plants of a hydroelectric power station in Hŭich'ŏn in the northern Chagang province started operation. The combined generating capacity of all the plants is supposed to reach 300,000 kilowatts. On 25 April, a dedication ceremony for a meat and fish shop was held in Pyongyang with Kim Jong Un attending. On 3 May, KCNA reported the completion of a new port facility on the east coast in South Hamgyŏng province. This port, Tanch'ŏn, is particularly important for the shipping of mineral resources such as magnetite and zinc. On 20 June, KCNA report-

8 The interview can still be watched online at www.youtube.com/watch?v=T_uSuCkKa3k (accessed 6 June 2013).

ed that construction of Ch'angjŏn street in downtown Pyongyang near Mansudae hill was finished. By late August, the first stage of a joint project with China to build an International Commerce and Trade Centre covering about 40,000 sq m in the northeastern economic zone of Rasŏn was nearing completion. Funding was shared between North Korea's Rason Paekho Trading Corporation and a Chinese real estate development company in Qinhuangdao.

These were important achievements for the development of North Korea's economy. But it seemed that the focus of Kim Jong Un's efforts to win the hearts of his people was on entertainment, and in the space of 2012, one folk park—Pyongyang Folk Park in Mt Taesŏng—and three pleasure grounds—the Rŭngna People's Pleasure Ground on Rŭngna islet in the Taedong river in Pyongyang, Mangyŏngdae park, where Kim Jong Un had voiced his harsh criticism in May before entrusting the renovation to the army, and a pleasure ground located near Mt Taesŏng—were opened or re-opened, involving huge funds for a country that according to its own statements suffers from food and electricity shortages. The Arirang mass games, held first in 2002 and annually since 2007, started in August. They were scheduled to last until early September but were extended until the end of the month. Stories that these would be the last Arirang games were later proven wrong. A newcomer in the entertainment field was the female music group, the Moranbong Band, first shown in July and said to be the personal creation of Kim Jong Un. Its members caught attention with their short, Western-style dresses and modern hairstyles. It was at one of their performances that Ri Sol Ju, the leader's wife, was first seen in public.

In contrast, the 64th anniversary of the establishment of the DPRK on 9 September and the 67th anniversary of the founding of the Party a month later were relatively modest celebrations.

North Korean participation in the London Olympics and in the Paralympics—the latter another first for the country—was hugely successful and was celebrated accordingly in the media. The 56 North Korean athletes won four gold and two bronze medals, the best gold tally since the 1992 Barcelona Olympics, earning them 20th place in the medal standings. North Korea had in the years before increased its efforts at promoting sports as a source of soft power, thus catching up with a practice that socialist countries such as the GDR (East Germany) had exhibited routinely.

On 19 November, Kim Jong Un made a field visit to a military unit, on which occasion he ordered the refurbishment of the unit's horse-riding training ground into a club for teenagers and workers. Also seen on photographs released by the state media was the leader's sister Kim Yo Jong.

It remains to be seen whether such measures will be able to generate and sustain the public support that the new leader is obviously hoping for.

6 Personnel

6.1 *Appointments*

No dictator can lead his country single-handedly. As soon as Kim Jong Un took over in December 2011, observers wondered whether he would be a figurehead, who the team was behind him, how he would deal with the top leadership group inherited from his father, and whether he would adopt a more collective leadership style.

The year 2012 brought a number of major developments and insights in this regard. It seems that in particular during the first half of the year, other leading figures in the North Korean administration received increased public attention. Among them was Premier Choe Yong Rim, whose guidance tours to a number of key economic facilities across the country were accorded detailed media coverage. The titular head of state (by virtue of heading the SPA presidium since 1998), Kim Yong Nam, is a remarkable man as he is among the very few who have served almost uninterruptedly at the very top of North Korea. He became a politburo member in 1980, at the same Party congress at which Kim Jong Il was officially announced as successor to Kim Il Sung. He is one of the few who have received modest media coverage even under Kim Jong Il. A particularly steep ascent was achieved by Choe Ryong Hae, son of the late Choe Hyon, a former minister of the People's Armed Forces. Choe, who is in his early sixties, was named as a four-star general and a member of the Party's Central Military Commission in 2010. In April 2012, he became a member of the presidium of the KWP Political Bureau, vice-marshal, and vice-chairman of the KWP Central Military Commission.

A series of relatively quick promotions and demotions, as well as the reorganisation of administrative and military units indicates that an intense process of power-building took place in 2012. A number of posts shifted; often we can only note these changes without being able to provide much detail on the background.

In February 2012, former Trade Minister Ri Kwang Gun became head of the Committee of Investment and Joint Venture, obviously in an effort to intensify activities in this crucial field. In March, Ri Jong Guk was appointed minister of machine-building industry, a post previously held by Vice-Premier Jo Byong Ju. In the same month, Jon Yong Nam was appointed as first secretary of the youth league during the 47th plenary meeting of its Central Committee, replacing Ri Yong Chol. The youth organisation has a membership of about five million North Koreans between the ages of 14 and 30. Hong Kwang Sun, who served as director of a movie studio affiliated with the military, replaced An Dong Chun as the country's new culture minister.

Table 2 Regular and alternate (*italic*) members of the politburo as announced by KCNA on 11 April 2012

CHOE Ryong Hae	Director of the General Political Bureau of the KPA since April 2012
KIM Jong Gak	Minister of the People's Armed Forces since April 2012
JANG Song Thaek	Vice-chairman of the DPRK National Defence Commission and director of the Administration Department of the KWP's Central Committee since June 2010
PAK To Chun	Secretary of the KWP's Central Committee since September 2010
HYON Chol Hae	First vice-minister and director of the General Logistic Bureau of the People's Armed Forces since April 2012
KIM Won Hong	Minister of state security since April 2012
RI Myong Su	Minister of people's security since April 2011
KWAK Pom Gi	Secretary of the KWP's Central Committee since April 2012
O Kuk Ryol	Vice-chairman of the DPRK National Defence Commission since February 2009
RO Tu Chol	Vice-premier of the cabinet and chairman of the State Planning Commission since April 2009
RI Pyong Sam	Director of the political bureau of the Korean People's Internal Security Forces and chief secretary of its party committee since May 2009
JO Yon Jun	First vice-departmental director of the Organizational Leadership Department of the KWP's Central Committee since Jan 2012

Source: www.kcna.co.jp, 11 April 2012.

Major changes in the North Korean leadership occurred during the fourth conference of the KWP and the annual session of the SPA in April. The new composition of the KWP's politburo is outlined at Table 2.

This reshuffling of the politburo is remarkable, if we consider that this instrument was hardly used at all under Kim Jong Il. Only in 2010, when the need to build the succession became more pressing, did the Party's highest organ recover some of the importance that would be regarded as standard, for example, in countries such as China.

Other newly appointed Party officials were Kim Kyong Hui and Kwak Pom Gi as secretaries of the Central Committee, Hyon Chol Hae, Ri Myong Su and Kim Rak Gyom as members of the Central Military Commission, and Kim Yong Chun, Kwak Pom Gi and Pak Pong Ju as departmental directors of the Central Committee.

During the SPA session, Choe Ryong Hae, Kim Won Hong and Ri Myong Su were elected members of the NDC at the proposal of Kim Jong Un. The composition of the NDC after April 2012 was thus as follows:

Table 3 Composition of the National Defence Commission after the April 2012 SPA session

Eternal chairman	Kim Jong Il
First chairman	Kim Jong Un
Vice-chairmen	Kim Yong Chun, Ri Yong Mu, Jang Song Thaek and O Kuk Ryol.
Members	Pak To Chun, Kim Jong Gak, Ju Kyu Chang, Paek Se Bong, Choe Ryong Hae, Kim Won Hong and Ri Myong Su

Source: KCNA, www.kcna.co.jp, 13 April 2012.

Thae Hyong Chol became secretary-general of the SPA presidium. Ri Sung Ho and Ri Chol Man were named as vice-premiers of the cabinet and Kim In Sik as vice-premier and chairman of the Capital Construction Commission. Pak Thae Dok, chief secretary of the North Hwanghae provincial committee of the KWP, and Jon Kyong Nam, president of the University of National Economics, were elected as members of the Legislation Committee of the SPA.

Further personnel changes were to follow. In August, Jon Sung Hun, minister for the metal industry, was appointed a vice-premier, increasing the number of holders of this title to 11. Along with Pak Pong Ju, Ro Tu Chol and Kwak Pom Gi, Jon Sung Hun was among the key officials responsible for economic reforms in the period around 2002/2003. Their reappointment to top posts has been interpreted as a sign of an imminent new round of economic reforms. Kwak Pom Gi was later appointed as chair of the SPA's budget committee.

In October, Hwang Min was appointed agriculture minister, replacing Ri Kyong Sik. In the same month, the ministers of the electronics industry and for physical culture and sports were replaced as well. Lastly, in late November Kim Kyok Shik replaced Kim Jong Gak as minister of the People's Armed Forces. This was of particular interest, as it seems that Hyong Yong Chol, who had been promoted to vice-marshal in July, was downgraded to four-star general again. Kim Jong Gak had only been promoted to the ministerial post in April.

6.2 *Comment*

As ever, we are usually left to speculate on the reasons for these reshuffles. Explanations range from reasons such as health to alleged lack of allegiance to the leader and even rumours of a failed military coup against Kim Jong Un.

The latter might well be true or a product of wishful thinking. Experience tells us that in a dictatorship, it is always dangerous for top officials to stick out too far. If they fail to master the task of continuously and reliably reassuring the leader of their loyalty, they can be removed from their posts very quickly. Given the dynamics of the year 2012, we can expect a few more personnel changes at the top in 2013. The high age of top officials will also play a role, enabling Kim Jong Un to fill key posts with new, perhaps younger and more pragmatically oriented technocrats.

The case of Ri Yong Ho shows that not only steep promotions, but also plunging falls from grace are possible under Kim Jong Un. In July, Ri's dismissal from all his posts was announced by the North Korean media. The politburo 'decided to relieve Ri Yong Ho of all his posts including member of the Presidium of the Political Bureau, member of the Political Bureau of the C.C., KWP and vice-chairman of the Central Military Commission of the KWP for his illness' (KNCA, 16 July 2012). Only two days later, Kim Jong Un became a marshal, and Hyon Yong Chol was promoted to the rank of vice-marshal to take over Ri's post. The demotion was of particular interest because Ri Yong Ho himself had become a central figure in the North Korean power elite only three years before, at the age of 67. He was one of eight top officials, including Kim Jong Un and Kim's uncle Jang Song Thaek, who escorted the funeral car of Kim Jong Il. After Kim Jong Il's death, Ri was seen as a key figure in securing the succession process. His abrupt and rather unusual dismissal triggered rumours about a power struggle or purge, and about potential instability in Kim Jong Un's leadership. Analysts in Seoul also pointed at a possible rivalry between Ri Yong Ho and Choe Ryong Hae (*T'ongilnews*, 16 July 2013).[9]

South Korean sources show a particular interest in the field of personnel. The South Korean Yonhap news agency in January 2012 reported on a dense network of family-based connections that extends into each and every aspect of the DPRK's administration. Several relatives of Jang Song Thaek, brother-in-law of the late leader Kim Jong Il, are involved in North Korea's diplomatic and trade relations. They include Jang Yong Chol and Jon Yong Jin. Jang Yong Chol is the second son of Jang Song Thaek's eldest brother and was appointed ambassador to Malaysia in 2010. Jang Yong Chol's elder brother is on a North Korean committee handling economic co-operation with foreign countries. Jon Yong Jin, North Korean Ambassador to Cuba, is the husband of Jang Song Thaek's elder sister and previously served as the DPRK's top envoy to Sweden and Iceland. Children of Party secretary Kim Yong Il and Vice-Premier Kang Sok Ju have been dispatched to North Korean overseas diplomatic missions. According to an unnamed source, Ri Son Il, son of Ri Yong Ho, and Cha Dong Sup, son-in-law of Kim Yong Chun, minister of the People's Armed Forces, are active either in earning foreign currency or in attracting foreign investment (Yonhap North Korea Newsletters Nos 192 and 194, 12 and 26 January 2012).

An interesting analysis of the origins of North Korea's elite has been provided by the South Korean Ministry of Unification (quoted in

---

[9] *T'ongilnews*, 16 July 2012. Online: www.tongilnews.com. (accessed 21 February 2013).

Yonhap North Korea Newsletter No. 219, 19 July 2012).[10] According to the report, which analysed the background of 106 top officials, about 35.5 percent of key government and Party figures are alumni of Kim Il Sung University, while the army-oriented Kim Il Sung Military University is the alma mater for 17.7 percent of them. Women accounted for only 5.7 percent of those surveyed. The female component in the North Korean cabinet stood at 2 percent. The average age of cabinet members was 63, while the average for key party members was 72, indicating a higher proportion of technocrats in the cabinet.

7 Budget

As each year, a report on the state's budget was presented during the parliamentary session in April. The presenter in 2012 was Finance Minister Choe Kwang Jin. As usual since 2003, no absolute numbers were provided. In March 2002, the last time North Korea announced a budget in monetary terms, planned revenue for 2002 was around 22 billion won. Despite their somewhat unorthodox structure and wording, these budgetary reports nonetheless represent the only available official information on the status of the North Korean economy. Given that the state owns the economy, the state budget comes close to resembling the North Korean gross domestic product (GDP), minus the sectors that are treated separately including, as is widely suspected, a large part of the military economy.

A look at Graph 1, updated on the basis of the 2012 budget report, shows that after a recession following the economic reform period, the DPRK seems to be catching up—at least in terms of its own statistics. Growth has been steady. It is also apparent that growth rates of planned expenditure (planned E) have been higher than those for planned revenue (planned R) since 2009. This is somewhat more expressive than the typically socialist announcements of achieved revenues (achieved R) having grown faster than planned, although the two curves seem to narrow towards the end. It implies that North Korea is either calculating with higher-than-expected income growth, or deliberately factors in some debt. The sources thereof are very limited. If

[10] Yonhap news agency North Korea Newsletters may be viewed on www.yonhapnews.co.kr.

the numbers below are to be trusted, then speculation can be voiced about China providing loans to the North Korean state.

According to the budget report, the official 'growth rate' of the North Korean economy in 2011 was 8.6 percent (in 2010 it was 7.7 percent), as this was the rate at which state budgetary revenue had grown compared to the previous year.

Graph 1 Economic growth in North Korea according to the DPRK budget (growth rates in %)

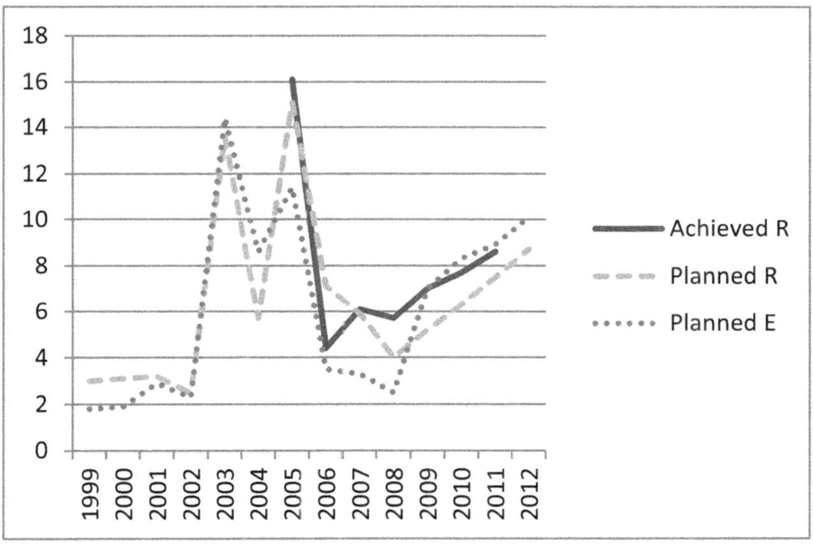

Source: Author's calculations based on www.kcna.co.jp.

The key data of the report are summarised in Table 4, which provides the numbers for the previous three years for comparison.

A general report on the budget by Premier Choe Yong Rim started with a rare announcement of a growth rate of industrial output of 2 percent. For other products of the economy such as electricity, iron ore, electrolytic zinc, power generators, fertilisers, magnesia clinker, etc., in a more typical vein 'remarkable growth' was reported. The improvement of the people's standard of living was once again identified as the most important target of economic policy. Light industry and agriculture were to stand at the centre of the cabinet's efforts. For light industry, full utilisation of existing capacities, innovation and quality

Table 4 Comparison of state budgets 2009–2012 in %

	Plan for 2009	Achieved in 2009	*Plan for 2010*	Achieved in 2010	*Plan for 2011*	Achieved in 2011	*Plan for 2012*
State budgetary revenue	*+5.2*	101.7 + 7	*+6.3*	+7.7	*+7.5*	101.1 +8.6	*+8.7*
Transaction tax							*+7.5*
Profits of state enterprises	*+5.8*		*+7.7*		*78.5*		*+10.7*
Profits of co-operative organisations	*+3.1*		*+4.2*		*+3.8*		*+5.3*
Fixed asset depreciation	*+6.1*		*+2.5*		*+1.4*		*+2.3*
Real estate rent	*+3.6*		*+2*		*+0.7*		*+1.9*
Social insurance	*+1.6*		*+1.9*		*+0.4*		*+1.7*
Local budgetary revenue		'over-fulfilled'			*16.1*	18.16 (+12.8)	
State budgetary expenditure	*+7*	99.8	*+8.3*	+8.2	*+8.9 83.9*	99.8	*+10.1*
National defence	*15.8*	15.8	*15.8*	15.8	*15.8*	15.8	*15.8*
Priority sectors of the national economy (metal, power, coal, railway)	*+8.7*	'huge investment'	*+7.3*	+8.0	*+13.5*		*+12.1*
Development of science and technology	*+8*	+7.2	*+8.5*	+8.1	*+10.1*		*+10.9*
Agriculture	*+6.9*	n.a.	*+9.4*	+9.4	*+9.0*		*+9.4*
Light industry	*+5.6*		*+10.1*	+10.9	*+12.9*		*+9.4*
City management/capital construction	*+11.5*		*+8.6*	+12.9	*+15.1*		
Popular policies			*+6.2*	+6.0	*n.a.*		
Education	*+8.2*						*+9.2*
Culture and arts	*+3.2*						*+6.8*
Public health	*+8*						*+8.9*
Sports	*+5.8*						*+6.9*
Social insurance and social security							*+7*

Source: KCNA. See earlier editions of *Korea: Politics, Economy, and Society* for budget data before 2009.

were particularly stressed. In the field of agriculture, the per hectare grain yields were to be increased, which hints at efforts to intensify agricultural production instead of expanding it.

Exports, as in 2010, received strong emphasis. The premier stressed that related 'production bases should be built under a long-term plan and the development of economic and trade zones and joint venture and contracts be vigorously undertaken and the technological cooperation in economy with other countries be boosted' (KCNA, 13 April 2012). In a side note, the KCNA report indicated the education reform of September 2012: 'Centers for training talents and schools at all levels should be built well, educational contents and methods be improved to meet the requirements of the developing situation.'

A number of projects received particular attention, such as the Taedonggang combined fruit processing factory, which is known for its apple products. Other explicitly named projects were the Kwaksan tideland project, the Hŭich'ŏn power station, and nonferrous metal production bases including those in the Tanch'ŏn area with the newly built Tanch'ŏn port (see Section 5). The Hŭngnam fertiliser complex, the February 8 Vinalon complex, the Namhŭng youth chemical complex, and Hŭich'ŏn precision machine plant were technologically updated.

In general, it may be said that the budget figures look more optimistic than in earlier years, that new details were reported, in particular the industrial growth rate, and that the focus on light industry and agriculture was maintained.

8 The North Korean economy

8.1 *Demographics and GDP*

A report on demographics issued by the UN Economic and Social Commission for Asia and the Pacific (ESCAP) suggests that the population of the DPRK is projected to increase to about 26.18 million by 2030 from 24.45 million in 2011. Total fertility rate is estimated to be around 2.0 as of 2012 (South Korea: 1.4). The urban population accounts for about 60 percent (South Korea: 80 percent), while average life expectancy is 68.8 years (ESCAP Statistics, March 2013).[11]

[11] ESCAP Statistics. Online: www.unescap.org/stat/data (accessed 9 March 2013).

The South Korean think-tank, Hyundai Research Institute, claims that North Korean GDP (see the estimates in Section 7 above) has grown by about 4.7 percent, reaching US$ 720 per capita.[12] Highlighting the great uncertainty about such kind of quantitative data, the South Korean Bank of Korea (BOK) saw a 0.8 percent growth in 2011. The biggest growth was estimated in the agricultural and fishery industry (+5.3 percent) and in construction (+3.9 percent). BOK estimated the overall gross national income of North Korea at US$28.5 billion in 2011.[13]

8.2 *Food and agriculture*

Ever since the famine of the mid-1990s, known as the 'Arduous march' in North Korea, the food situation in the DPRK has been the subject of keen interest from both humanitarian organisations and strategists who try to estimate the domestic pressures on the North Korean government.

In January 2012, the (South Korean) Korea Meteorological Administration agency reported that during the period 1981–2010, the average temperature in North Korea was 4 degrees lower than in the South, while the North has experienced a smaller amount of annual rainfall (report quoted in Yonhap North Korea Newsletter No. 195, 2 February 2012). About 60 percent of the precipitation was summer rain. This corresponds with older studies, which conclude that despite the relatively short distance between North and South Korea, conditions for farming are much less favourable in the North, with a shorter growth period and higher risks of floods and droughts.

In April and May 2012, the rice-planting season, North Korea was hit by a severe drought. According to KCNA (27 May 2012), most western regions of the country recorded the driest May since 1962. A few weeks later, KCNA reported an unchanged situation: 'There has been no rainfall from late April in Kangnam County in Pyongyang City, Anak County in South Hwanghae Province, Songrim City and Junghwa County in North Hwanghae Province, Ryonggang County and Kangso District in Nampho City and Unchon County in South Hwanghae Province' (KCNA, 12 June 2012). Starting in late June, the

[12] Hyundai Research Institute. Online: www.hri.co.kr (accessed 10 March 2013).
[13] Bank of Korea. Online: www.bok.or.kr (accessed 10 March 2013).

drought was replaced by floods, which, according to KCNA, left 169 people dead, 144 injured and 400 missing. They made 212,200 people homeless. At least 65,280 hectares of arable land were washed away, buried and inundated across the country (KCNA, 4 August 2012).

Except for the construction of more pig farms, no major agricultural policy initiatives were reported for the year. Despite unfavourable conditions, North Korea's agriculture achieved a record harvest in 2012. According to the World Food Programme (WFP), the country produced 4.9 million tons of rice or rice equivalent, which is only 0.2 million tons short of what is regarded as the subsistence level. Individual food rations in December 2012 stood at 400 grams of cereals per day, 'the highest level...compared to the previous years'. However, uneven distribution means that it is still to be expected that vulnerable parts of the population will suffer from malnutrition or famine. The WFP also pointed out that the quality of food has been reduced; in particular the intake of protein seems to have dropped.[14]

8.3 *Telecommunications*

North Korea's telecommunications sector has for many years been the subject of outside interest, since mobile phones in particular are associated with a certain amount of individual freedom, progress and affluence. By February 2012, the number of subscribers to the services of Orascom Telecom, the Egyptian partner of Koryolink, reached one million. South Korean sources also reported on a growing use of Android-based smart phones. Overall investment by Orascom in North Korea's telecom business since 2008 had reached US$150 million by 2012. The Egyptian firm also invested US$180 million in the completion of the Ryugyŏng hotel in Pyongyang, which had remained unfinished since the late 1980s (Yonhap North Korea Newsletter No. 236, 15 November 2012). The Kempinski Group has shown interest in managing the hotel.[15]

---

[14] United Nations World Food Programme, 'Nutrition Support for Women and Children in the DPRK', PRRO 200114 Report, Oct.–Dec. 2012. Online: www.wfp.org.

[15] It now seems that Kempinski has withdrawn from this project in reaction to the security crisis of March and April 2013.

8.4 *Minerals*

Estimates of the value of the DPRK's mineral resources vary, but it seems clear that their importance as a source of hard currency income is increasing. In August 2012, Yonhap quoted the Seoul-based North Korea Resource Institute's assessment that put the overall value of deposits at US$9.7 trillion. The figure increased in 2012 over previous estimates because of rising world market prices. Over the past decade, North Korea's exports of mineral resources recorded a 33-fold jump. China was the biggest importer, in particular of iron ore and coal. According to the Korea Trade and Investment Promotion Agency, North Korea's mineral exports reached $1.65 billion in 2011, accounting for 59.4 percent of the country's total exports (Yonhap North Korea Newsletter No. 230, 4 October 2012).

The joint development of mines continued in 2012. The North Korean Committee of Investment and Joint Venture reported the signing of contracts on the development of one gold mine and two iron ore mines. China holds a 51 percent stake in North Korea's biggest copper mine in Hyesan, and 50-year mining rights over another major mine in Musan, North Hamgyŏng province.[16] The Chinese mining firm Xiyang Group of Liaoning claimed it lost a huge amount of money it had invested in the joint venture with Korea's Ryŏngbong Corporation. The North Korean side countered that the Chinese group had fulfilled only 50 percent of its obligations (KCNA, 5 September 2012).

9 Economic changes and reforms

A new, young leader; a country with many systemic problems; the success model of China: the combination of these factors suggests that economic reforms are not only needed, but almost inevitable. What has been done in this regard in 2012, and what are the prospects?

---

[16] Yonhap, 9 August 2012, accessed 29 May 2013 at http://english.yonhapnews.co.kr/news/2012/08/09/0200000000AEN20120809004600315.HTML.

9.1 *Foreign investment and its legal foundation*

In late January, North Korea's state media reported the amendment of laws on foreign-funded businesses, focusing on labour and financial management. Foreign investment laws were enacted in 1992 and subsequently revised in 1999 and 2004. KCNA did not provide much detail, except that the law on labour in foreign-funded businesses breaks into 51 articles in eight chapters, including employment of labour, conclusion of labour contract, work and rest, labour safety, social insurance and social security. The revised law on financial management in foreign-funded businesses is made up of 72 articles in ten chapters, while the law on accounts in the same businesses consists of 59 articles in four chapters (KCNA, 30 January 2012).

A few weeks later in February, the revision of a number of laws related to foreign investment was announced, although it seems to have taken place in late 2011. The Law on registration of foreign-funded businesses consists of 34 articles in six chapters and deals with the registration of business set-ups, residence, taxation and customs. Amendments were also made to the Law on foreign-funded businesses and foreigners' tax payment and the Law on insolvency of foreign-funded businesses. The Law on foreign-funded banks has been amended as well, leaving it with 32 articles in five chapters that deal with the classification, residence, property right and independent management of foreign-funded banks. It 'stipulates that the banks with 10 or more years of banking activities shall be exempted from paying income tax for the first-year profits. It also provides that business taxes shall not be levied on the interest receipts from loans that were credited to local banks and businesses in their favor' (KCNA, 9 February 2012). In March, KCNA quoted a vice-departmental director of the DPRK Committee for Investment and Joint Venture as saying: 'Contracts on joint venture and joint collaboration have been on increase with the investment environment changing for the better. Rare earth abundant in the country and infrastructure projects lure foreign investment in the DPRK' (KCNA, 23 March 2012).

An investment insurance firm was established in an apparent bid to reduce the risk of investing in North Korea. In June, an international insurance seminar on 'Dynamics of insurance coverage arrangement and rate application responding to recent catastrophes and disasters' was held in Pyongyang in co-operation with the Federation of Afro-Asian Insurers and Reinsurers. So Tong Myong, chairman of the Korea National Insurance Corporation Executive Committee of Management gave an opening speech at the seminar, the contents of which were reported in great and unusual detail. Paper topics included earthquakes and the relevant insurance in China; opportunities in the emerging reinsurance market in Russia; recent natural disasters in the DPRK, their insurance coverage and measures ahead; arbitration clauses in international arbitration contracts; general principles relating to the conduct of loss surveys and claim adjustments following catastrophic events; and on contingent business interruption (KCNA, 11-12 June 2012).

After inter-Korean relations soured with the end of the Roh Moo-hyun presidency, China remained the DPRK's only major economic partner and thus also a major source of incoming foreign direct investment. Numerous measures were taken to intensify this co-operation, such as the 2nd Rasŏn International Trade Fair in late August 2012. Trade fairs have been held regularly in Pyongyang in spring and autumn. The Rasŏn trade fair has been established in connection with the upgrading of the area, formerly known as Rajin and Sŏnbong, in the northeastern part of North Korea, into a special economic zone in 2010. The North Korean Rasŏn Paekho Trading Corporation, which is believed to be the key trading unit of the military, has been particularly active in attracting investment to the zone and has also been responsible for running the Mt Kŭmgang tourism project in co-operation with Chinese partners after the South Korean firm Hyundai Asan had been kicked out.

In February, China secured the rights to build three new piers in the Rasŏn special economic zone and use them for 50 years. It will also build an airfield and a thermal power plant, as well as a 55-km railway track between the northeastern Chinese city of Tumen and Rasŏn. The two countries had reached an agreement in 2011 to build infrastructure with Chinese investment of about US$3 billion (Yonhap North Korea Newsletter No. 197, 16 Feb. 2012).The acceleration of the joint development of economic zones was the subject of an agreement between China and North Korea, signed in August 2012 by Chen Deming, the Chinese minister of commerce, and Jang Song Thaek for the DPRK. In addition to Rasŏn, a zone is to be developed on the islands of Hwanggŭmp'yŏng and Wihwa in the western section of the Yalu river. A certain division of labour between the two zones seems to be planned. The Rasŏn Economic and Trade Zone will focus on the development of raw materials, equipment, high-tech products, light industry, the service sector and modern agriculture. The Hwanggŭmp'yŏng and Wihwa Islands Economic Zone will focus on the development of the information industry, tourism, modern agriculture and garment manufacturing. The third meeting of the DPRK–China Joint Guidance Committee for the joint development and management of the Rasŏn Economic Trade Zone and Hwanggŭmp'yŏng and Wihwa Economic Zones, in mid-August, mapped out a master plan for developing the zones, and there was discussion of the transmission of electricity from China and of a number of infrastructure projects such as railroads and port facilities. The Rajin–Wŏnjŏng highway, originally a UN Development Progamme project,[17] was finally opened in October (KCNA, 26 October 2012). It was also reported that foreigners would from 2013 be allowed to own residential houses in the zone, that the Chinese yuan would be allowed to circulate freely, and that the establishment of both domestic and Chinese banking institutions in the zones would be permitted.

In late September, North Korea and China held an investment seminar in Beijing to promote Chinese investment opportunities in the DPRK's special economic zones. Reportedly, 43 projects were introduced. The Chinese ministry of commerce said it will actively encourage both domestic and foreign enterprises to invest in the North Korean economic zones. Chen Jian, vice-minister of commerce, was quoted as saying: 'We will support (such investment) with strength, willingness and sincerity. We will work together to create a better tomorrow for the economic and trade cooperation between China and the Democratic People's Republic of Korea' (Yonhap North Korea Newsletter No. 230, 4 October 2012).

An unusual case of investment occurred when Associated Press, a US news agency, formally opened a bureau in North Korea in January 2012, making it the first Western news organisation with a full-time presence in North Korea.

In an unexpected move, the Unification Church, based in South Korea, was said to be in the process of selling its joint auto-making venture with North Korea called P'yŏnghwa (Peace) Motors after a decade of operations. The background seems to be growing cooperation between North Korea and China in the automobile sector.

---

[17] For a project outline, see www.tumenprogramme.org/data/upload/download/Rajin-Wonjong%20Road%20Feasibility%20Study/Rajin-Wonjong%20Roa%20Feasibility%20Study.pdf.

The business is likely to be sold to the North Korean state (Yonhap North Korea Newsletter No. 238, 29 November 2012).

A major move for improved DPRK international economic relations was a debt adjustment pact the country signed with Russia in September. After years of negotiations, roughly US$10-11 billion, about 90 percent of outstanding North Korean debt from the Soviet era, was written off. The remaining 10 percent is to be invested in joint education, medical and energy projects in North Korea (KCNA, 18 September 2012).[18] Debts to Western countries remain unpaid.

9.2 *Education and sports*

The promotion of Kim Yong Jin, chairman of the Education Commission, to a vice-premier of the cabinet in January early on indicated a certain emphasis on education by the new leader. The unexpected second session of the North Korean parliament on 25 September approved as its main result the extension of compulsory education from 11 to 12 years. The goal was to improve and strengthen secondary general education and further consolidate the socialist education system 'to meet the requirements of the developing revolution and the times'. Importantly, the focus of the additional year is not on ideology, but on general basic knowledge and basic knowledge of modern technologies. In particular, the need to strengthen education in computer technology and foreign languages as well as in mathematics, physics, chemistry and biology was stressed. Knowledge is supposed to be applicable; teachers are supposed to use information technology. New and substantial educational methods are to be created, and tests will be developed to assess the abilities of the students. Educational institutions were asked to 'analyze and systematize scientifically and theoretically the new and advanced teaching methods and experience' (KCNA, 25 September 2012). The emphasis on applicability carries a faint reminder of a reform movement in the late Chosŏn dynasty, called *silhak* or 'practical learning'. The new leader seems to understand the need to develop human resources for the modernisation of the economy, and that ideology plays a still important but secondary

---

[18] See also Miriam Elder, 'Russia writes off $10bn of North Korean debt', *The Guardian*, 18 September 2012. Online: www.guardian.co.uk/business/2012/sep/18/russia-writes-off-north-korea-debt (accessed 29 May 2013).

role here. In a letter to two prestigious local schools (Mangyŏngdae Revolutionary School and Kang Pan-sok Revolutionary School) on the occasion of their 65th founding anniversary, Kim Jong Un in October stressed the importance of education in economic subjects, without however forgetting the need for a firm ideological training (KCNA, 13 October 2012).

During an expanded meeting of the politburo in November, it was decided to turn the DPRK 'into an economic power and sports power'. To this purpose, the State Physical Culture and Sports Guidance Commission would be inaugurated to 'control the overall sports work of the country in a unified manner' (KCNA, 4 November 2012). This is not necessarily extraordinary; other socialist countries had long before discovered sports as an important strategic field, and even in North Korea, related efforts had increased in the past years. What was remarkable, however, was the composition of the commission. It is headed by Jang Song Thaek, and the list of its vice-chairmen and other members reads like a who's who of the North Korean power hierarchy. It includes names such as Ro Tu Chol, Choe Pu Il, Ri Yong Su, Choe Thae Bok, Pak To Chun, Kim Yang Gon, Kim Yong Il, Kim Phyong Hae, Kwak Pom Gi, Pak Pong Ju and many others.

9.3 *Other developments*

Western media in August reported on lecture meetings held for each labour group, party cell and factory regarding the introduction of what was called the 'June 28 new economic management system'. The new scheme required factories and companies to independently produce and set prices and sales methods without state plans. In agriculture, the state would take 70 percent of what was produced from farmland, while the remaining 30 percent would go to farmers (Radio Free Asia, 9 August 2012). No official confirmation ever followed; going by previous experience, however, it cannot be excluded that indeed some measures were under preparation. In late August, analysts detected an increasing number of publications on monetary reform.

The slogan 'have your feet on your own ground but look out at the world' (*chagi ttange parŭl put'igo nunŭn segyerŭl pora*) had already been popular under Kim Jong Il (an example appeared in *Rodong*

Sinmun, for 1 September 2010).[19] During a number of public appearances, Kim Jong Un, too, stressed the need to catch up with global trends. His emphasis on international standards has been interpreted by South Korean analysts as yet another sign of the new leader's reform-oriented outlook. This impression was supported by the fact that the country's main newspaper, *Rodong Sinmun*, had increased the frequency of its economic reporting and also upgraded the visibility of related articles. In September, it carried a number of economy-related articles on its front page, in a hitherto unseen move (Yonhap North Korea Newsletters Nos 218, 220, and 228, 12 July, 26 July and 20 September 2012). A culinary nod to global tastes was the addition to already existing Western-type restaurants of a Viennese coffee shop, located at Kim Il Sung square right in the heart of Pyongyang.

10 Conclusion and outlook

In hindsight, the year 2012 witnessed a new leader who was much more active than originally expected. He quickly established himself as a public figure, shuffled positions in the various branches of the administration, adjusted ideology and its icons, and was fortunate enough to see the successful completion of major projects such as the construction of new apartments or the launch of a three-stage rocket. However, he has not yet shown his potential as a reformer. Despite the many new developments including his emphasis on the improvement of the living conditions of his people, an educational reform, and his more open public image, he has in many fields continued the policies of his predecessors. The logic of his political ambitions in combination with the systemic constraints of North Korea suggests that in 2013 the chances for substantial changes in the general direction of economic development are high.

[19] *Rodong Sinmun*, 1 September 2012. Online: www.rodong.rep.kp.

RELATIONS BETWEEN THE TWO KOREAS IN 2012

Sabine Burghart

1 INTRODUCTION

In 2012, relations between the Republic of Korea (ROK—South Korea) and the Democratic People's Republic of Korea (DPRK—North Korea) were marked by continuous flexing of rhetorical muscles and military provocations, but no deadly military clashes were reported. Both countries underwent leadership transitions,[1] but if optimists had hoped for a turning point in inter-Korean relations such hopes quickly faded away. The DPRK was focused on a smooth dynastic transition, and the transaction costs of a shift in policy were apparently perceived as too high. The DPRK leadership seemed confident that time would play into their hands: the South Korean president Lee Myung-bak had already entered the lame-duck period of his term and progressive political forces were gaining ground in the polls. Instead, both sides were trapped in a vicious cycle of defamation, accusations and provocations. Apart from the Kaesŏng Industrial Complex (KIC) and a few other small-scale projects, exchanges between the two sides remained frozen. For the first time in almost fifteen years, no North Korean citizen visited the South.[2] The ROK's inter-Korean co-operation fund was primarily used to support South Korean businesses, while humanitarian aid to vulnerable groups in the DPRK was further curtailed.

---

[1] To be more precise, the new president of the ROK was elected on 19 December 2012 and took office on 25 February 2013. However, the transition team of Park Geun-hye was able to exert influence on Saenuri lawmakers to support an increase in the annual budget of the ministry of unification (MOU).

[2] Compared to an average of 1,000 persons per year during the Roh Moo-hyun administration; from the ROK side, 110,116 persons travelled across the border in 2012, 99.8 percent of whom went to the KIC.

2 SLAMMING THE WINDOW OF (N)OPPORTUNITY

After the death of DPRK leader Kim Jong Il, some observers in the ROK saw an opportunity to 'reset' the policy towards the North. However, official statements by the two governments proved little conducive to a fresh start in inter-Korean relations. North Korea's major print media greeted the New Year with a joint editorial[3] that failed to carry any positive tone about relations with the South. Moreover, it included aggressive language against the Lee administration, calling it a 'group of traitors' (*yŏkchŏk p'aedang*) and the South Korean president a 'rat' (*Ri Myŏng Pak chwi saekki*).[4] The Saenuri Party was called a 'source of disaster' (*chaeang kŏri*) and of 'all misery' (*ongat pulhaeng*) for the Korean nation; even the party's chairwoman and presidential contender, Park Geun-hye, who had met Kim Jong Il in 2002, was not spared from verbal attacks.[5] ROK government officials did not hesitate to hit back; their rhetoric was much more subtle but carried a lot of criticism against the North Korean system and its (failed) policies. For example, the DPRK was openly criticised for spending a large amount of money on missile launches instead of improving the living conditions of the ordinary people. The need for agricultural reform in the North was also publicly addressed by ROK government officials. Lee expressed little understanding for the DPRK's decision to choose 'the path of isolation' and 'to prevent the current of change from flowing in'.[6] He called it 'an outdated way of thinking' and stressed that its provocative acts will put the North in 'greater danger'.[7] Lee also denounced the DPRK media's attempt to influence the elections in the South by dividing South Korean society. He stressed that the 'way for the North to survive is to voluntarily dismantle its nuclear weapons and to cooperate with the international

---

[3] Published by *Rodong Sinmun* (Workers' Party), *Chosŏn Inmingun* (People's Army) and *Ch'ŏngnyŏn Chŏnwi* (Youth League).

[4] Korea Central News Agency (KCNA), 23 April 2012. Online: www.kcna.co.jp/calendar/2012/04/04-23/2012-0423-035.html (accessed 15 May 2013).

[5] KCNA, 3 November 2012. Online: www.kcna.co.jp/calendar/2012/11/11-03/2012-1103-013.html (accessed 15 May 2013).

[6] See Ch'ŏngwadae, 2012, 'The way for the North to survive is to voluntarily dismantle its nuclear weapons and to cooperate with the international community through reform and open-door policies', Speeches, 16 April 2012. Online: http://english.president.go.kr/...vity/speeches/speeches_view.php?uno=6639&board_no=E03&search_key=&search_value=&search_cate_code=&cur_page_no=1 (accessed 4 May 2012).

[7] Ibid.

community through reform and open-door policies'.[8] In a rare move, President Lee in his New Year's speech explicitly addressed 'the brothers [and sisters] in the North' (*pungyŏk' tongp'o yŏrŏbun*) and emphasised that the 'window of opportunity [to restart inter-Korean dialogue] was open' (*urinŭn kihoiŭi ch'angŭl yŏrŏnok'o issŭmnida*).[9] However, what might have looked like extending an olive branch towards the North was little more than a repetition of previously stated invitations with conditional strings attached. The Lee administration did not move away from its demand that any rapprochement was on condition that the DPRK apologised for the sinking of the *Cheonan* (*Ch'ŏnan*) and the attack on Yeonpyong (Yŏnp'yŏng) island in 2010. Hence, this window of (n)opportunity remained unacceptable to the DPRK leadership. In the eyes of the latter there was little to gain and much to lose from engaging with an administration that was approaching the end of its term. Representatives of the Korean Workers' Party (KWP) were optimistic that 2012 would bring a change in political majorities and consequently a shift in policies in South Korea.[10] However, these hopes were disappointed after the parliamentary elections on 11 April 2012, in which the conservatives secured a (slim) majority of seats.[11] The fact that the liberal-progressive political forces, particularly the more radical United Progressive Party (UPP), had regained lost ground in terms of mandates prompted President Lee to warn against domestic pro-North Korea groups called 'chongbuk forces' (*chongbuk seryŏk*).[12] In a radio address, he considered them as 'more problematic' than North Korea (*uri naebuŭi chongbuk seryŏgŭn tŏ k'ŭn munje*).[13]

---

[8] Ibid.

[9] Ch'ŏngwadae, '2012 nyŏn sinnyŏn kukchŏng yŏnsŏl 'wigirŭl nŏmŏ hŭimangŭro' [2012 New Year's speech on state of affairs (in Korea) 'Overcoming the crisis with hope'], 1 January 2012. Online: www.president.go.kr/kr/president/news/news_view .php?uno=1725&article_no=367&board_no=P01&search_key=&search_value=&sear ch_cate_code=&order_key1=1&order_key2=1&cur_page_no=1&cur_year=2012&cu r_month= (accessed 2 January 2012).

[10] Personal conversation with the author in Pyongyang, November 2011.

[11] See the overview by Patrick Köllner on 'South Korea in 2012: politics, economy and social issues', Section 2, in this volume.

[12] In October 2012, the ROK ministry of defence defined pro-North Korean groups in the ROK as 'enemies' and 'anti-state organisations' and a 'malicious virus'. In 2010, the Supreme Court had defined the DPRK as an 'anti-state entity seeking to build a communist society in the South'.

[13] *Sŏul Sinmun*, 'Pukhan poda naebuŭi chongbuk seryŏki tŏ k'ŭn munje' [Compared to North Korea the domestic pro-North Korea forces are a bigger problem], 29 May 2012. Online: http://www.seoul.co.kr/news/newsView.php?id=20120529031010 &spage=19 (accessed 28 May 2013).

3 PLAYING WITH FIRE

Over the year verbal attacks, defamations and military provocations reached a new level of escalation. On several occasions the Lee administration stressed that it would 'strongly respond' to provocations from the North, but in practice it had already exhausted almost all non-military countermeasures ranging from resolutions to economic sanctions. The ROK's military defence capabilities and joint military drills with the United States (US) were expanded, both in quantity and quality.[14] The KIC was the last inter-Korean prestige project that, despite grievances, appeared to have withstood the deterioration in inter-Korean relations. Closing the KIC would have hurt the DPRK government; but it would have primarily hurt South Korean small- and medium-sized companies. There were no sticks left.

Neither side seemed willing to take a first step towards solving the impasse. Instead, both governments reconfirmed their non-negotiable positions and engaged in a vicious cycle of provocations.[15] The ROK government, on the one hand, strongly criticised the North's 'South Korea bashing' (*han'guk ttaerigi*).[16] Official language in the DPRK, on the other hand, put the responsibility for the deterioration in inter-Korean relations exclusively with the Lee administration.[17] In March, the DPRK's ministry of foreign affairs threatened a 'sacred war' andshortly afterwards declared that it was 'fully ready for both dia-

[14] See the overview by James E. Hoare on 'Foreign relations of the two Koreas in 2012', Section 1.1, in this volume.

[15] There were reports about electronic jamming signals allegedly coming from Kaesŏng that led to disruptions of GPS signals in civilian aeroplanes and ships. See *Chosun Ilbo*, 'N. Korea's GPS jamming is terrorism pure and simple', 11 May 2012. Online: http://english.chosun.com/site/data/html_dir/2012/05/11/2012051101175.html (accessed 29 May 2013).

[16] T'ongil yŏn'guwŏn, 'chinbuhan pukhanŭi taenampibang sŏnjŏn'gongseŭi paegyŏng: "choguk p'yŏnghwa t'ongilwiwŏnhoe sŏgiguk chinsanggobaljang" mun'gŏnŭl chungsimŭro' [Korea Institute for National Unification (KINU), 'The background to North Korea's outdated aggressive propaganda toward South Korea: focusing on the document "Truth indictment bill by the secretariat of the Committee for the Peaceful Unification of the Nation"'], Online Series 12-32, 7 August 2012, p.6.

[17] The DPRK adopted a 'Bill of truth indictment' (*chinsanggobaljang*) that accuses the South of being responsible for the deterioration in inter-Korean relations. The statement is based on four main arguments: (1) 'provocations against efforts to improve inter-Korean relations by denying the June 15 declaration and other actions', (2) 'provocations nurturing conflict between government administrations', (3) 'extremely dangerous military provocations', (4) 'egregious provocations against the supreme dignity'. In a reaction, a publication by KINU calls the claims and accusations by the DPRK a 'distortion of facts [based on] one-sided arguments' (*sasilgwan'gyeŭi waegok ddonŭn ilbangjŏk chujang*). KINU, 7 August 2012, p. 6.

logue and war'.[18] The tense atmosphere was further aggravated when the DPRK launched what it described as a rocket to put a satellite into orbit. The missile launch officially announced by the North constituted a violation of United Nations Security Council (UNSC) resolutions. If the DPRK leadership had hoped that their provocations would be conducive to a progressive win in the parliamentary elections, it was not well advised. The ROK government strongly condemned the (failed) satellite launch and the National Assembly adopted a resolution that warned the North against further provocative behaviour. The Lee administration lauded its own military capabilities and stressed that its 'cruise and ballistic missiles were capable of a precision strike on the window of Kim Jong Un's office in Pyongyang'.[19] The DPRK's reactions were prompt: the (North) Korean People's Army threatened to take 'special actions' (*t'ŭkpyŏl haengdong*), which were also directed against major (conservative) South Korean media and broadcasting stations accused of defaming the DPRK leadership. Loudspeakers in the streets of Pyongyang called for unconditional protection of the DPRK leadership and revenge against President Lee. The threats combined with the DPRK authorities' restricted information policy led to heightened nervousness among North Koreans.[20] In South Korea, several precautionary measures were taken and security tightened.

In an attempt to ease provocations ahead of the presidential elections, the Lee administration deployed policemen to the southern border area of the Demilitarised Zone (DMZ) to prevent human rights activists from sending balloons into DPRK territory. Shortly before, on 9 September, when the DPRK celebrated its national day, South Korean activists sent 200,000 balloons carrying leaflets, DVDs and one thousand US$1 bills into the North. According to media reports, for the first time in a decade, DPRK propaganda leaflets criticising the political leadership in the ROK and its 'anti-*chongbuk*' education were also found on the southern side of the DMZ.[21]

---

[18] Yonhap News Agency, 'South Korea urges North Korea to come forward for talks', 8 March 2012.

[19] KCNA, 23 April 2012; and Kim Kyu-wŏn, 'Seoul pledges retaliation to North Korea's threat to cancel armistice agreement', *Hankyoreh*, 7 March 2013. Online: www.hani.co.kr/arti/politics/politics_general/534880.html (accessed 8 May 2013).

[20] Based on the author's personal observations in Pyongyang in April 2012.

[21] Yonhap News Agency, 'North Korea resumes sending propaganda leaflets after 12-year break', 2 August 2012.

The presidential election campaign was in full swing in South Korea when the DPRK fired a second long-range missile to put the satellite Kwangmyŏngsŏng-3 into orbit in December. In a first reaction, Moon Jae-in, the presidential candidate fielded by the liberal-progressive camp, said that the missile launch constituted a clear violation of the UNSC resolution and that he firmly opposed North Korea's behaviour, which threatened peace on the Korean peninsula. In the same breath, Moon criticised the conservatives for misusing important security issues in the election campaign.[22] Park Geun-hye strongly denounced the North's missile launch as a provocative attempt to influence the presidential election; she expressed confidence that this kind of behaviour would 'not shake the South Korean people'.[23] President Lee's successor also announced a more flexible policy towards the North.

Table 1 Comparative statistics of Lee Myung-bak administration's policy towards the North and that of Roh Moo-hyun administration

	Lee government	Roh government
Total inter-Korean trade (US$)	8.94 billion	5.62 billion
KIC (US$)	6.695 billion	957 million
Number of authorised ROK companies doing business with the DPRK	108	370
Number of cultural exchanges with DPRK approved	5	121
Total humanitarian assistance (public and private) provided to DPRK (in US$)	227.9 million	1.13 billion
Number of North Korean defectors arriving in the ROK	12,350	9,130
Number of reunited family members	1,774	14,600

Source: IFES, NK Brief, 23 January 2013 and Ministry of Unification, 'Data and statistics'.[24]

---

[22] *Chosŏn Ilbo*, 'Mun Jae-in "Puk rok'et palsa, anbori kyŏlŭi wiban … tanhohi pandae"' [Moon Jae-in 'firm opposition against North (Korea)'s rocket launch, violation of SC resolution'], 12 December 2012. Online: http://news.chosun.com/site/data/html_dir/2012/12/12/2012121201643.html (accessed 29 May 2013).

[23] *Chosŏn Ilbo*, 'Pak Kŭn-hye "puk, taesŏn ap'tugo paslbŏdungch'yŏdo kungmin hŭndŭlliji anhŭl kŏt"' [Park Geun-hye 'North (Korea), with the presidential elections ahead the people will not be shaken even if North Korea is restless'], 12 December 201. Online: http://news.chosun.com/site/data/html_dir/2012/12/12/2012121201233.html (accessed 29 May 2013).

[24] Ministry of Unification, 'Data and statistics'. Online: http://eng.unikorea.go.kr/CmsWeb/viewPage.req?idx=PG0000000541 (accessed 2 May 2013).

Table 1 gives an overview of the outcome of the Lee administration's policy towards the North compared with that of the Roh Moo-hyun government in terms of economic, humanitarian and social exchanges with the DPRK.[25]

4 Searching for a new North policy: old wine in new bottles?

It seemed that the Lee administration's 'principled' North policy (the term chosen by the government), labelled a 'policy of mutual benefits and common prosperity', was tangled up in a multitude of conditional strings: a precondition for discussing further exchanges and food aid was the resumption of inter-Korean dialogue; however, the South would have only agreed on higher-level talks if the DPRK had officially apologised for the *Cheonan* sinking and the Yeonpyeong shelling; the North's apology would have also led to a lifting of the 5.24 measures.[26] The DPRK, on the other hand, first demanded an apology for not having sent an official delegation to the funeral of the North Korean leader and a withdrawal of sanctions before it would agree to any meeting with the South.

To solve this deadlock, a study by the Hyundai Research Institute called for a 'flexible policy' towards the North and recommended that the ROK government should engage in 'more forward-looking talks' with the North. During the election campaigns in the South, the political parties presented what they believed an appropriate North policy (*taebuk chŏngch'aek*). The conservative Saenuri Party under Park's leadership pledged to pursue a more 'flexible North policy' (*yuyŏnhan taebuk chŏngch'aek*)[27] integrated in a 'trust process' to normalise relations with the North. A closer look at the party's basic policy document reveals calls for the initiation of confidence-building measures in the field of politics and the military and for a 'comprehensive

[25] Based on IFES, 'A Review of the last five years of People-to-people exchanges and inter-Korean economic cooperation under the Lee Myung-bak government', NK Brief, 23 January 2013.

[26] On 5 January 2012, Yu Woo-ik, ROK minister of unification, re-confirmed that the ROK government had no intention of lifting the 5.24 measures, imposed in reaction to the *Cheonan* incident of 26 March 2010. The measures had the effect of suspending and curtailing inter-Korean co-operation and exchanges.

[27] *Kyŏnghyang Sinmun*, 6 April 2012, p.5.

strengthening of defence capabilities' and 'deterrence assets'.[28] Central issues such as the repatriation of abducted South Koreans, POWs and their families as well as the adoption of a North Korean human rights law remain of 'highest priority'.[29] The pledges made by Park Geun-hye regarding humanitarian assistance point at a continuation of the current practice. Park announced that the inter-Korean co-operation fund would be increased under her presidency, but transparency of aid deliveries (i.e. strict monitoring), limitation of assistance to the most vulnerable groups in society, and provision of assistance through multilateral organisations such as the World Food Programme, UNICEF, etc., would be continued. In an attempt to show more flexibility Saenuri chairman Hwang Woo-yea urged the ROK government to consider the resumption of flood aid to North Korea after typhoon Bolaven had devastated large parts of the peninsula.[30] The North policy emerging from the Liberty Forward Party (LFP, *chayusŏnjindang*) demanded a firm response to North Korean military provocations and emphasised the investigation and improvement of human rights conditions in the DPRK, as well as strengthening monitoring humanitarian aid. In contrast, the Democratic United Party (DUP, *minjut'onghapdang*) pledged to stick to and fulfil the 6.15 Joint Declaration and the 10.4 Declaration[31] as well as holding regular summit meetings. In addition, the progressives promised to abolish the 5.24 measures and to resume Mt Kŭmgang tourism. The radical UPP went much further and proposed a kind of package deal consisting of denuclearisation, a peace treaty and the establishment of diplomatic relations between the DPRK and the US. Furthermore, the party

---

[28] Saenuri Party: '*Trustpolitik* and a new Korea: foreign affairs, national security, and unification policies', November 2012. Online: www.saenuriparty.kr/web/eng/gnpPolicy/readPolicyView.do?bbsId=EBD_000000000358109 (accessed 28 April 2013).

[29] Ibid.

[30] According to DPRK media reports, Bolaven killed about fifty persons and injured many more; about 7,000 houses were reportedly destroyed by the typhoon.

[31] The 6.15 Joint Declaration was the outcome of the first inter-Korean summit between Kim Dae-jung and Kim Jong Il in 2000. Both sides agreed to solve the issue of unification on their own (i.e. independently from external powers), to promote unification towards some form of (con)federation, to resolve humanitarian issues (particularly, the reunion of families and political prisoners in the ROK), and to support inter-Korean economic co-operation and exchanges in various fields. The second summit agreement reached by Roh Moo-hyun and Kim Jong-il in October 2007 was much more detailed. The 'Declaration on the advancement of South-North Korean relations, peace and prosperity' included concrete objectives and actions such as establishing a peace regime, expanding inter-Korean economic co-operation and establishing a 'special peace and cooperation zone' in the West (or Yellow) Sea.

pledged that it would suspend the ROK–US military drills, abolish the Proliferation Security Initiative, immediately remove the 5.24 measures, and resume family reunions.[32]

With regard to the new (old) majorities in the ROK's National Assembly, informed observers in South Korea suggested that under a conservative government chances for bipartisan support of a more flexible policy would be higher. The progressive minority would be likely to support (at least it could not block) even small steps towards rapprochement. Such a situation would pre-empt paralysis in the legislative process. By contrast, things would be different under a progressive president facing a conservative majority in the legislature. DPRK officials, however, seemed less optimistic about the renewal of conservative rule in the South. In a personal conversation with the author in Pyongyang, a representative of the international department of the KWP Central Committee expressed both dissatisfaction and concern about what a continuation of conservative politics in the ROK would bring. In his view, a victory by the Saenuri Party would mean gloomy prospects for inter-Korean relations.

Probably in an attempt to tailor its North policy, analysts of the ROK ministry of unification completed a two-year development project of a so-called North Korea condition index (*pukhan chŏngse chisu*) that can measure levels of (in)stability in North Korea. At the time of writing neither the methodology nor the index itself have yet been made public, with reasons of sensitivity and accuracy cited. What can be learned from media reports is that the North Korea condition index is a 100-point scale index that analyses three key variables—risk of instability, regime change, and crisis at the political, economic, social and military level.[33]

5 Economic exchanges

ROK statistics show that after a drop in 2011, inter-Korean economic exchanges increased by 15 percent in 2012 to the level of 2010 (see

[32] Based on *Kyŏnghyang Sinmun*, 6 April 2012, p. 5.

[33] Yonhap News Agency, 'Pukhan puran chŏngsŏng, ch'aejae pyŏnhwa, wigisujun ch'ŭkchŏnghanda' [Measuring North Korea's instability, change of system, level of crisis], 29 January 2013. Online: www.yonhapnews.co.kr/bulletin/2013/01/29/0200000000AKR20130129106700043.HTML (accessed 15 February 2013).

Table 2). The trade volume increased and reached almost US$2 billion in 2012, compared to US$1.7 billion in 2011.[34]

Table 2 Inter-Korean trade (2001–2012) (in US$ million)

Year	2001	2002	2003	2004	2005	2006
KIC	-	-	-	41.7	176.7	298.8
Other trade	403.0	641.7	724.2	655.3	879.1	1,050.9
Total trade	403.0	641.7	724.2	697.0	1,055.8	1,349.7

Year	2007	2008	2009	2010	2011	2012
KIC	440.7	808.4	940.6	1,442.9	1,697.6	1,961
Other trade	1,357.2	1,012.0	538.5	469.4	16.3	1.0
Total trade	1,797.9	1,820.4	1,679.1	1,912.3	1,713.9	1,971

Source: Ministry of Unification, 'Data and statistics'.

While other inter-Korean trade almost diminished, it seemed that the KIC would be able thus far to withstand the political and military tensions on the Korean peninsula. In 2012, production output at the KIC increased by 17.5 percent to an estimated US$470 million.[35] Contrary to other South Korean small and medium enterprises (SMEs), KIC companies were not directly affected by the 5.24 measures that paralysed or interrupted most other inter-Korean business projects. They were doing relatively well: they had moved up to black (from def-icit) and reported for the first time an operating profit averaging US$50,000. The annual wage increases of 5 percent for the 53,448 North Korean workers had meanwhile become institutionalised. However, new demands by the DPRK authorities cast a cloud of troubles over the joint economic zone: the KIC Management Council representing the South Korean SMEs was informed about new tax by-laws for tax fraud as well as additional taxes such as corporate income tax, sales tax and others.[36] KIC companies were also obliged to provide all kinds of internal documents about the costs of raw materials used,

[34] Ministry of Unification, 'Data and statistics', accessed 5 May 2013.

[35] Yonhap News Agency, 'Output from Kaesong complex jumps 17.5 pct on-year in 2012', 10 January 2013.

[36] Amendments or a partial revision of bylaws require agreement between the North's Central Special Direct General Bureau (chungang t'ŭkku kaebal chido ch'ongguk) and the Kaesong Management Council. Hence, any unilateral amendment of a by-law constitutes a violation of the Kaesong Industrial District Law.

financial transactions and so on to the DPRK authorities. In a letter of protest the council called the new rules 'excessive' and one entrepreneur was quoted as saying that 'we have to expose our business secrets, which is hard to accept'.[37] A few weeks later, the DPRK unilaterally imposed additional taxes on eight out of the 123 companies operating at the KIC.

Not only the KIC but also the Mt Kŭmgang resort was faced with new tax regulations.[38] (The resort has been closed to visitors from the South since a South Korean tourist was shot dead by a North Korean guard when entering a restricted area in July 2008.) These regulations are part of the 'Law on Mount Kŭmgang Special Tourism Zone' (*Kŭmgangsan kukche kwan'gwang t'ŭkku pŏp*), which was passed in 2011.[39] The DPRK authorities also included a clause regarding the safety of tourists and opened the resort to international (mainly Chinese) tourists, which was considered a violation of the exclusive rights of Hyundai Asan, the South Korean tour operator.

On the 14th anniversary of the opening of the tourist resort a ceremony attended by Hyundai Asan President Kim Jong-hag and DPRK officials was held. But there was little to celebrate: for Hyundai Asan and the ROK government, the suspension of the tours has resulted in financial losses of about US$1.6 billion.[40] Although neither delegation was in a position to negotiate, both sides agreed to take the necessary steps for the resumption of tours 'if chances are offered in the future'.[41] Local governments in Kangwŏn province were also affected by the suspension of the tours resulting in a decrease of 12.5 percent in tax revenues.

---

[37] Yonhap News Agency, 'Kaesong park firms protest against N. Korea's fine raise', 20 September 2012.

[38] According to media reports, the presidium of the DPRK Supreme People's Assembly adopted the regulations in June 2012. See IFES, NK Brief, 'North Korea enacts new tax regulations in Mt Kŭmgang Tourist Zone', 21 March 2013. Online: http://ifes.kyungnam.ac.kr/eng/FRM/FRM_0101V.aspx?code=FRM130321_0001 (accessed 22 March 2013).

[39] For further details see Sabine Burghart, 'Relations between the two Koreas in 2011', *Korea: Politics, Economics and Society 2012*, p. 74.

[40] The sum is based on an estimated 2.56 million tourists who would have visited the resort in the past four years.

[41] Yonhap News Agency, 'Seoul urges N. Korea to end tours for foreigners to Mount Kumgang', 22 November 2012.

6 Humanitarian aid and exchanges

The year 2012 saw a further drop in both public and private humanitarian aid to the DPRK. As Table 3 shows, humanitarian aid provided by the ROK government and NGOs amounted to US$2.1 million and US$10.9 million respectively. Overall, humanitarian aid reached its lowest amount within 16 years: under the Lee administration, total aid amounted to US$220 million, which constitutes about 20 percent of the funds provided by the previous progressive governments.[42]

Table 3 Overview of humanitarian aid provision (in US$ million)

	2007	2008	2009	2010	2011	2012
Government aid	208.9	39.9	24.2	17.8	5.7	2.1
Non-governmental aid	95.7	64.7	28.6	17.5	11.7	10.9
Total aid	304.6	104.6	52.8	35.3	17.4	13.0

Source: Ministry of Unification, 'Data and statistics', May 2013.

Similarly to previous years, about US$65.2 million or less than 10 percent of the budget annually earmarked for the inter-Korean co-operation fund was spent for inter-Korean projects. Most of the money was allocated to South Korean businesses, particularly for construction projects and in form of financial subsidies for domestic companies; about US$2 million (3 percent) were spent for humanitarian aid projects in the DPRK.

Regarding direct aid, the ROK government offered rice shipments to the DPRK on condition that the latter apologised for the two deadly attacks in 2010, but the North did not respond.[43] In addition, the Lee administration provided funds for multilateral and international organisations including UNICEF and the International Vaccine Institute. The latter received US$2.1 million for an encephalitis vaccination programme targeting North Korean children that had been suspended for several months. Moreover, after a two-year interruption due to

[42] See also IFES, NK Brief, 'Lee Myung Bak administration sets lowest record for assistance to North Korea', 31 January 2013.

[43] Not all aid comes in form of grants. Between 2000 and 2007, the ROK governments provided loans of rice and corn to the DPRK, totalling US$720 million. The first repayment instalment was due in June 2012 (about US$5.8 million), but the DPRK failed to repay.

political tensions a hepatitis B vaccination programme funded by the ROK (US$2.37 million) and run by Caritas Germany, in which 3.7 million North Korean children were involved, was completed.

As Table 3 shows, non-governmental aid constituted the larger share of the total aid but it has also been decreasing over the past years. The ROK authorities adopted stricter criteria of eligibility on humanitarian projects and further limited the items that were authorised for sending to the North. While medical supplies, vaccines, infant nutrition, powdered milk, soy milk and flour were included in the list rice, fertiliser or construction materials did not receive the necessary government clearance. For example, the Korea Peace Foundation was authorised to send 180 tons of flour to a primary school and a day care centre in Kaesŏng. Furthermore, X-ray equipment and tuberculosis-related medicines worth US$70,000 provided by Nanum International and the Eugene Bell Foundation also received the necessary clearance by the MOU. Several South Korean NGOs criticised the increased governmental scrutiny in the selection of projects. Particularly after typhoon Bolaven had hit the Korean peninsula causing considerable damage in the North, the provision of emergency aid was hampered by 'excessive red tape' set up by the ROK government. Aid deliveries from South Korean civil organisations were only authorised on condition that the DPRK authorities could provide a comprehensive distribution plan. However, as a representative of World Vision put it, 'requiring a distribution plan in a flood relief aid case cannot help fulfil the purpose of emergency assistance'.[44] In September 2012, World Vision and the Korea NGO Council for Cooperation with North Korea (KNCCK, *taebuk hyŏmnyŏk min'gan tanch'e hyŏbŭihoe*) each sent 500 tons of flour (worth about US$230 million). Faced with increasing administrative hurdles imposed by the ROK authorities, more and more civil organisations decided to send their aid through an intermediate organisation. For example, the South Korean National Council of Churches provided 153 tons of flour via the Chinese Amity Foundation to its North Korean counterpart, the DPRK's Christian Federation.

The drop in humanitarian aid was not only a result of administrative restrictions and a reduced provision of matching funds from the inter-Korean co-operation fund; the DPRK government also contributed to the decrease by refusing to accept certain forms of aid or dis-

---

44 Quoted in *Korea Times*, 'Saenuri party leader calls for Bolaven aid to North Korea', 5 September 2012, p. 4.

tribution modalities. For example, the South's offer to send flood aid in the form of flour, instant noodles and medicine worth US$8.9 million was declined.[45] The issue of monitoring continued to be a bone of contention between South Korean NGOs and DPRK authorities. Opposition lawmakers criticised both the Lee administration for unilaterally deciding on the needs of the DPRK people, and the DPRK government for not accepting flood aid.[46]

With regard to humanitarian exchanges between the two Koreas, particularly the reunions of separated families, no progress was achieved in 2012. The proposal by the South to hold Red Cross talks was rejected by the North, which demanded an apology over the South's failure to send an official government delegation to attend the funeral of Kim Jong Il.

7 Defectors: Exclusionary Integration?

A high unemployment rate and an increase in reported illegal activities among the almost 25,000 North Korean defectors (*pukhan it'aljumin*)[47] who had entered the South up until 2012 have prompted the ROK government to review its resettlement policy. The publicly subsidised programmes that constitute half of the MOU's annual budget have proved insufficient and ineffective when it comes to the inclusion of this marginalised group into South Korean society in general, and the labour market in particular.[48] A survey conducted by the North Korean Refugees Foundation (*pukhan it'aljumin chiwŏn chaedan*) revealed that more than 30 percent of the interviewees earn less than US$900 per month (compared to an average US$2,430 for ROK (male) employees).[49] The unemployment rate among North Ko-

[45] Yonhap News Agency, 'South aid groups to send flour aid to North Korea this week', 20 September 2012.

[46] *Korea Times*, 'Opposition slams gov't over NK's refusal to accept flood aid', 13 September 2012, p. 2.

[47] According to the act on the protection and settlement support of residents escaping from North Korea, the correct term for North Korean defectors is *pukhan it'aljumin*, literally 'citizens who have escaped from North Korea'.

[48] Yonhap News Agency, 'Gov't overhauls subsidies for NK defectors', 16 September 2012.

[49] In South Korea, women earn on average 30 percent less than their male colleagues because of wage discrimination. ROK Ministry of Employment and Labour, 'Major Statistics'. Online: www.moel.go.kr/english/statistics/major_stati stics.jsp (accessed 18 May 2013).

rean defectors is reported to be three times higher compared to the South Korean working population, 12.1 percent versus 3.7 percent. Although the ROK government provides financial incentives for companies that employ defectors,[50] these turn out to be only a temporary solution. Once public subsidies stop, most employers fire their North Korea-born workers. This leads to a situation in which the defectors stay ten months on average in the same job.

Despite these poor outcomes, especially in the improvement of capacities among North Korean defectors, the ROK ministry of finance and strategy announced an increase in the settlement fund. The new regulation that comes into effect in 2013 provides a 5.5 percent increase in the US$17,000 of basic settlement subsidy. In addition, the South Korean government plans to provide financial incentives in the form of a one-time payment of US$19,000 to those persons who integrate 'smoothly'.[51] This decision can also be seen as a response to the criticisms of defector organisations that public subsidies for the reset

Table 4 Number of DPRK defectors entering the ROK

	Until 1998	1999–2001	2002	2003	2004	2005
Female	116	479	632	810	1,272	959
Male	831	565	511	472	624	423
Share of females (in percent)	12.2	45.9	55.3	63.2	67.1	69.4
Total	947	1,044	1,143	1,282	1,896	1,382

	2006	2007	2008	2009	2010	2011	2012
Female	1,510	1,977	2,196	2,258	1,813	1,909	1,107
Male	512	571	608	671	589	797	402
Share of females (in percent)	74.7	77.6	78.3	77.1	75.5	70.5	73.4
Total	2,022	2,548	2,804	2,929	2,402	2,709	1,509

Source: Ministry of Unification, 'Data and statistics', May 2013.

[50] Usually half of the wages are paid from public funds.

[51] Yonhap News Agency, 'Gov't marks up settlement fund for N. Korean escapees', 9 January 2013. Apart from the MOU's budget, other government agencies provide additional resources to support the resettlement of defectors, among them the ministries of health and welfare, public administration and security, and gender equality and family, and regional municipalities, 'pushing the total amount to an uncalculated figure' (Yonhap News Agency, 16 September 2012).

tlement of refugees are often not reaching the target group. Instead, the money benefits a relatively new branch of business composed of several intermediary organisations and agents that have mushroomed in the last years; some of them are criticised for providing unsustainable assistance or conducting 'redundant research projects'.[52]

In 2012, the number of North Korean defectors dropped by almost half to 1,509 persons, down from 2,706 persons in 2011. This represents the lowest number in seven years, and one can only speculate about the reasons. Some observers point to tighter border controls at the DPRK–China border, while others suggest that an increasing number of North Koreans is more likely to take the risk and settle down in China rather than taking the dangerous 'underground railway' to the South. The majority of defectors continue to be female, and this situation has prompted the ROK authorities to adopt a gender-based approach to provide better tailored programmes. While the first resettlement education centre Hanawŏn in Kyŏnggi province will host only young and female defectors, in the future male defectors will be accommodated in a new facility. The second resettlement centre, providing space for 500 men, has been opened in Hwach'ŏn-gun in Kangwŏn province. Moreover, the Seoul education office has also announced the establishment of a public school exclusively for North Korean defectors.

8 Outlook

Few observers doubt that it was a strategic mistake by the Lee administration to withdraw from inter-Korean business projects and to impose conditions on the DPRK that the latter would hardly accept. However, the DPRK leadership has done little to ease the tensions on the Korean peninsula and beyond. On the contrary, abuse, verbal threats and military provocations continued, leaving no chance for improving relations. Even the last remaining and most successful economic inter-Korean project, the KIC, was put in jeopardy by the DPRK's violation of the Kaesong Industrial District Law.[53]

[52] Yonhap News Agency, 'N. Korean defectors suffer from inefficient state support programs', 16 September 2012.

[53] At the time of writing in May 2013, the KIC was closed; North Korean workers and South Korean managers withdrew from the complex and production stopped.

In the current situation it seems an almost impossible task to engage seriously in dialogue and start a cool-headed phase of trust-building. It remains to be seen whether a more flexible North policy or—as termed by Park Geun-hye—*trustpolitik* can bear fruit in the foreseeable future. A radical reappraisal of the ROK government's policy towards the North is not to be expected, and the extent to which the new administration will be willing (and able) to implement the 6.15 and the 10.4 summit declarations is difficult to predict. Nevertheless, in anticipation of improved inter-Korean ties the National Assembly approved the presidential transition team's increase in the inter-Korean co-operation fund and the MOU's budget by about 10 and 5 percent respectively. Behind the political scene there are moves towards exploring new business opportunities in the DPRK. Informed observers suggest that some of the largest South Korean companies are making preparations to engage in joint ventures with the North as soon as the political situation allows. In practice, this would mean first and foremost a removal of the 5.24 measures.

In 2013, both countries are going to commemorate the 60th anniversary of the end of the Korean War and the signing of the armistice agreement. There are hopes that these events may provide new opportunities for a rapprochement between the Koreas.

FOREIGN RELATIONS OF THE TWO KOREAS IN 2012

James E. Hoare

1 INTRODUCTION

This was the year of successions. The Democratic People's Republic of Korea (DPRK—North Korea) jumped the gun, with Kim Jong Il's death in December 2011 and the succession of his youngest son, Kim Jong Un. In the Republic of Korea (ROK—South Korea), the presidential election began to cast its shadow well before Park Geun-hye's election as the country's first female head of state in December. Further afield, new leaders in China, Russia and Japan, and the return of United States President Barak Obama for a second term, all had implications for the peninsula and for the foreign policies of the two Koreas. And if there were no major changes in 2012, there were signs that there might be some in 2013.

2 REPUBLIC OF KOREA

2.1 *Relations with the United States*

ROK President Lee Myung-bak continued the active commitment to good relations with the United States (US) that had been a characteristic feature of his presidency. He prided himself on having repaired the damage to the relationship that he believed had been caused by his immediate predecessors. He hosted the Second Nuclear Security Summit in March (see Section 1.4) and had several meetings during it with US President Obama, who was making his third visit to the ROK. As always, the personal chemistry between the two presidents seemed to be good, and it was clear that they saw eye to eye on most matters, especially where the DPRK was concerned. Also in March, the long-delayed ROK–US Free Trade Agreement (FTA) came into force. Under its terms, 80 percent of existing tariffs were to be abolished immediately, and 95 percent within five years. In both countries, however, opposition remained from groups that thought their interests would suffer under the new arrangements. In the ROK, the main protests came from farmers, despite government pledges of financial support for those affected. For a time, some opposition politicians said that they would jettison the agreement if elected, a somewhat illogical stand since the negotiations for it had begun under President Roh Myoo-hyun and some of those involved had helped negotiate the original agreement. Farmers in the US also protested, arguing that much of the ROK's agriculture remains protected. US automobile makers continued to express concern at increased competition from ROK manufacturers. In the event, ROK–US trade, which had breached the US$100 billion level in 2011, saw a relatively small rise in 2012 to US$101.3 billion, with the balance of trade continuing heavily in favour of the ROK. US agricultural products did particularly well.[1] No doubt complaints will continue but the incoming ROK president, Park Geun-hye, is strongly in favour of the FTA and is unlikely to support any attempts at renegotiation. There was a brief flurry over the safety of US beef in May, but it soon passed. As well as competing for mobile telephone and tablet users, the ROK's Samsung Group and the US computer giant fought each other in the courts of several countries over alleged Samsung infringements of Apple patents. Apple won in the US, although an appeal is likely, while Samsung was successful in Japan, the United Kingdom and the ROK.

As usual, the year saw a regular series of ROK–US military exercises, beginning with a joint submarine exercise in the Yellow Sea in February, and continuing with Key Resolve/Foal Eagle from the end of February until the end of April, Max Thunder, an air exercise, in May, a joint ROK–Japan–US exercise in June, and Ulchi Freedom in August. These were of course defensive in nature but one can perhaps understand that the DPRK did not see it that way. Despite the reassurances provided by such exercises, the ROK remained worried that the 2011 re-ordering of US international priorities (the pivot to Asia) meant less commitment to defending the ROK. The US agreed in October to an increase in the ROK's missile capability, which may provide some form of reassurance. As ROK–Japan exchanges over the

[1] Statistics from the US Census Bureau: International Trade. Online: www.census.gov/foreign-trade/balance/c5800.html#2012 (accessed 25 May 2013).

Tokto/Takeshima issue became sharper in the course of the year (see Section 1.3), the US kept resolutely out of the quarrel, just as it tried to avoid being drawn into other Asian territorial disputes.

On the whole, the election of the conservative Park Geun-hye will have served to still US apprehensions over ROK policies. There may well be some concern, nevertheless, that President Park's wish to improve relations with the DPRK, as indicated in her election manifesto, might lead to differences of approach and emphasis between the two sides.

2.2 *Relations with China*

Relations with China were up and down. China is a major neighbour and an important regional power. It is of great economic importance to the ROK and is also seen as the one country able to exert influence on the DPRK. That it does not do so in the way that the ROK wants is a source of much angst. There is also concern about China's long-term intentions on the peninsula, although this has receded somewhat, at least in public statements. China's refusal to stop returning DPRK refugees and clashes over fishing added to the frustration.

The year began with President Lee's state visit to China to mark the 20th anniversary of the establishment of diplomatic relations. Coming soon after Kim Jong Il's death in December, it will also have provided a welcome opportunity for Lee to discuss with Chinese President Hu Jintao prospects for the DPRK under the new and untested leadership of Kim Jong Un and the implications for the ROK. The two presidents were able to hold further discussions in the margins of the March nuclear summit in Seoul, and met at a number of other meetings during the year. A number of bilateral and multi-lateral meetings brought together the ROK and Chinese foreign and trade ministers, there were defence minister meetings, and the first-ever visit by a Chinese minister of public security took place in July. The minister, Meng Jianzu, held discussions on immigration and consular issues, which may have included the treatment of DPRK refugees, and he opened a Chinese consulate on Cheju island. In an apparent goodwill gesture to mark the visit, the Chinese released the South Korean former student activist turned anti-North Korean campaigner, Kim Young-hwan, who had been in detention in the border city of Dandong since March.[2]

Trade with China dropped back 2.5 percent on 2011's figures, which had shown a rise of 17 percent on 2010. The reason was sluggish trade worldwide. Chinese goods using South Korean components found it harder to secure markets. Total trade was US$215 billion, with the balance heavily in the ROK's favour. ROK exports were $134.3 billion, and imports $80.7 billion.[3] During the year, talks began both on a bilateral free trade agreement and on a trilateral China–Japan–ROK trade agreement, although these were complicated by the growing territorial dispute between China and Japan over the Senkaku/Daiyutai islands. Total ROK investment in China reached $524 billion, while Chinese investment in the ROK was about one billion dollars. The ROK is the seventh largest foreign investor in China and its investments continue to grow. Wang Chao, the Chinese deputy minister of commerce, visited in November, seeking to increase ROK investment even further. Tourism between the two countries continues to grow, with the number of Chinese visitors to the ROK rising faster than those from any other country.

All this indicated that at some levels, links between the two countries were in good shape after twenty years of diplomatic relations. Yet there were problems. Often-expressed ROK government hopes that China would exercise its influence over the DPRK proved unfulfilled once more. China's leaders made clear that they were not happy with many aspects of DPRK behaviour, and appeared willing to join in the drawing up of the additional United Nations' sanctions that were imposed after the failed April and successful December rocket launches; a Chinese official was a member of the UN body monitoring the sanctions. They regularly expressed the wish that the DPRK would return to the Six Party Talks on denuclearisation. The authorities did not stop think-tanks and some newspapers from speculating about whether close Chinese relations with the DPRK were good or bad for China. While it may have a long way to go in Western eyes, China is a

---

[2] If Kim's release had been a positive gesture, some of the shine was taken off it by his allegations that he had been tortured while in detention and by an ROK demand for an investigation. *New York Times*, 26 August 2012, p. A5. See www.nytimes.com/2012/08/24/world/asia/korean-activist-kim-young-hwan-ex-supporter-of-north-plots-his-next-move.html?pagewanted=all&_r=0 (accessed 26 May 2013).

[3] Trade figs accessed 26 May 2013 from www.mofat.go.kr/ENG/policy/bilateral/asiapacific/index.jsp?menu=m_20_140_10.

society now much more tolerant about the discussion of dissenting ideas—within limits. The mistake is to think that such discussion indicates a change of policy. The Chinese did not do agree, however, that isolating the DPRK was a good policy and they appeared to do little to implement the sanctions, to the frustration of the ROK, the US and other countries that hoped for more robust Chinese action. Instead, Chinese trade and investment in the DPRK continued, apparently without any problems. As the detention of Kim Young-hwan and others showed, the Chinese authorities were not very pleased at anti-DPRK activities along their borders and they continued to track down and send back those caught fleeing from the DPRK, despite pleas from the ROK, other governments and human rights' groups for a change of policy.

Then there were the fishing disputes in the Yellow (West) Sea. The Chinese captain who killed a South Korean coastguard during a clash in December 2011[4] went on trial in Inch'ŏn in April. He received a 30-year sentence and was fined 20 million won (US$17,600). Chinese vessels continued to intrude in ROK waters, however, and there were several incidents in the course of the year, including one in October in which the ROK coastguards fired rubber bullets and killed a Chinese sailor. While there are periodic apologies, each side accuses the other of excessive force, and such clashes seem likely to continue as the demand for seafood continues to grow, sustained by increased Chinese wealth.

2.3 *Relations with Japan*

History continued to complicate ROK–Japan relations all through the year. In January, Japan asserted its claim to Tokto/Takeshima, the island group in the East Sea claimed by both Koreas as Korean and by Japan, and reiterated its assertion in one form or another throughout the year.[5] As noted above, there were meetings involving China, Japan and the ROK to discuss both security and trade matters, but there was

[4] See James E. Hoare, 'Foreign relations of the two Koreas in 2011', in: *Korea: Politics, Economy and Society 2011*, p. 85.

[5] Background can be found in James E. Hoare, 'Foreign relations of the two Koreas', in: *Korea Yearbook 2008: Politics, Economy and Society*, p. 62, footnote 5b. Later in August 2012, the Japanese government proposed referring the issue to the International Court of Justice. The ROK rejected the proposal.

little progress. A proposed agreement between the ROK and Japan that would have allowed the sharing of classified military secrets, and which had the backing of President Lee Myung-bak, collapsed in the face of parliamentary opposition at the end of June just before it was due to be signed. The president was accused of being pro-Japanese and a traitor like those who agreed to the 1910 annexation treaty that ended Korea's independence. As a consequence, Kim Tae-hyo, senior secretary for national security strategy in the Blue House, who was widely regarded as the architect of the agreement, was forced to resign.

Thereafter, as the year went on and as Lee Myung-bak neared the end of his presidency, he played the history card. Lee laid much stress on the plight of the ageing 'comfort women', the term used for women who were forced into prostitution during World War II, in his address on 1 March, the anniversary of the 1919 uprising against Japan, and it was a theme that he returned to several times in the course of the year. On 8 August, he became the first-ever ROK president to visit Tokto; Japan recalled its ambassador in protest. A week later, on 15 August, the anniversary of Japan's surrender in 1945, which is celebrated as liberation day in both Koreas, Lee dismissed the possibility of a visit by the Japanese emperor unless he 'sincerely apologised' to the families of 'deceased independence fighters'.[6] Also on 15 August, the ROK government protested at the proposed visit by two Japanese cabinet ministers to Tokyo's Yasukuni Shrine, which honours Japanese war dead including some of those convicted at the International Military Tribunal for the Far East after the war. Members of the ROK National Assembly visited Tokto in the autumn, and the year ended with an ROK reassertion of its claim in its annual defence white paper, followed by an equally predictable Japanese rejection.

Many outsiders assume that common concerns about the DPRK and about the growing importance of China would bring the ROK and Japan closer together. Both are US allies, and the US would like to see more co-operation, especially on defence matters. There have been some joint exercises but the ROK remains wary, since such co-operation is viewed with great suspicion by many. Even the problems with the DPRK do not necessarily lead them to see eye to eye. The ROK was concerned at the end of the year to learn that the Japanese

---

[6] *Korea Herald,* 15 August 2012. Online: www.asianewsnet.net/news-35066.html (accessed 27 May 2013).

and North Koreans had been talking in Mongolia. The odd contact between senior representatives did take place; the two foreign ministers spoke on the telephone following the DPRK December 2012 rocket launch, according to a Japanese Ministry of Foreign Affairs' press release. But it was hardly the full-blown co-operation that some foreign commentators hoped for.

Whatever the spats over history, the economic interdependence between the two countries continued, although it was reported that there was a drop in tourism. Total trade also fell, reflecting the general downturn in Japan's trade in 2012. In 2011, total trade had grown by 16.8 percent, but it was down by 4.4 percent in 2012, at US$103.2 billion. ROK exports were $388.5 billion, and imports $643.5 billion.[7]

The caravan has moved on. In Japan there has been a new prime minister since December, Abe Shinzo, who previously held the post in 2006–07. He is on the right of the political spectrum and has in the past rejected Korean criticisms of Japan's historical record. He may be more careful this time around, but the signs are not good. On the ROK side, the incoming President Park Geun-hye has to cope with the Japanese ties of her father, Park Chung-hee. It does not look likely that these two new leaders will bring a fresh approach to ROK–Japan relations.

2.4 *Other relations*

In May, President Lee visited Burma, the first ROK president to do so since the attack on then President Chun Doo Hwan in October 1983, which killed three cabinet ministers, fourteen other Koreans and four Burmese. Lee met President Thein Sein and Aung San Suu Kyi. One aim of the visit was to send a message to the DPRK about the benefits of abandoning isolation. Thein Sein in turn visited the ROK in October. Lee's visit was also part of the projection of the ROK as a 'middle power', a somewhat nebulous concept, that has been much pushed in recent years by the ROK government. Other facets of the same programme include the staging of major international meetings in the ROK. In 2012, as well as the Second Nuclear Security Summit held in Seoul in March with some fifty world leaders attending, there was a

[7] Trade figures accessed 26 May 2013 from www.mofat.go.kr/ENG/policy/bilateral/asiapacific/index.jsp?menu=m_20_140_10.

meeting of the International Union for the Conservation of Nature on Cheju island in September, and the decision by the United Nations (UN) Green Climate Fund to establish its secretariat in Seoul. The opening of the ROK's first Korean Cultural Centre in South Asia, in Delhi, in December, could be seen as another aspect of the same approach.[8]

President Lee and other senior government officials did much travelling as usual, often associated with big international meetings, another tie-in to the 'middle power' concept, or with the vitally necessary resource diplomacy. The ROK's need for resources such as oil clashed with its international commitments at one point during the year, when it admitted that it had imported Iranian oil despite an undertaking not to do so because of sanctions. However, it committed itself to maintaining troops in Afghanistan until the end of 2013 and staged a Proliferation Security Initiative exercise. The latter was held well away from the DPRK, although it was presumably staged with it in mind.

As noted in the account of ROK domestic affairs, the ROK did well in the London Olympics, and almost as important, the video 'Gangnam Style' by the South Korean rapper Psy (Park Jae-sang) became YouTube's most watched video ever in December. Psy was immediately taken up by the government as a symbol of the ROK's international success. Less headline catching, though equally pleasing to many in the ROK, was the selection of Seoul-born Dr Jim Yong Kim as president of the World Bank. It all helps to project what the government calls 'Global Korea'.

3 Democratic People's Republic of Korea

The vast international media frenzy that marked the death of Kim Jong Il and the coming to power of Kim Jong Un in December 2011 quickly faded away once it became clear that the DPRK was not on

---

[8] For an account of the ROK as a 'middle power' by an ROK diplomat, see Dong-min shin, 'The concept of middle power and the case of the ROK: a review', in: *Korea: Politics, Economy and Society 2012*, pp. 131–51. It is also closely associated with 'branding', the effort to make the ROK better known and recognised in the world. See Alena Schmuck, 'Nation branding in South Korea: a modern continuation of the development state', in: *Korea: Politics, Economy and Society 2011*, pp. 91–117.

the point of instant collapse and that there was to be no obvious objection to the new arrangements in place. Although there were many calls for a change of policy on the part of the DPRK, no real attempt was made to reach out to the new DPRK leader. Even the normal courtesies on the death of a national leader were only followed by a few states. Developments during the year indicated that hopes for major changes in policy were not to be met. Faced with DPRK defiance of the attempts to counter its nuclear and missile projects, the international response was more sanctions. It was not unsurprising, therefore, that by the end of 2012, the DPRK seemed less inclined than ever to heed calls for it to become 'less isolated'.

3.1 *Rockets, the nuclear issue and relations with the United States*

Yet at the beginning of the year, hopes that the new leadership might move away from confrontation rose in February, when the US and the DPRK appeared to have reached agreement on a moratorium on missile launches and further nuclear development, in return for US 'nutritional assistance', aimed at women and children. The talks had begun in autumn 2011, and in an echo of 1994 and the agreed framework negotiations, had only paused for Kim Jong Il's funeral. On 29 February, they appeared to have come to fruition, with parallel announcements. In return for 'substantial' food aid, the DPRK would cap its highly enriched uranium programme and stop testing missiles. The International Atomic Energy Agency would also be allowed back in, to check on the status of the DPRK nuclear programme. The talks also seem to have covered a resumption from March of the US army's missing in action (MIA) programme to investigate service personnel and others unaccounted after the Korean War (1950–53).[9] But the agreement collapsed almost immediately. Since 2011, the DPRK had indicated that it intended to launch a satellite to mark Kim Il Sung's 100th anniversary and on 16 March, it announced that such a launch would take place between 12 and 16 April (Kim Il Sung's birthday was on 15 April). Protests that the launch would breach the new agreement were met with the argument that the agreement covered

---

[9] The programme had been suspended in 2005; see C. Kenneth Quinines, 'The US-DPRK 1994 Agreed Framework and the US Army's return to North Korea', in: *Korea Yearbook 2008: Politics, Economics and Society*, pp. 199–229.

military launches but that this would be a peaceful launch for civilian purposes. To emphasise this, the DPRK formally notified the relevant international authorities and issued guidelines on areas for shipping and aircraft to avoid during the launch period. The US response was that there was no technological difference between a satellite and a missile launch and that such an action was not allowed. Speaking at a joint press conference in Seoul on 25 March, presidents Obama and Lee stated that any launch would be in breach of UN sanctions.

The launch went ahead, in the presence of foreign observers. Although it was unsuccessful, it was still condemned as a provocative act in breach of UN sanctions dating from 2006 and 2009. The US declared the 29 February agreement cancelled and that the MIA programme would not restart. The DPRK protested that it had not agreed to a prohibition on the peaceful use of rocket technology and that it was discriminatory to single it out as the only country in the world that was not allowed to engage in space exploration, a position it would maintain throughout the year. Following the launch, a unanimously agreed UN Security Council presidential statement condemned the DPRK action. This carried less force that a resolution, but a fresh round of UN sanctions was imposed in May. The DPRK responded that this was an 'act of war' and demanded that the sanctions be lifted. They were not, but there was evidence that the DPRK had little difficulty in evading them, mainly because not all countries interpreted them in the same way. At the end of the year, preparations were seen for what was again billed as a satellite launch. This time the launch was a success, in that a satellite seems actually to have gone into orbit. However, although the DPRK claimed total success, observers reported the satellite was in a tumbling orbit that prevented it transmitting. The DPRK rejoiced, but as the year ended, negotiations were under way to reach agreement on yet another UN condemnation. Rumours surfaced from time to time during the year that the DPRK was on the point of conducting a third nuclear test, but these proved unfounded. They were kept alive by signs of activity at a known test site and by a DPRK statement following the May sanctions that it would 'boost' its nuclear development. No doubt it had taken note of a passage in President Obama's speech at Hankuk University in March during the Seoul nuclear summit that the US would continue to provide a nuclear cover for its allies, and that it had 1,500 deployed nuclear weapons and 5,000 warheads; even Obama admitted that this was too many.[10]

By the end of 2012, the DPRK had, therefore, succeeded in launching one rocket that successfully put a satellite into space. It had not demonstrated that it had developed a rocket that could truly be a missile, able to re-enter the atmosphere and hit a target. Neither had it shown that it had been able to attach a suitable warhead to such a rocket. No doubt its scientific and technical staff are working on such matters and may one day be able to achieve success. But much of the media coverage, especially in the US, assumed that they could already do so and that the US was now within the range of a DPRK attack.

In January, the US-based Associated Press (AP) news agency opened a bureau in Pyongyang, joining Xinhua and Itar-Tass. AP had been trying to do this for some years and would have opened in 2011 but for Kim Jong Il's death. Some criticised the move, arguing that there would be no operating freedom for the bureau and that it would be dependent on DPRK media handouts. The AP response was that you had to start somewhere.

There was a moment's excitement in June. Speaking at a defence conference in Tampa, Florida, Brigadier General Neil Tolley, commander of US special forces in Korea, appeared to say that the US and the ROK special forces operated intelligence-gathering missions in the DPRK, something hitherto always denied. Tolley claimed that his words had been misinterpreted. The issue caused some debate for a time but eventually faded away. In what was described as a routine career move, Tolley was replaced in the autumn.

US concern over North Korean human rights continued. A bill calling for bipartisan efforts on the issue, and which provides the authority for funding for radio stations broadcasting to the DPRK and for the US North Korean human rights' special representative, was approved by the Senate in August.[11] In September, the US House of Representatives passed a 'North Korean Refugee Adoption Act'. The effect of this is likely to be minimal. The US, like most other Western countries, has been reluctant to accept North Korean refugees as permanent settlers.

---

[10] 'Remarks by President Obama at Hankuk University', 26 March 2012. Online: www.whitehouse.gov/the-press-office/2012/03/26/remarks-president-obama-hankuk-university (accessed 28 May 2013).

[11] Yonhap Newsletter, no. 22[illegible], 2 August 2013, accessed 29 May 2013 at http://english.yonhapnews.co.kr/northkorea/2012/08/08/95/0401000000AEN20120808011500325F.HTML

Indeed, the State Department had announced in July that the US accepted a total of 135 North Korean refugees between 2006 and 2012.[12]

During his visit to Burma in November, President Obama offered to reach out to all those who would unclench their fists, which was an invitation to countries such as the DPRK that the US would respond if they changed their ways. The 'Burma route' has now clearly replaced the 'Libya route' that was regularly suggested to the DPRK before the 'Arab spring'. Knowing what happened to Colonel Gaddafi, the DPRK seems unlikely to run the risk.

To complicate matters further, in November the DPRK announced that it had arrested a US citizen, Kenneth Bae. Bae, whose Korean name is Pae Jun-ho, was born in Seoul but became a US citizen over twenty years ago. He was operating as a tour operator, bringing groups into the Rasŏn area. No charges were made public until May 2013, but it was widely known that Bae was using his tour operator role to cover other activities as a Christian minister.[13]

3.2 *Relations with China*[14]

It is hard to overlook the massive influence China has on the DPRK. While this does not necessarily mean that the DPRK does what it is told by China, the relationship is as close as it is asymmetrical. It has its own dynamics and is not easily exploited by others. The relationship may be changing, however. Kim Il Sung spoke Chinese, apparently held a Chinese Communist Party (CCP) membership card before he had a Korean one, and he fought together with CCP guerrilla units in the 1930s. The Chinese intervention in the Korean War saved both the North Korean state and Kim himself. He may have objected to Chinese pressure but, as his frequent official and unofficial visits to the country showed, he had a close involvement with many of its leaders. Kim Jong Il's relationship with China was different. He spent part of the Korean War there and he too was a frequent visitor. Again,

---

[12] Yonhap Newsletter, no. 218, 12 July 2012, accessed 29 May 2013 at http://english.yonhapnews.co.kr/northkorea/2012/07/11/23/0401000000AEN20120711007100325F.HTML.

[13] In May 2013, a DPRK court sentenced him to 15 years hard labour.

[14] Much of this section and the following one on relations with Russia were originally drafted by Rüdiger Frank as part of his survey of the DPRK's political and economic development in 2012.

he may not have liked some Chinese policies and no doubt resented such pressure as the Chinese would sometimes apply. But there were real links and contacts.

Kim Jong Un seems to have none of these links. His foreign experiences appear to be limited to a few years' schooling in Switzerland. It is not even clear that he has visited China. His views and knowledge of China are likely to be very different to those of his father and grandfather, and also from those of many of the people about him. The lack of any personal involvement may explain why Kim Jong Un has not visited China since taking over from his father. Given China's major economic involvement with the DPRK and its political support, the lack of such a visit is surprising. There is another new and unknown factor at play, with a new leadership in China. Some have speculated that this group, led by Xi Jinping, are lacking the personal involvement with the DPRK that many Chinese leaders have had in the past, a shift that may lead to a change of policy. No such development had taken place by the end of the year, however, and at least one member of the new team, Zhang Dejiang, who joined the CCP politburo in 2012, does have North Korean connections. Zhang comes from Liaoning province, which borders on the DPRK, studied Korean at Yanbian University and then studied economics at Pyongyang's Kim Il Sung University. His career began in another border province, Jilin, where he dealt with the refugee/defector issue. His views on the DPRK are unknown but he will at least have a close personal understanding of some of the issues [15]

The Special Economic Zone at Rasŏn (formerly Rajin-Sŏnbong) in the far northeast of the DPRK began to enjoy a new lease of life with Chinese investment. Work continued also in tandem with the Chinese on the new economic zone based on islands in the Yalu river at the western end of the border near the cities of Dandong (China) and Sinŭiju (DPRK).[16] The joint development of mines with China continued in 2012;[17] and tourism continued to develop, with more and more

---

[15] Biographical details from the China Vitae website Online: www.chinavitae.com/biography/Zhang_Dejiang/bio, and from https://en.wikipedia.org/wiki/Zhang_Dejiang (both accessed 29 May 2013).

[16] For a detailed discussion of Chinese investment in these two economic zones, see the overview by Rüdiger Frank. 'North Korea in 2012', Section 9.1, in this volume.

[17] For details see Rüdiger Frank's overview, 'North Korea in 2012', Section 8.4, in this volume.

Chinese visitors replacing the now departed South Korean visitors in the Diamond (Kŭmgang) mountains.

Trade between the two countries kept growing at a high pace, surging 40 percent year on year in the first quarter of 2012 alone to reach US$1.37 billion. This growth rate slowed a little in the course of the year but remained high at an increase of about 25 percent over the previous year's figures. Iron ore was the DPRK's leading export item, while the Chinese customs office said that China exported crude oil and construction machinery. Given the reduction in inter-Korean trade, China's share of overall DPRK trade grew to an estimated 80 percent.[18]

Support also extended to the field of capacity-building. DPRK government officials and scholars went to China and received training on ways to operate, manage and attract investment to special economic zones. According to the Shanghai *Oriental Morning Post*, as quoted by Yonhap News Agency, a total of 100 officials in charge of managing economic zones participated in the training programme, which was sponsored by Beijing's Ministry of Commerce.[19]

However, not everything went well in economic relations. In a rare move, the DPRK media openly criticised a Chinese partner for misbehaviour, and Chinese media for not correctly reporting the incident. The Chinese mining firm Xiyang Group in Liaoning claimed it had lost a huge amount of money it had invested in a joint venture with the Ryŏngbong Corporation. KCNA responded on 5 September that the Chinese group had fulfilled only 50 percent of its obligations. The fact that such a conflict has been reported by the state media indicates a decision by the DPRK government to explicitly safeguard its independence, and at the same time points at the overwhelmingly and uncomfortably huge influence of Chinese businesses in the North Korean economy.[20] Reports of North Korea's markets being swamped with Chinese goods fit well into this picture. In particular, local producers,

---

[18] Figures from Korea Trade and Investment Promotion Agency at www.kotra.or.kr, accessed 28 May 2013.

[19] Yonhap North Korea Newsletter No. 218, 12 July 2012, accessed on 29 May 2013 at http://english.yonhapnews.co.kr/northkorea/2012/07/11/23/0401000000AEN20120711007100325F.HTML.

[20] Adam Cathcart, 'The plot thickens: documenting the DPRK-Xiyang spat' in: Sino-North Korea: Northeast Asia With A China-North Korea Focus, 6 September 2012. Online: http://sinonk.com/2012/09/06/documenting-dprk-xiyang-spat/ (accessed 29 May 2013). A complication in following this story is that some of the web links appear to have disappeared.

the great hope for economic revival, suffer from the cheap Chinese competition. Against that, the DPRK apparently became less dependent on Chinese grain imports. According to ROK figures, these were down some 26.8 percent, at 257,931 tons compared with 2011, the result of increased DPRK production from better harvests. But it can also be seen as an effort at reducing the one-sided dependence.

Politically, China has continued to be the DPRK's main international supporter, although it often appears that the support comes through gritted teeth. The Chinese have made it clear that they do not want nuclear weapons on the Korean peninsula and have given no encouragement to the DPRK's rocket/missile programme. At the same time, however, they argue that the DPRK is an independent state and has rights as an independent state, and they also express concern at pushing its leaders into a corner. They claim to see the nuclear problem as not just something created by the North Koreans but one that others, in particular the United States, have also contributed to and should take responsibility for solving. However, as outlined above (Section 1.2), the Chinese went along with the UN's condemnation of the DPRK rocket launches and the additional sanctions imposed. They also allowed a wider public debate than usual over the country's policy towards the DPRK. This perhaps defused criticism of government actions but may also have been intended to send notification to the DPRK that if it did not modify its policies, China's policies might change.

In other ways, relations between the two countries continued along much the same pattern as recent years. Kim Jong Un may not have visited China but others, including his uncle Jang Song Taek, widely believed to be a major power behind the throne, did so. Jang led an economic and development delegation in August. This discussed special economic zones among other matters. There were defence and public security contacts; the last may have looked at the refugee/defector issue. If it did, there was no discernable change in policy. DPRK and Chinese senior officials met in the margins of a number of international events as usual. One disturbing element for the Chinese was an incident in the Yellow Sea in May, when seven Chinese fishing boats were seized and held to ransom. Four were released, apparently after paying, but the other three and their crews were held for a time before they too were let go. It was not clear if a ransom was paid. At first suspicion fell on pirates but later it seemed that DPRK officials were involved and there were negotiations between Chinese and

DPRK authorities. According to Leonid Petrov, such incidents are not uncommon, and there was nothing to indicate that the incident was officially sanctioned. But whether officially sanctioned or private enterprise, it was hardly a positive development.[21]

3.3 *Relations with Russia*

DPRK–Russia relations have grown cooler since the early 2000s, when Kim Jong Il became a regular visitor. Russia then seemed to have greater influence than China. Partly, perhaps, this was another product of Kim Jong Il's personal experience. Although the official myth has his birth and upbringing in Korea, in reality he was born in Russia and appeared to retain an affection for the country. He regularly visited the Russian embassy. It was on his personal initiative after a visit to Irkutsk in 2002 that Pyongyang got a Russian Orthodox church in 2006. Yet although Russia, like China, was cautious in its criticism of some of the DPRK's policies, the political relationship seemed to fade gradually. In recent years, Russia has been more critical.

Nevertheless, Russia remains a significant economic partner, with influence on the DPRK's domestic developments. While Russia serves less as an example for reforms in the way that China does, it provides an important counterweight to China's influence and opens alternative sources of co-operation in the fields of technology, trade and investment. In February 2012, the Itar-Tass News Agency reported that a group of North Korean railway specialists had been dispatched to Russia to receive training.[22] In April, KCNA announced that a cross-border cargo train service between Rajin and Khasan would start from October 2012 (KCNA, 2 April 2012). This service is significant, as China and Russia have for many years been fighting over the route by which the Korean peninsula, and later also Japan, would be connected to Europe. In fact, the service may not have start-

---

[21] Leonid Petrov, 'North Korea, China and the abducted Chinese fishing boats', in: *East Asia Forum*, 6 June 2012. Online: www.eastasiaforum.org/2012/06/06/north-korea-china-and-the-abducted-chinese-fishing-boats/ (accessed 29 May 2013). In May 2013, a similar incident occurred. See Tania Branigan, 'North Koreans seize Chinese fishing boat', in: *The Guardian*, 20 May 2013. Online: www.guardian.co.uk/world/2013/may/20/north-koreans-seize-chinese-fishing-boat (accessed 29 May 2013).

[22] Yonhap North Korea Newsletter no. 199, 1 March 2013, accessed 29 May 2013 at http://english.yonhapnews.co.kr/northkorea/2012/02/29/23/0401000000AEN20120229007100325F.HTML.

ed as scheduled but work continues.[23] Trade between the two countries increased by 50 percent in the first half of 2012, although it remained at a low level with a turnover of below US$100 million annually. Settlement of the DPRK's outstanding debt to Russia, contracted during the Soviet era, was finally achieved in September 2012.[24]

3.4 *Relations with Japan*

Relations with Japan remained in the doldrums, with the issue of abducted Japanese citizens dominating Japanese thinking on the DPRK. Japan was a firm supporter of continued sanctions on the DPRK, and its own bilateral sanctions went beyond those imposed by the UN over the two rocket launches in 2012. Pressure continued on Chongryong, the pro-DPRK group in Japan, which found its activities increasingly circumscribed.

It was not all gloom, however. In a move with implications for the issue of abducted Japanese, following the first meetings for ten years, the DPRK and the Japanese Red Cross organisations reached an agreement in August to allow relatives to visit graveyards where Japanese soldiers had been buried in World War II. The first such visits since the end of the war in 1945 took place in September and October.[25] In another unusual development, Japanese media were allowed into the DPRK to cover the visits.

In November, it was made public that talks at senior foreign ministry level were under way in the Mongolian capital, Ulaanbaatar, between DPRK ambassador Ho Song Il and Sugiyama Shinsuke, director-general for Asia at the Japanese ministry of foreign affairs. The talks had apparently been brokered during a visit to Pyongyang by a senior aide to then Japanese Prime Minister Noda.[26] The advent of a

---

[23] KCNA, 2 April 2012, text available online at: www.nkeconwatch.com/category/dprk-organizations/state-offices/ministry-of-railways/ (accessed 29 May 2013).

[24] For details see Rüdiger Frank's overview, 'North Korea in 2012', Section 9.1, in this volume.

[25] Adam Westlake, 'Second delegation visits North Korea to pay respects at wartime graves, in: *Japan Daily Press*, 3 October 2012. Online: http://japandailypress.com/second-delegation-visits-north-korea-to-pay-respects-at-wartime-grave-sites-0314319 (accessed 29 May 2013).

[26] Reported on the InfoMongolia.com website at www.infomongolia.com/ct/ci/5229 (accessed 29 May 2013); and the globalpost website at www.globalpost.com/dispatch/news/kyodo-news-international/130523/ex-pm-noda-aide-visited-pyongyang-fall-break-impasse-s (accessed 29 May 2013).

more conservative Japanese government may have implications for the continuation of these efforts.

3.5 *Other relations*

The apparently better harvests did not stop appeals for international food aid for the DPRK. The famine conditions of the 1990s may now be a memory, but reports of stunting among children and general malnutrition point to the country's continued inability or unwillingness to feed its population adequately. The contrast between appeals for food and expenditure on nuclear developments and missiles was frequently noted. Floods in August added to the problem, with the World Food Programme appealing for international assistance and announcing that it would send corn as emergency aid.[27]

The DPRK sent 51 athletes to the London Olympics. They won four gold medals and two bronze, making them 20th overall. For the first time, DPRK athletes participated in the Paralympics, with assistance from the British embassy in Pyongyang.[28] The British embassy also enjoyed some unwanted publicity when a member of staff was spotted on a fairground ride sitting behind Kim Jong Un. The rather solemn British official explanation that the incident had no significance was no doubt true but came across as a bit flat-footed.[29]

In May, the DPRK's Unhasu Orchestra played a concert with the Radio France Philharmonic Orchestra in Paris, under the latter's South Korean conductor Chung Myung-whun. In the first half of the concert, the 75 Unhasu musicians performed North Korean pieces including works for traditional stringed instruments, the *haegŭm*, and the zither-like *kayagŭm*, and the joint ensemble performed works including Brahms's Symphony No 1 and Bizet's Carmen.[30]

---

[27] *New York Times*, 4 August 2012, quoting Reuters News. Online: www.nytimes.com/2012/08/05/world/asia/emergency-food-aid-for-north-korea-after-severe-floods.html?_r=0 (accessed 29 May 2013).

[28] Yonhap News Agency, North Korea Newsletter, no. 209, 10 May 2012. Online: http://english.yonhapnews.co.kr/northkorea/2012/05/09/43/0401000000AEN20120509001100325F.HTML (accessed 29 May 2013),

[29] James Meikle, 'It was British diplomat enjoying amusement park ride with Kim Jong-un British chargé d'affaires Barnaby Jones is revealed as mystery man in photo with North Korean leader', in: *The Guardian*, 2 August 2012. Online: www.guardian.co.uk/world/2012/aug/02/kim-jong-un-british-diplomat-ride (accessed 29 May 2013).

[30] Reported by BBC News Asia-Pacific, 15 March 2012. Online: www.bbc.co.uk/news/world-asia-pacific-17379127 (accessed 29 May 2013).

HOW TO PROMOTE A FREE TRADE AGREEMENT: UK TRADE & INVESTMENT AND THE EU–KOREA FTA

Judith Cherry

ABSTRACT

This article considers key challenges facing national governments within the European Union (EU) that have been seeking to promote the recently implemented free trade agreement (FTA) with South Korea. Governments have to promote the deal to companies that have often been unaware of, or lacked interest in, the content of the FTA and the specific benefits that it can offer. They also need either to raise awareness of Korea—an important trading partner for the EU but described by some executives as a 'forgotten' or 'unknown' market—or, paradoxically, to address negative perceptions of Korea, its business environment and culture. This article uses a case study of the promotional work done by UK Trade & Investment to examine these challenges and suggest ways in which practitioners in government and business within the EU and beyond might successfully promote the EU–Korea FTA and other such agreements with East Asian trading partners.

Key words: South Korea, European Union, UK Trade & Investment, free trade agreement, trade, foreign direct investment

1 INTRODUCTION

On 19 July 2011, the British Foreign Secretary William Hague hosted a reception at the Foreign and Commonwealth Office (FCO) in London to mark the implementation of a free trade agreement between the European Union (EU) and South Korea.[1] The FCO press release noted that the agreement had the potential to double bilateral trade between the EU and Korea to more than €154 billion over the next two decades and to benefit the UK economy by €580 million annually. Mr Hague told the press:

[1] Hereafter 'Korea'.

> [The EU–Korea FTA] is the most ambitious trade agreement ever negotiated by the EU. The UK was the champion of this agreement and we are, and will remain, the leading advocate of free trade in the EU (Foreign and Commonwealth Office 2011).

The EU–Korea free trade agreement (FTA) was the first to be negotiated under the European Commission's (EC's) 'Global Europe' strategy and, according to the EU's chief negotiator Ignacio Garcia Bercero, is likely to serve as a model for other FTAs negotiated between the EU and Asian countries (Agence France Presse 2011). With all free trade agreements, once a deal is negotiated and signed, and even before it is ratified, it is important for national governments and trade-related organisations to sensitise domestic companies both to the general benefits of free trade agreements and to the specific advantages of the deals they have struck.

However, in terms of FTA promotion, Korea presents additional challenges that may offer timely lessons for the EU regarding further deals with East Asian nations. Despite the fact that Korea is a major economic player and trading nation and a desirable FTA partner in the eyes of the EC, it remains an unknown, overlooked or misunderstood market in the eyes of many EU corporations. In addition, the 'soft' socio-cultural barriers identified by EU executives and officials in earlier studies, which include problems relating to policy implementation, regulatory consistency, transparency and predictability, education, labour and attitudes towards globalisation, will continue to have an impact on the Korean business environment, the successful implementation of the FTA and the operations of EU-owned companies in Korea, even when 'hard' barriers such as tariffs, duties and regulations have been eliminated (Cherry 2007; 2012). Thus, in order to maximise the potential benefits of the FTA, national governments and trade promotion agencies need to sensitise companies to the Korean business environment and culture as well as to the deal and the opportunities it creates.

This article seeks to fill a gap in the existing academic literature on free trade agreements, which has thus far focused on the effects of, motivations for, and potential impediments to these arrangements. Taking a practical approach and using the United Kingdom's export support and inward investment agency, UK Trade & Investment (UKTI), as a case study, it examines the challenges facing national governments in promoting the EU-Korea FTA and offers a timely analysis of the activities undertaken to address these issues. It highlights the generic and specific issues relating to the promotion of this free trade agreement that can give food for thought to, or serve as a model for, other EU member states seeking to maximise the benefits from the EU–Korea FTA and pursue similar future agreements with other countries. Similarly, it can provide useful information for countries beyond the EU that are seeking, negotiating or implementing free trade agreements with key trading partners in East Asia. The article begins with a brief overview of the academic literature relating to free trade agreements, before analysing the EC's motivations for pursuing an FTA with Korea and the benefits that it anticipates from that deal. This will provide the context for the subsequent discussion of the promotion of free trade agreements by national governments and trade promotion agencies, focusing on the activities of UK Trade & Investment.

2 THE ACADEMIC DEBATE

Recent years have seen a proliferation of bilateral and regional free trade agreements, which Dent (2007: 458) defines as:

> A negotiated set of preferential market access concessions, trade-related rules and protected industry interests forged between signatory parties.

The rapid growth in free trade agreements reflects, to a great extent, increasing doubts about the prospects for a successful conclusion of the Doha Development Agenda talks and the capacity of the World Trade Organisation (WTO) to regulate world trade adequately (Cho 2001: 91–92). Following the implementation of the North America Free Trade Agreement in 1994, the deepening of Asian regionalism and the wave of FTAs among Asian countries in the wake of the 1997 financial crisis, there has been a growing trend for governments of developed and developing countries to pursue bilateral and regional trade arrangements, while maintaining a commitment to the WTO-led multilateral process. The increase in free trade agreements has generated a substantial body of academic literature on the motivations for, and potential impediments to, these trading arrangements.[2]

[2] Earlier versions of the background sections of this article have appeared in Cherry (2011, 2012).

2.1 *Free trade agreements—motivations*

Key economic motivations for governments to enter into bilateral and regional trade agreements are to improve or safeguard access to foreign markets (by reducing existing trade barriers and restricting their partner's ability to erect new ones), to enhance export opportunities for domestic firms, and to expand production and boost efficiency (as exports increase and economies of scale can be achieved). The entry of foreign companies into the domestic market increases competition and thus stimulates local firms to strengthen their competitiveness. In times of economic recession, declining domestic demand, rising unemployment and falling profits, governments may seek the benefits accruing from forming or joining FTAs with countries whose key industries are not a threat to domestic firms, and they may seek to address public concerns about market opening by restricting imports from countries with whom agreements have not been signed (Urata 2002: 25; Mansfield 1998: 525–26).

As free trade deals proliferate, there is an increasing incentive for states that have not entered into any deals to develop and implement an FTA policy in order to avoid being at a competitive disadvantage in global markets. Baldwin identifies the phenomenon of the 'domino effect', clearly demonstrated by the cases of the creation of the Single Market in Europe and the signing of a free trade agreement between the United States and Mexico. In such cases, countries that were previously content to remain outside an economic bloc may be prompted to consider membership as integration deepens. The enlargement of an existing trade bloc to encompass an even greater number of markets increases the cost disadvantage to non-member countries and may prompt a government that has previously been ambivalent towards seeking membership of the bloc to assume a more positive and proactive stance (Baldwin 1994: 32–33). Mansfield (1998: 523, 527) also identifies a demonstration effect, as states and companies see the benefits that competitors derive from such arrangements and seek to conclude their own deals.

In addition to the potential economic benefits to be gained from entering into FTAs, there are other features of these agreements that prompt governments to pursue them with key trading partners. A report published by the Asian Development Bank in 2002 observed that it was easier for governments to win public support for bilateral rather than multilateral arrangements, and smaller-scale negotiations allowed more leeway for protecting sensitive sectors. From an international perspective, FTAs provided an opportunity to raise a nation's diplomatic profile and strengthen its influence in the international arena (Asian Development Bank 2002; Urata 2002: 27). Given that they are concluded on a bilateral or regional basis, free trade agreements are 'more manageable and more effective' than multilateral agreements and can be tailor-made to suit the needs of all the parties concerned (Andreosso-O'Callaghan 2009: 148). Another attraction of FTAs is the opportunity to go beyond the scope of the global agenda and negotiate 'broad band' or 'WTO-plus' agreements covering issues such as the environment, investment and labour (Nicolas 2009: 33).

2.2 *Free trade agreements—impediments*

In his work on free trade agreements in the Asia-Pacific region, Dent identifies what he terms 'deficient capacity' as a potential problem for developing countries wishing to engage effectively with bilateral trade agreements. Dent argues that insufficient numbers of trained and experienced technocrats able to analyse, negotiate and implement free trade agreements, a lack of coherence in foreign economic policy formulation, insufficient local industrial capacity to exploit the opportunities in new or expanded FTA markets, and the inability of domestic legal and socio-cultural frameworks and institutions to implement the agreement can serve to frustrate efforts to implement such deals fully and maximise their net welfare effects (Dent 2006: 57–58).

In his view, developed countries like the United States (US) and regions like the EU may choose as potential FTA partners more advanced developing countries with the technocratic, industrial and institutional capacity to accommodate the 'broad band' measures they seek relating to market access issues such as financial services liberalisation, competition policy and government procurement (Dent 2006: 247–51). Korea, which has signed FTAs with both the US and the EU, has relatively strong capacity functions in terms of its pool of experienced and talented technocrats and the ability of its major export industries to adapt to new market conditions; it is in the area of institutional capacity that problems may arise. Dent (2006: 247) defines such capacity as:

> The ability of the nation's institutional frameworks (e.g. legal, socio-cultural) to accommodate the various policy-related commitments incorporated into the FTA, such as on intellectual property rights and competition policy. Examples of 'institutions'...mainly relate to agencies...and associated laws and rules devised to enforce legislation once enacted.

Weak institutional capacity functions may hinder a developing country's ability to implement and enforce key requirements of an FTA, a situation that can be exacerbated by the continuing existence of social and cultural barriers to trade and investment and outdated 'software' that hinders the ability of agencies to enforce the provisions of the free trade agreement.

Moving beyond the tariff and non-tariff barriers that FTAs seek to address and remove, I have highlighted elsewhere the importance of a third class of barriers: social, cultural and institutional barriers to trade with and investment in Korea that cannot be legislated for under the EU-Korea free trade agreement but that can serve as 'hidden stumbling blocks' to its implementation and effectiveness (Cherry 2012). I have argued that the phenomenon of 'mismatched globalisation' (in which economic globalisation outpaces cultural globalisation) is still apparent in Korea, as evidenced by the continuing existence of these 'soft' barriers, which include the gap between policy and implementation, the lack of predictability, consistency and transparency in the regulatory environment (including the protection of intellectual property rights), education systems, labour militancy, and attitudes towards globalisation (Cherry 2007).

My findings resonate with Dent's argument (2006) that 'deficient capacity' in terms of technocracy, industry and/or institutional arrangements can pose problems for developing countries seeking to negotiate and implement bilateral trade agreements with more developed countries. In the case of Korea, the long-term 'soft' social and cultural barriers identified and discussed in my earlier writing act as a constraint on the country's institutional capacity functions and thus have the potential to hinder the full and effective implementation of the EU–Korea free trade agreement and reduce the economic benefits that the signatory parties hope to gain from it.

3 THE EU–KOREA FREE TRADE AGREEMENT

In 2006, the European Commission announced a new phase in its external trade policy with the publication of *Global Europe: Competing in the World: A Contribution to the EU's Growth and Jobs Strategy*. The rationale for the new strategy was the fostering of open markets through the pursuit of a 'new generation' of bilateral and regional trade agreements that would boost trade and investment and thus contribute to economic growth and job creation within the EU by acting as a 'powerful stimulus to competition, innovation and productivity growth' (European Commission 2006). While offering assurances that it remained committed to the multilateral process led by the WTO and the successful conclusion of the Doha Round, the EC announced its intention to achieve maximum benefits for the EU by negotiating 'deep' bilateral or regional agreements that went beyond the simple elimination of tariffs, and included non-tariff barriers such as those relating to standards, certification and testing, intellectual property rights), and regulatory transparency (Barfield 2007: 2; Rollo 2008: 2; Guerin et al. 2007: ii–iv).

There were three key commercial motivations for the 'Global Europe' strategy: to minimise the negative impact of FTAs signed by trade partners and third countries (especially the potential trade diversion effects in favour of the US); to forge strategic links with countries already experiencing high rates of growth or forecast to do so in the future; and to ensure the implementation of international commercial regulations such as those pertaining to the protection of intellectual property rights (Woolcock 2007: 4). The priority markets selected as potential FTA partners under the strategy were ASEAN, South Korea and Mercosur (comprising Argentina, Brazil, Paraguay, Uruguay and Venezuela). In making its selection, the EC considered market potential (in terms of current and future market size and growth); the level of protection faced in the market by European exporters and investors; and the likelihood that European firms might be shut out or disadvantaged by bilateral agreements already being negotiated or considered with other trading partners. The focus on Asia reflected the growth in trade flows between Europe and Asia and the EC's desire to strengthen and enhance European links with the region (Barfield 2007: 2–3; Gavin and Sindzingre 2009: 9).

Judged by all the above-mentioned criteria, South Korea was an obvious priority country for the new strategy. In 2007, the year in which negotiations got underway, Korea was the EU's eighth most important trading partner and the EU ranked as Korea's fourth most important trading partner (Guerin et al. 2007: ii). The level of protection faced by European investors in the Korean market encompassed not only tariffs and duties but also a variety of non-tariff barriers and social, cultural and institutional challenges that were raised annually by the EU business community in Korea and by the European Chamber of Commerce in Korea (EUCCK 2010) in its report *Trade Issues and Recommendations*.[3] Finally, the signing of an FTA between Korea and the US on 30 June 2007 provided an important stimulus for the EC to commence talks with the Korean government.

The FTA signed by the EU and Korea was intended to create new trade opportunities for EU companies in goods and services worth €19.1 billion, most notably in the chemicals, pharmaceuticals, iron and steel, auto parts, footwear, spirits and medical equipment sectors. New sectors in the service industry would be opened up, including financial and legal services, telecommunications, environmental services and shipping, and EU exporters would benefit from a reduction of €1.6 billion in the duties levied annually on their products. The FTA would also result in the dismantling of non-tariff barriers to trade, including technical standards and certification, and provide greater transparency and predictability on regulatory issues such as intellectual property rights protection (EUCCK 2010; Europa 2010). The EC also reported the inclusion in the FTA of significant provisions relating to the liberalisation of investment in the manufacturing and service sectors, including telecommunications, satellite broadcasting, express delivery services and legal services (European Commission Trade 2010b: 1, 7).[4] Negotiations for the EU–Korea free trade agreement began in May 2007 and the FTA was signed on 15 October 2009.

4 Promoting the EU–Korea Free Trade Agreement

The following analysis of the challenges inherent in promoting the EU–Korea free trade agreement is based on a series of interviews with members of the EU business community in Seoul in September 2009,

[3] For more detail, see Cherry 2007.
[4] For the full text of the agreement, see European Commission Trade 2010a.

and with UKTI officials in September 2009, May and July 2011. Although the main aims of the interviews in Seoul were to assess corporate expectations of the FTA (Cherry 2011) and to identify the socio-cultural impediments to the smooth implementation of the agreement (Cherry 2012), there was also discussion of issues relating to the promotion of the FTA among companies in Europe and the role that national governments and trade-related organisations could and should play in that task. In total 23 EU expatriates working for a wide range of companies and institutions were interviewed; some of the interviewees were existing contacts and others were introduced by staff at the European Chamber of Commerce in Korea or by the interviewees themselves. All the interviews, which were conducted in English, were semi-structured and based on a range of questions prepared in advance, but with the flexibility to explore interesting issues that arose in conversation. In addition, interviews were held in Seoul in May, and London in July 2011 with members of staff of UK Trade & Investment, discussing the planning, execution and outcomes of the FTA promotion initiatives in the United Kingdom. All but five of the executives and officials were interviewed individually; the one-on-one interviews lasted between one and two hours, and the group interview lasted for two hours.

When discussing the issue of promoting the EU–Korea FTA in 2009, interviewees in the EU business community in Seoul expressed concerns that, in addition to a lack of knowledge among EU businesses about the benefits and advantages of free trade agreements in general, there was also insufficient awareness about the Korean market and the specific current and future opportunities it offered to them. There was a consensus that, before and after the FTA went into effect, there would be a need for education and training, including information about the concept of an FTA. In addition, interviewees felt that there was a clear 'mismatch' between Korea's status in the global economy and in the eyes of those negotiating the FTA, and its profile and image in business circles. The education and training should, therefore, also include the Korean business environment and business culture, especially in the case of small- and medium-sized enterprises with little or no experience of doing business in Asia.

Paradoxically, there were also concerns about a potential 'rush to market' by firms believing that the FTA would remove all barriers to trade and create a problem-free business environment. There was, interviewees felt, a danger that companies motivated to explore or enter the Korean market by the headline news of the elimination of tariffs, opening of market sectors, easing of trade- and investment-related regulations and the creation of new business opportunities would be unaware of important underlying issues that could have a negative impact on the success of their venture.

A key issue as regards impediments to success in the Korean market was the persistence of socio-cultural barriers that needed to be understood by foreign business executives, as they could not be legislated for and would take time to change. Some of the most important potential stumbling blocks to the implementation of the FTA had their roots in Korean culture, which would not be changed by an FTA. The interviewees' message was unequivocal: while the signing and implementation of the EU–Korea FTA would lead to the dismantling of many important tariff and non-tariff barriers, it would not per se turn Korea into an easy place to do business overnight. In order to take full advantage of the opportunities offered by the FTA and to achieve or sustain success in the market, traders and investors had to develop an understanding of Korea's political, social, cultural and institutional environments, adapt to the challenges they presented, and develop a strategy for dealing with those barriers.

In view of this, there was a general consensus on the need for national governments and trade promotion agencies to be proactive and 'sell' the FTA—it would not be enough for governments to sign and ratify the agreement and then move on to the next pressing issue in the belief that companies would pick up on the new opportunities. There was a need for a significant amount of education, public relations (PR) work and awareness-raising to introduce the market opportunities and dispel the myths and negative perceptions that had accumulated about South Korea (particularly in respect of the situation with North Korea) in order to gain support from corporate headquarters for approaching the market.

In order to delve further into the issue of promoting the EU–Korea FTA, the author conducted interviews with staff at UKTI Seoul in September 2009, May 2011 and September 2012, followed by additional interviews with members of staff at UKTI headquarters in London in July 2011. The interviewees included: Douglas Barrett (Seoul, May 2011 and September 2012, Head of Trade and Investment), Christine Leaver (London, July 2011, Head of Emerging Markets and Policy Team), and Richard Webster (London, July 2011, Head of EU–Korea Strategic Trade Development). The aim of the interviews was to analyse the activities undertaken by the UK government to ensure the success of the trade agreement which the UK had championed and of which the UK government was, in its own words, the 'leading advocate' (Foreign and Commonwealth Office 2011).

4.1 *The government's role—UK Trade & Investment*

The campaign to promote the EU–Korea FTA was a joint effort between various departments within UK Trade & Investment: UKTI headquarters in London, the regional offices in the UK, and the UKTI section of the British Embassy in Seoul. The International Group in UKTI headquarters HQ is divided into several sections that focus on specific markets with different resource allocations depending on the significance of the market, particularly in terms of potential for achieving high rates of growth. The teams have responsibility for the bilateral trading and investment relationship with their allocated markets, arrange visits for ministers and government officials, and liaise with the FCO and other parts of government as necessary on the wider relationship.

A key section within the International Group is the Emerging Markets and Policy Team, which was established in 2006 to commission research that would bring in fresh thinking and new ideas to fill knowledge gaps. Additional resources were to be allocated to high-growth and emerging markets to enable UKTI to reach out to UK businesses and make them more aware of new opportunities in those markets (Leaver, July 2011). With specific reference to Asia, the Emerging Markets and Policy Team is responsible for the Asia Task Force, a group that carries out outreach and sensitising events across the UK for markets in Asia. These events include Asia-specific events under the banner 'Doing Business in Asia' which aim to sensitise UK companies to the opportunities offered by the Asian markets, covering countries east of India, including China, Japan and Korea; Business Development Visits, in which trade officers from the embassies participate in exhibitions, give lectures and meet companies on a one-to-one basis or as part of an event; and the more general Explore Exports events, which are often run by UKTI's regional offices with the aim of promoting UK exports.

Trade and investment promotion and support work in the UK regions is carried out by offices that subcontract to private organisations such as chambers of commerce. They use the resources, materials, reports, and information provided by UKTI London and British embassies around the world to promote trade, provide face-to-face export and investment support for local companies and, in some cases, organise trade missions to specific markets. The link to the market is provided by the overseas UKTI offices, which supply market information and carry out commission-based Overseas Market Introduction Service (OMIS) work on behalf of prospective UK traders and investors. OMIS work includes preparing market reports, identifying potential partners in the overseas markets, arranging meetings and providing support in the local market.

In summary, UKTI offices overseas provide information to the UKTI London and regional offices that their staff members can convey to UK business through outreach activities, publications and sensitising events. The overseas offices of UKTI receive details of companies that have attended these events and registered an interest in the market, and then begin to provide feedback to, and develop a relationship with, those companies that will, it is hoped, lead to activity in the market.

4.2 *Putting the case for Korea*

With its global remit to promote trade and investment, UKTI uses limited resources to cover a broad range of markets, 17 of which, including Korea, are categorised as 'high growth' (Webster, July 2011). Leaver observed that, although the most popular markets (in terms of patterns of demand for outreach and sensitising events) were China, India, Hong Kong and Singapore, the team had noticed a gradual increase in interest in Korea, a market that was less well known to UK business. In September 2009, the year in which the EU–Korea FTA was signed and almost two years before it went into force, UKTI staff in Seoul felt that the time was right to prepare for the FTA and were already looking at ways to highlight the opportunities for British business that the trade deal would create. The most important message that they wished to convey was that Korea was a 'rich market of possibilities': the fourth biggest economy in Asia and, according to 2007 figures, as big as all the combined economies of countries in Southeast Asia. With good levels of disposable income, a centralised, well-educated and increasingly internationalised population, and high demand for quality foreign goods, Korea was an attractive package for potential exporters (Barrett, May 2011).

Thus in 2009, UKTI Seoul staff began exploring options with the resources available to them, in the expectation of increasing the resources once the deal was in place. In their opinion, the best approach would be a process of 'evangelising' the FTA through the existing UKTI network within the United Kingdom.

> We are preparing. We have lined up a team to analyse what is in the text and we want to make sure we are ready to go the moment the flag drops. The British Embassy will be analysing what the new opportunities are and trying to bring those opportunities to British companies.[5]

In July 2009, Douglas Barrett took up the post of Head of Trade and Investment in the British Embassy Seoul; part of his remit in going to Seoul was to ensure that British companies got the best out of the proposed EU–Korea FTA. One month later, when the Emerging Markets Group asked for bids for funding to carry out research to support trade promotion, Barrett applied for funding to commission a report highlighting the top 100 opportunities that the FTA would create for British business. The report was envisaged as a 'snapshot' of the most promising opportunities that matched the strengths, expertise and competitive advantage of UK business, rather than a detailed account of the free trade agreement document and all the changes that the deal would bring about. The report would form part of a campaign that included sensitising events about the FTA and the Korean market and the creation of channels of communication to relay key information to potential traders and investors.

The main body of the work was contracted to IRC, a Seoul-based consultancy firm that was well known to the British Embassy; a major part of the brief for IRC was to highlight the specific opportunities where it was clear that that the UK had 'capability and interest' (Leaver, July 2011). Asked why Barrett's bid was attractive to her team, Leaver replied:

> It was a mixture of things—one is definitely that Korea is a high priority; also it was the opportunity to do some new research, unique research particularly focused on UK companies. For us it was really quite a compelling case because there will only be one EU–Korea FTA and so

[5] As I have been unable to contact the UKTI staff member interviewed in 2009 to obtain consent to be identified in this article, I have not given a name or attributed the comments provided.

> this seemed a good opportunity to do some in-depth research, but we needed to make the research practical. The key thing for us how do we make it operational—how do we take what could be quite an academic subject matter and turn it into something that actually means something to our business audience? This was a tool to help us address both questions—'What is an FTA?' and 'Where is Korea?'

Leaver's group was responsible for bringing the FTA research together, putting together a team that included experts in Korea, trade policy colleagues, and representatives from the Confederation of British Industries. The overall message was clear: the EU-Korea free trade agreement would radically alter the way Britain did business with Korea. Most tariffs would be eliminated within three years and some would fall away on implementation. It was the perfect time to do business in Korea (UK Trade & Investment 2011).

In the eyes of the UKTI staff, the EU–Korea free trade agreement was 'the strongest hook that you can have from a PR angle', and would enable staff to spotlight Korea among the 17 high-growth markets and present UK business with real and tangible opportunities. The FTA provided UKTI staff in Seoul, London and the UK regions with a new message and a fresh impetus for Korea-related promotional activities, highlighting a specific, short-term, first-to-market opportunity that gave UK businesses a competitive advantage over major competitors such as the US and Japan, which did not yet have FTAs in place and operational.[6]

Once the message had been formulated, the next challenge was to create a variety of robust communication channels to disseminate the news to the people who could most benefit from it. The channels included sensitising events: a total of 30 were held between March 2010 and October 2011 in various formats that were either FTA-specific or piggy-backed on more general events such as Doing Business in Asia and Explore Exports events, Business Development Visits and regional events in the UK that were held to recruit members for trade missions to Korea. These events combined presentations, case studies, clinics, and one-on-one sessions between exporters and trade advisors. The presentations included elements such as historical, political and economic background, bilateral trade, the benefits of the FTA, information on key sectors, and rules for success (incorporating cultural issues). After the FTA went into effect in 2011, UKTI organised a

[6] The KORUS free trade agreement went into effect on 15 March 2012

reception for Korean and UK business representatives at the Foreign and Commonwealth Office on 19 July to celebrate and promote the new trade deal. A key element of many of the sensitising events was the presence of high-level government officials, including the then British ambassador to Korea at promotional events, the then trade minister at the launch event in March 2010, and Foreign Secretary William Hague at the reception to celebrate the implementation of the EU–Korea FTA in July 2011.

The report that Leaver's group had commissioned was published in March 2010; an updated version was released in March 2011, once it became clear that the FTA would go into effect in July 2011 rather than January 2011, as had been originally envisaged. The revised 2011 report, entitled *South Korea Open for Business: 100^{PLUS} Opportunities for UK Companies in South Korea Following the EU-South Korea Free Trade Agreement*, incorporated additional opportunities for British business and was made available via the UKTI website. In addition, a hard copy of the report was mailed out to UK companies; both the hard copy and an e-version—a USB stick that also housed a short film entitled *Doing Business in Korea* and 17 sector-specific flyers[7]—were also handed out at the sensitising events. The flyers included a sector overview, analysis of the influence of the FTA on that specific sector focusing on tariffs and timescales, key opportunities and factors for success, including cultural issues (Webster, July 2011).

In addition to bidding for funding for the research report, Barrett also put in a bid to have a trade officer assigned to the Seoul team under the Overseas Attachment Scheme, which gives UKTI staff work experience overseas. Richard Webster was seconded to the team in Seoul to help them both to promote the FTA and the report, and to enhance their marketing efforts. Webster developed the sector flyers and also took the lead on setting up an e-newsletter and a blog specifically to raise awareness about Korea and to address negative preconceptions about the country and market. The e-newsletter from the Seoul embassy comprises six sections including the topic of the month, a sector overview, a case study, upcoming events and cultural issues. According to Webster, the click-through rate (the proportion of readers who click on a link in a story to access a related website) was

[7] The sectors selected were: advanced engineering, construction, consumer goods, cosmetics, design, e-learning, education, energy, environment, fashion, financial services, food and drink, global sports, ICT, legal services, life sciences, and water.

75 percent, considerably higher than the average of 50 percent in e-newsletters sent out by the UKTI regional offices to companies on a variety of topics.

The new initiatives fed into the existing system at UKTI for tracking contacts and building relationships with UK business. The details of any company registering for, or expressing an interest in, Korea at a UKTI event were entered into a database, and were fed through to the Seoul UKTI office, where staff would begin the process of creating a working relationship with the company. The follow-up process from the events also included placing the companies on the e-newsletter mailing lists to ensure that up-to-date market information continued to be channelled to them after they had attended the event.

According to Barrett and Webster, UKTI staff were unaware of any outreach activity on a similar scale by their counterparts in the other 26 EU member states. This was confirmed (by Webster) in a conversation with an EU official in Seoul in 2010 who commented that 'You [the British] are the only people treating the FTA seriously'—although it had to be acknowledged that, for some of the member states, the opportunities were less exciting than for the UK (Barrett, May 2011).

4.3 *Confronting the challenges*

At one of the EU–Korea FTA sensitising events held in the UK, a company executive commented that the speakers faced a double challenge in promoting the trade deal; firstly, explaining what an FTA was and the benefits it offered, and, secondly, explaining why Korea was an important market for UK business. Although the expatriate executive interviewees in Seoul were equally concerned that companies back at home did not understand the workings and benefits of an FTA, the UKTI staff members felt that, in general, companies were not interested in free trade agreements per se and did not need detailed explanations of how such agreements worked. In Leaver's view, it was not the UKTI's job to promote the FTA as a whole; their role was to promote specific opportunities for UK companies, both those that existed before the deal went into effect and specific ones created by the FTA.

In the case of the EU–Korea FTA, the document ran to 1,200 pages contained in an 8.6 megabyte PDF file (European Commission,

2010)—far too much information for companies to digest easily and evaluate in terms of business opportunities. This prompted the UKTI to focus on the top 100 opportunities for UK business, while still retaining the capability to deal with individual enquiries about other sectors.

> Companies don't care about an FTA—they care about the opportunities for their company. Flicking through the FTA it's quite funny what you can export. If you want to, you can export live bears to Korea. That illustrates the far-reaching nature of [the FTA] and the way that [you] can turn this stuffy document that means not a lot to very many people into something that, from a company perspective, [can be explained] in a really factual and quantitative way when they are sitting there looking at their balance sheets and thinking 'Where is our next market?' (Webster, July 2011).

In contrast, the potential negative impact of the lack of awareness of the current and future opportunities presented by the Korean market that had been highlighted by the Seoul interviewees was also a matter of concern to staff at UKTI:

> The biggest challenge has been getting people interested in Korea and actually telling them what it is like and making them interested in Korea. Some people already have got it...others really don't get it and because Korea has been forgotten for so long you are almost starting from scratch (Barrett, May 2011).

For too many companies, Korea was a forgotten or overlooked market with a negative reputation that dated back to previous decades when the Korean government sought to restrict and control trade and inward investment. Indeed, Webster referred to Korea as a 'market that people bump into', and thus the biggest challenge for the UKTI team was getting people excited about Korea as a market of opportunity. Thus the FTA gave UKTI the perfect opening to 'sell' Korea to UK business, to try to overcome nervousness about approaching such an unknown market and attempt to dispel negative perceptions of the country, its business environment and inter-Korean relations.

However, the team were realistic about the prospects for success in these endeavours, in that they could provide an up-to-date and honest picture of the current situation, but did not have sufficient resources to tackle the bigger problem of changing deeply entrenched attitudes. All they could do was give people accurate information and point them in a direction, but only if that was the direction in which they wanted to go. UKTI staff were well aware that there were situations where they could be saying: 'There are great opportunities in this market', and the company would reply: 'Yes...but what about this other market?' (Webster, July 2011).

Both sides were also agreed on the importance of culture when doing business overseas. The UKTI staff saw culture as an issue common to all foreign markets, observing that there were even cultural differences between countries as apparently similar as the UK and the US, and emphasised that cultural awareness was an essential element of successful trading or investing overseas. Thus culture was an integral part of UKTI events and an important feature of their newsletters. While there were key etiquette issues involved (such as handling name cards in Asia), cultural awareness was a 'far more sophisticated and nuanced idea' encompassing issues as diverse as management, negotiations, decision-making, networks and relationships (Leaver, July 2011).

Company responses to information about cultural awareness varied from being unconvinced that culture was an issue in certain markets (the US being a good example), to an assumption that cultural issues were identical in countries located within the same region or cultural zone (such as Hong Kong and Singapore in Asia, or Europe and the US in the Western world), to genuine concern about unfamiliar markets such as Korea. Thus, there would be a wide variety of responses, depending on the country in question, and cultural sensitising had to be a 'very bespoke service' rather than a generalised approach (Webster, July 2011).

The sense among interviewees in Seoul that small and medium enterprises either were more in need of help, or needed a different kind of help to multinationals was not, in general, borne out by the experiences of the UKTI staff. Although in some cases the needs were the same, they also felt that it was easy to assume that large companies knew everything and needed little help because they were already in many other markets. However, there were well-publicised cases, such as Walmart and Carrefour investing in, and then pulling out of, Korea, that proved that the assumption was sometimes false. Similarly, there was little concern at UKTI about a potential 'rush to market' in Korea by inexperienced companies, as entering a new and unfamiliar market was a significant commitment for any company, requiring careful consideration in terms of capacity, risk, resources and business culture. Indeed, Leaver observed that, far from rushing in unprepared, some companies almost needed a push to go into these markets.

4.4 *Measuring success*

With any publicly-funded initiative, there is a need to track its progress and assess the outcomes. Once the FTA message was formulated and the communication channels were established, a key issue for UKTI was monitoring the success of the initiatives in terms of promoting Korea as a market for trade and investment; as Leaver observed: 'The bottom line will be—does it lead to business?' The biggest measure of success within UKTI is the level of OMIS commissions and the attainment of targets set for each country (Leaver, July 2011). UKTI's monitoring systems enabled staff to determine whether the OMIS commissions, which were highly likely to lead to business activity in Korea, were directly attributable to the EU–Korea FTA promotional initiatives.[8] The OMIS target for UKTI Seoul was set at £44,000 in 2009; this was increased to £63,000 in 2010 and further to £106,400 in 2011, reflecting a sharp increase in 'footfall' through the UKTI offices. There were other gauges of the extent to which interest in and awareness of Korea was increasing: the numbers of people attending events, beginning to develop a working relationship with UKTI, clicking through on the e-newsletter, and so forth. All of these would give an indication as to whether awareness about market opportunities in Korea had been raised.

In an internal e-gram written in October 2011 and entitled 'Korea—How to promote a Free Trade Agreement', Barrett reported on the success of the various promotional initiatives: 700 USB sticks had been distributed by October 2011, the Korea team had given 'significant' help to more than 500 UK companies in 2010, they were on target to help more than 700 firms in 2011, and there had been an increase in trade missions to the market. In 2010, OMIS commissions for UKTI Korea totalled £111,730—or 177 percent of the target set for the staff—making UKTI Seoul the 11th highest income generator in the world per full-time employee, and the highest in the Asia-Pacific region. In terms of lessons learned from the initiatives to promote the EU–Korea FTA, Barrett warned his colleagues in government not to underestimate the scale of the task of promoting such a

[8] It should be noted that, while a good proportion of this OMIS income was attributable to the events that UKTI had organised, staff acknowledged that the effects of the research and the promotional activities could take time to filter through. Especially in economically difficult times, putting resources into entering a new market would not be an overnight decision for most companies.

deal, especially if they were promoting trade with 'one of the less popular markets'. Although it would take time, the effects of the sensitising events and the reports would filter through and would result in converting business contacts into business success (Barrett 2011).

5 Discussion and conclusions

In terms of the EC's motivations and expectations, the free trade agreement between the European Union and the Republic of Korea that went into force on 1 July 2011 aligns with the theories put forward in the existing academic literature. In pursuing an FTA with Korea, the EC was seeking to dismantle tariff and non-tariff barriers and thus boost bilateral trade and investment, while also raising the profile of the European Union in Korea and the East Asian region. We have discussed elsewhere a third category of barriers to trade and investment in Korea that have their roots in Korea's society and culture and that members of the EU business community fear may slow down the successful implementation of the FTA (Cherry 2011; 2012). However, the existing literature does not cover the practicalities of promoting free trade agreements or offer advice on the action that national governments and trade agencies can take to ensure that the anticipated benefits actually materialise.

The EU–Korea FTA provides an excellent case study of promoting FTAs in that Korea is an important trade and investment partner in the eyes of some EU member states and yet remains an 'unknown' or 'forgotten' market in the eyes of many EU companies. Another interesting dimension of this case is that, while FTAs concluded by the EC on behalf of the European Union's 27 member states are negotiated on behalf of all members, once the agreement goes into force, the states that have the most to gain from the enhanced trading conditions become competitors, striving to gain an advantage over all the other countries that signed the same deal. Even before the deal was ratified and went into effect, it was clear that, having successfully negotiated the FTA, national governments seeking to maximise its benefits would have to take an active role in publicising the deal and its benefits for EU business. The socio-cultural differences between the Korean and EU business environments added another dimension to the challenge facing EU governments: educating potential exporters and investors about such problems and barriers and helping them to develop coping strategies.

There are several important lessons that can be taken from the UKTI initiatives. Firstly, it is essential to begin preparations for promoting the FTA well in advance of ratification and implementation: a two-year head start enabled UKTI staff to commission research, plan events, weave the FTA-related activities into their existing trade promotion structures and processes, and create robust communication channels for the findings of the research they commissioned. In the eyes of the UKTI staff, the free trade agreement was invaluable as a 'hook' for promoting more intensively a market in which there were signs of increasing interest among UK companies. The advantages offered by the FTA might only be short term in nature, dependent on the speed with which their competitors negotiated and signed similar deals; it was vital to capitalise on this advantage and be ready 'before the flag dropped'.

Secondly, the FTA has to be presented to domestic business in an accessible way, and UKTI staff were quick to recognise the challenges inherent in presenting and selling the FTA to British business. Generalisations or theoretical discussions about market expansion, trade creation, competition enhancement and the effects of collaboration would mean little to potential exporters. Equally, broadbrush overviews highlighting the lowering or elimination of tariff and non-tariff barriers and the general benefits to EU business were likely to be of scant interest to British companies that were not focused on Korea and had negative perceptions of, or no knowledge about, the market. A document of the length and complexity of a free trade agreement is not user-friendly as far as the deal's intended beneficiaries are concerned. UKTI staff and IRC turned the document into a concise and accessible format through which UK companies could easily understand the impact of the deal on selected sectors and the specific opportunities it would create. From the EU–Korea free trade agreement, which was negotiated on behalf of the whole region, UKTI staff identified and extracted the specific sectors that played to the strengths and competitive advantages of UK business, producing a clear picture of the first-to-market opportunities that would be available. In short, UKTI tailored the information to potential exporters and provided demonstrable and concrete benefits for their companies that had the potential to impact on their bottom line.

Thirdly, it is essential to recognise the particular challenges presented by a given market and take steps to address them: in the case of Korea these related to a general lack of information about the market, negative perceptions of the country and concerns over the unfamiliar business culture. UKTI staff realised that, when presenting the opportunities to potential exporters to stimulate interest in the Korean market, they faced the dual challenge of changing perceptions and raising awareness. As some companies would need reassurance that help was available to deal with this unknown market, it was important to provide accurate and up-to-date information about the country, the market and the business culture, both in the narrower sense of everyday etiquette and in the broader sense of adapting to the market, business culture and environment.

Fourthly, the promotion of an FTA requires a variety of robust communication channels. In addition to producing the research report in hard copy and USB formats, UKTI developed new communication channels to feed specific information through to companies expressing an interest in the Korean market, including an e-newsletter and FTA-related blogs. Fifthly, success requires the development and maintenance of close relationships with potential exporters. UKTI staff afforded high priority to this aspect of FTA promotion, immediately feeding contacts made at the UK-based sensitising events through to post in Korea to ensure prompt feedback and effective communication between UKTI Seoul and potential clients. Finally, as Barrett emphasised in his review of the UKTI initiatives and best practice in promoting FTAs, a wide range of promotional events and high-level support from government at those events is an important factor. UKTI organised a variety of sensitising events on a large scale, taking in every region in the United Kingdom, and the support and presence of senior government officials underlined the significance of the deal for UK business. Barrett also warned that it would take time for the hard work to pay off; patience would be needed while the effects of the various promotional efforts turned into recordable and measurable business activity (Barrett 2011).

Over the past three years, staff at UK Trade & Investment have developed a successful model of FTA promotion that can be followed or adapted by other EU member states or governments pursuing or implementing FTAs, particularly in East Asia. The model will be especially useful in the case of partner countries that share some or all of the challenges presented by Korea: a lack of awareness of or interest in the market, negative perceptions of the country, and socio-cultural issues that can serve as barriers to successful business operations. Just as the EC views the EU–Korea FTA as a model for other deals in East Asia, national governments can draw upon UKTI's experience in developing promotional activities to 'sell' a free trade agreement to their corporate sector and thus reap the benefits that are anticipated from these trade deals.

6 Postscript—September 2012

In an interview conducted in Seoul in September 2012, just over a year after the implementation of the EU–Korea free trade agreement, Douglas Barrett reflected on the 'huge benefits' that the UK and UK businesses had gained from the trade deal. Exports to Korea had risen steadily through the first decade of the 21st century, increasing from £1.29 billion in 2001 to £2.20 billion in 2010. In 2011, the year in which the EU–Korea free trade agreement went into effect, exports increased by 12.6 percent year on year to £2.48 billion. In the first six months of 2012, however, exports from the UK to Korea jumped by 124 percent to £2.38 billion, boosted by a surge in oil exports from £2.8 million in January–June 2011 to £1.2 billion in the same period in 2012. The surge in oil sales to Korea, which accounted for 84 percent of the increase in export sales, could be attributed directly to the FTA, as the removal of the 3 percent tariff on North Sea oil made Brent crude oil prices more competitive, at a time when Korea was having problems buying oil from Iran and in the Dubai spot market. In the same period, exports of power-generating machinery increased by 161 percent from £32.6 million to £85.1 million; sales were boosted by Korea's promotion of 'green growth' and contributed 3.8 percent to the UK's first half export increase. Sales of inorganic chemicals were the third largest contributor, rising by 486 percent to £52.2 million (from £8.9 million) as tariffs fell by 6 to 8 percent, contributing 3.1 percent to the overall increase in exports. Electrical machinery and road vehicles both increased by 2 percent compared with the same period in 2011.

However, the UK's traditional top five export sectors performed less well in 2012; sales of general industrial machinery fell by 19 percent, and exports of electrical machinery declined by 7 percent as the Korean economy continued to experience slower growth. A general belt-tightening among consumers in Korea and a switch in alcoholic beverage preferences from whisky to wine contributed to an increase of just 0.2 percent in beverage exports to £36.9 million. Exports of medicinal and pharmaceutical products edged up by 0.1 percent, reflecting concerns among foreign drugs companies that domestic market prices for their goods, which are controlled by the National Drug Administration, do not reflect the time, effort and capital they invest in research and development. Exports of road vehicles saw a similar increase of 0.1 percent in the first six months of the year.[9]

Despite the downturn in some of the UK's key export sectors and the possibility that the boom in oil exports would only last as long as prices remained in the UK's favour, Barrett was upbeat about the UK's performance.

> People don't have a lot of money in Korea right now so it's amazing that these things have happened. Against that background, we've done really well and for the first time in living memory, we are in a trade surplus with Korea. A lot of that is down to the oil...that's absolutely true...but a lot of that was down to the FTA tariff reduction. But strip that away and [exports] are still 15 percent up (Barrett 2012).

When asked about other factors that had contributed to the UK's ongoing export success, Barrett highlighted the continuing sensitising events, most notably a British lifestyle event in Seoul in March 2012, which attracted 25 UK firms and 400 Korean buyers. The 'Olympic effect', which prompted British promotions at major store chains in Korea, also helped UK retailers and was a case of 'good timing at a difficult period', according to Barrett. The events had continued in the UK too and there were plans for a Korea-unique event to be called 'Opportunity Korea' in early 2013, focusing on four big centres within the UK where UKTI activities can have the greatest impact.

> The events do work—there's no doubt at all in our minds. We see them as absolutely crucial to getting people to come here [Korea]. When we trace back the companies that come here and whether we saw them or not, you can pinpoint where you met them in the past.

The sector-specific report on the opportunities generated by the FTA and the promotional USB stick in Barrett's words 'continued to be

[9] In the first half of 2012, the UK's top six export sectors were: petroleum (49 percent of the total); general industrial machinery (5 percent); medicinal and pharmaceutical products (4 percent): power-generating machinery (4 percent); road vehicles (3 percent); and beverages (3 percent).

gobbled up by people'; although it was not easy to estimate accurately the impact of the FTA report, Barrett noted that visitors were better informed about tariff reductions than before the report was published, suggesting that the sectoral approach taken by UKTI made this specific information much more accessible to exporters. Footfall through the embassy in Seoul had also increased and there had been a concomitant increase in OMIS income: in fiscal year 2010–11, UKTI Seoul almost doubled its OMIS target of £63,000 with commissions of £111,730, and in fiscal year 2011– 2012 it was 45 percent over target, with commissions of £154,377 against a target of £106,400.

In summary, asked if the London head office was pleased with the results of the investment of the funding they had provided and the initiatives put in place by the Korean team, Barrett replied:

> We've done pretty well, really. If you try and sum it all up, the bottom line for us is…it's a success and it is seen to be a success, and it's really working well.

REFERENCES

Agence France Presse (2011), 'EU Sees S. Korea Trade Pact as Model for Asia'. Online: www.bilaterals.org/spip.php?article19721 (accessed 20 June 2011)

Andreosso-O'Callaghan, Bernadette (2009), 'Economic Structural Complementarity: How Viable is the Korea-EU FTA?', in: *Journal of Economic Studies*, 36 (2), pp. 147–67

Asian Development Bank (2002), 'Asian Development Outlook 2002: Preferential Trade Agreements in Asia and the Pacific'. Online: www. scribd.com/doc/49451448/Asian-Development-Outlook2002-Preferential-Trade-Agreements-in-Asia-and-the-Pacific (accessed 8 November 2012)

Baldwin, Richard E. (1994), 'A Domino Theory of Regionalism', Graduate Institute of International Studies, University of Geneva, Working Paper 4465. Online: www.nber.org/papers/w4465 (accessed 30 September 2011)

Barfield, Claude (2007), 'Europe (Re)joins the FTA Bandwagon', American Enterprise Institute, 12 January. Online: www.aei.org/outlook/foreign-and-defense-policy/regional/europe/europe-rejoins-the-fta-bandwag on/ (accessed 8 November 2012)

Barrett, Douglas (2011), 'Korea—How to Promote a Free Trade Agreement', draft e-gram, 13 October

Cherry, Judith (2007), Foreign Direct Investment in Post-crisis Korea: European Investors and 'Mismatched Globalization', Abingdon, Oxon, UK; New York: RoutledgeCurzon

Cherry, Judith (2011), 'Making Friends with the Hydra: European Expectations of the EU-Korea Free TradeAgreement', in: *European Journal of East Asian Studies*, 10 (1), pp. 59–83

Cherry, Judith (2012), 'Upgrading the "Software": The EU-Korea Free Trade Agreement and Socio-cultural Barriers to Trade and Investment', in: *Pacific Review,* 25 (2), pp. 247–68

Cho Whan-bok (2001), 'Globalization and Outlook for Korea's Economic Diplomacy', in: *Korea Focus*, 9 (2), pp. 89–98

Dent, Christopher (2006), *New Free Trade Agreements in the Asia-Pacific*, Basingstoke, UK: PalgraveMacmillan

Dent, Christopher (2007), 'Full Circle? Ideas and Ordeals of Creating a Free Trade Area of the Asia-Pacific', in: *Pacific Review*, 20 (4), pp. 447–74

EUCCK (European Chamber of Commerce in Korea) (2010), 'EUCCK Welcomes EU-Korea FTA'. Online: www.eucck.org/site/press_centre/euccknews.htm?mode=view&num=13 (accessed 28 June 2011; now removed from site)

Europa (2010), 'Free Trade Agreement with South Korea', 15 October. Online: http://europa.eu/rapid/pressReleasesAction.do?reference=MEMO/09/452&format=HTML&aged=0&language=EN&guiLanguage=en (accessed 28 June 2011)

European Commission (2006), 'Global Europe: Competing in the World'. Online: http://trade.ec.europa.eu/doclib/docs/2006/october/tradoc_1303 70.pdf (accessed 28 June 2011)

European Commission (2010), 'Free Trade Agreement Between the European Union and the Republic of Korea'. Online: www.eucck.org/popup/20100927/images/eu_all_of_text_e.pdf (accessed 28 July 2011; now removed from site)

European Commission Trade (2010a), 'EU-Korea Free Trade Agreement Online'. Online: http://eur-lex.europa.eu/LexUriServ/LexUriServ.do?uri=OJ:L:2011:127:FULL:EN:PDF (accessed 8 November 2012)

European Commission Trade (2010b), 'EU-South Korea Free Trade Agreement: A Quick Reading Guide'. Online: http://trade.ec.europa.eu/doclib/docs/2009/october/tradoc_145203.pdf (accessed 28 June 2011)

Foreign and Commonwealth Office (2011), 'UK Companies to Benefit from EU-Korea Free Trade Agreement'. Online: www.fco.gov.uk/en/news/ latest-news/?id=633131382&view=News (accessed 28 July 2011)

Gavin, Brigid, and Alice N. Sindzingre (2009), 'EU Trade Relations with Emerging Asia: Identifying the Issues', in: *Asia Europe Journal*, 7, pp. 9–22

Guerin, Selin. S., Heungchong Kim, Hongshik Lee, Guido Glania, Jurgen Matthes, Huw Edwards and Mahmut Tekce (2007), *A Qualitative Analysis of a Potential Free Trade Agreement Between the European Union and South Korea*. Brussels: Centre for European Policy Studies and Korea Institute for International and Economic Policy

Mansfield, Edward (1998), 'The Proliferation of PTAs', in: *Journal of Conflict Resolution*, 42 (5), pp. 523–43

Nicolas, Françoise (2009), 'Negotiating a Korea–EU Free Trade Agreement: Easier Said Than Done', in: *Asia Europe Journal*, 7, pp. 23–42

Rollo, Jim (2008), 'An EU-Korea Free Trade Area: Playing Catch-up or Taking the Lead?', *Chatham House Briefing Papers*, IEP/JEF BP 08/03, London: Chatham House

UK Trade & Investment (2011), *South Korea: Open for Business*, Seoul: UK Trade & Investment

Urata, Shujiro (2002), 'Globalization and the Growth in Free Trade Agreements', in: *Asia-Pacific Review*, 9 (1), pp. 20–32

Woolcock, Stephen (2007), 'European Union Policy Towards Free Trade Agreements', ECIPE *Working Papers*, 03/2007, Brussels: European Centre for International Political Economy

INTERVIEWS

Barrett, Douglas, interviewed at UK Trade & Investment, British Embassy, Seoul, in May 2011 and September 2012.

Leaver, Christine, interviewed at UK Trade & Investment headquarters, London, in July 2011.

Webster, Richard, interviewed at UK Trade & Investment headquarters, London, in July 2011.

FRAMING THE GLOBALISATION DEBATE IN KOREAN HIGHER EDUCATION

Stephanie K. Kim

ABSTRACT

The South Korean government has enacted a series of policy initiatives to recruit more foreign students as a means of generating more income for the country's universities. These internationalisation policies are a direct response to the phenomenon of global competition that is currently reshaping higher education. The case of South Korea is indicative of what is happening throughout Asia, where competition for student markets has become more pronounced as Asian universities devise incentives and mechanisms for enhancing the inflow of foreign students. By understanding how internationalisation policies arise out of the socio-economic realities of South Korea and create contentious issues in Korean higher education, we will better understand not only the globalisation process in South Korea but also how Korean higher education connects to the larger debates surrounding globalisation.

Key words: globalisation, higher education, South Korea, universities

1 INTRODUCTION

In a continuing neoliberal trend in higher education reform, the government of the Republic of Korea (ROK—South Korea, hereafter Korea) has enacted a series of policy initiatives to recruit more foreign students as a means of generating more income for its universities and thereby counterbalance a shrinking population of domestic students. In effect, this policy shift underscores the need for Korean universities to improve institutional quality and to create campus settings that better accommodate foreign students. Higher education is undergoing substantial changes under globalisation, and market forces are increasingly emphasised in educational decision-making. How to differentiate institutions and in what ways global competitiveness can be enhanced have become increasingly important issues in higher education. Furthermore, worldwide trends towards mass education and the marketisation of education have led to severe competition for funds, students and faculties. Reform measures have thus evolved into predominantly a search for student markets domestically and abroad. The purpose of this paper is to connect the internationalisation policies adopted by Korean universities to the broader discussion of globalisation and higher education, especially as globalisation gives rise not only to new economic dynamics but also to new social relations. Specifically, this essay offers a discussion of (1) the market forces flowing from globalisation that create global competition in higher education, (2) the contemporary landscape of internationalisation and student mobility in Asia as a product of this phenomenon of global competition, (3) the socio-economic realities of South Korea that lead to Korean policies of internationalisation, and (4) the contentious issues arising out of those policies as they relate to the broader issues of Korean higher education.

2 The Phenomenon of Global Competition in Higher Education

As globalisation has become the focal point of higher education, competition has become a central preoccupation. Competition is closely connected with a global free-market economy. Combined with the impact of globalisation and the development of the global knowledge economy, these competitive forces have resulted in the phenomenon of global competition that is currently reshaping higher education. Many developments characterise this trend in higher education, including the rise of global university rankings, a continuing neoliberal tendency towards academic capitalism, claims by nations to have a world-class university, and cross-border quality assurance practices.[1]

Since the 1960s, higher education has been pushed towards worldwide mass dimensions, producing a diversified and complex academic environment (Chan 2004). The inevitable result of a complex, mass system is a ranking procedure. The first international ranking project was undertaken by Shanghai Jiao Tong University Institute of Higher Education in 2003 with the title Academic Ranking of World Universities (ARWU) (ARWU 2003). It was followed by the *Times Higher*

[1] For a more in-depth discussion of the global competition phenomenon in higher education, see Rust and Kim (2012).

Education (*THE*)-QS World University Rankings, which appeared from 2004 to 2009.[2] Though both rankings designate the highest ranked universities primarily in North America and Western Europe, within these groupings there is quite a difference. For example, my institution, UCLA, was ranked 15th according to the 2003 Shanghai rankings and 26th according to the 2004 *THE* rankings. Furthermore, the first Shanghai rankings designate a much higher proportion of universities in the United States (US) with 60 of the top 100 in the US alone, while the *THE* rankings have a broader distribution that encompasses North America, Western Europe, Asia and Australia. Regardless of variation between rankings, both of these annual reports have 'triggered the transformation of world higher education' (Marginson 2010). The first reaction came from national leaders in China, Germany and France, who quickly initiated research and development policies that aimed to increase their higher education stature (Hazelkorn 2008). Rankings now influence attitudes and behaviour to the point that every nation is conscious of its global standing in higher education. In effect, these ranking are a byproduct of global competition; at the same time, they engender increased competition as universities clamour to make it to the top of the list, or to be represented at all.

A key feature in the global race is academic capitalism, where knowledge is no longer a public good but a private commodity, where higher education institutions are increasingly becoming suppliers and marketers of knowledge, and where students are increasingly treated as customers of knowledge (Slaughter and Rhoades 2004). In the evolving global system of higher education, being competitive becomes key, and global positioning is integral to competing with other nations and institutions (Marginson 2006). Some scholars claim that universities are currently in a 'reputation race' in which they compete for academic prestige (van Vught 2008). Arguments have been made

---

[2] The first *THE* rankings survey was published in the *Times Higher Education Supplement* in November 2004. In 2009, the *THE* split with its original partner, Quacquarelli Symonds, and created a new ranking methodology, compiling the information for its citation database in partnership with Thomson Reuters. Quacquarelli Symonds has continued to publish the QS World University Rankings. Currently, the *THE* rankings are aligned more closely to the Shanghai rankings and differ from the QS rankings in that they place less importance on reputation and heritage and give more weight to hard measures of research, teaching and knowledge transfer. The original 2004 rankings may be viewed at http://jobs.timeshighereducation.co.uk/hybrid.asp?typeCode=194 (accessed 15 May 2013).

that 'the more an individual university aspires to the top end of competition, the more significant global referencing becomes' (Marginson 2006: 27). Universities, and the countries in which they are located, thus seek to project the best image possible in order to be poised to compete for research funding, the best and brightest students, and star faculty members. Moreover, there is gravitation towards an ideal type of institutional model, what Kathryn Mohrman, Wanhua Ma, and David Baker (2008) call the Emerging Global Model of the top stratum of research universities in the quest to reach world-class status.

Philip Altbach (2004a) says it best: 'Everyone wants a world-class university. No country feels it can do without one. The problem is that no one knows what a world-class university is, and no one has figured out how to get one. Everyone, however, refers to the concept.' The one thing we do know is that among the tens of thousands of universities in the world, only a very few are world-class, and the most elite universities are located in only a small handful of countries. Still, higher education institutions, governments and organisations compete to have their institutions reflected in the rankings. The one common outcome of the ranking systems is the tendency to establish a single set of criteria that shapes institutions. Because the ranking systems heavily weigh top scholarly output as a measure of institutional quality, the highest ranked institutions are the large research and development universities. Many countries are making large commitments to developing world-class universities through their research and development capability, or are turning to private institutions to enhance their higher education status.

In this period of intense globalisation, quality assurance has become a priority. The proliferation of institutions, the rapid expansion of students, the mobility of students to travel outside of their home countries, and other factors have forced policymakers to pay attention to accountability and quality. In the past, the major focus of most countries has been to increase access and enrolment. Now the focus has begun to shift towards quality and achievement, not only amongst students but also amongst faculty and administrators. However, because institutions are rapidly emerging that fall outside the customary boundaries of control, where there is no mechanism for assessing these institutions, and because many countries have attempted or are attempting to establish accrediting agencies, these countries have turned to highly developed states and their institutions to help define quality. Quality assurance has thus become a contested issue. Some observers claim that it is nothing more than the cosmopolitan powers once again imposing their notions of quality on the rest of the world and universalising the criteria by which quality is to be determined (Ntshoe and Letseka 2010). This likelihood is made particularly acute as international forces confront local traditions when quality assurance standards involve a social as well as a technical dimension (Gertel and Jacobo 2010). Critics also point out that the reason countries such as the US and the UK possess the most highly ranked universities stems from much larger socio-historical trajectories—histories, wealth, ability to attract top scholars and students worldwide, strong traditions of academic freedom, and academic cultures based on competition and meritocracy—and their significant head starts create centres and peripheries based on a colonial legacy (Altbach 2004b; Altbach 2009). Post-colonial criticisms aside, Western principles of quality and assurance often take the form of marketisation of the university against the backdrop of international benchmarking and increased student mobility.

3 Internationalisation and Student Mobility in Asia

Internationalisation has become a premier topic of discussion in higher education. Knight (2004; 2010) and Altbach and Knight (2007) define internationalisation not as synonymous with globalisation but as representing choice-based actions and responses to globalisation. The methods through which higher education institutions respond to globalisation, and ultimately how they internationalise themselves, depend on the mission and competitive strategies an institution chooses to pursue (Knight 2010).

Asia has taken the internationalisation agenda very seriously. International benchmarking by way of global university rankings is the commonly adopted approach to assess university performance. To become more internationalised, Asian universities have begun to change their teaching and learning strategies and to restructure their curricula. Instead of the conventional teacher-centred approach, Asian universities have tried to train students to become independent and self-directed learners in a broader attempt to prepare them for the challenges of globalisation. In Hong Kong, for example, the University of Hong Kong now follows a common core curriculum that requires all undergraduate students to take six courses in four broad-based subject matters—humanities, global issues, Chinese culture, state and society, and scientific and technological literacy—that was loosely modelled after the liberal arts curriculum in the US (Mok and Cheung 2011). Asian universities are also forming international exchanges and joint programmes with Western counterparts. In fact, Chinese students now form the largest international student group in both the US and UK higher education systems. Chinese universities have also begun to adopt English as a medium of instruction alongside Standard Chinese. English-mediated instruction can easily be found in other Asian societies like Hong Kong, Taiwan, Singapore, Malaysia, Japan and South Korea. It is clear that internationalisation is considerably shaping the student experience in Asia.

Meanwhile, dynamics of student mobility in Asia are also rapidly changing. For the past three decades, our observations of student mobility have been largely unidirectional: students from Asia going to North America or Western Europe for education, training and degree acquisition. But things have begun to change. The number of students from Asian countries studying in other Asian countries reveals a sharp increase in student mobility within the region (see Table 1). Over 40 percent of tertiary-level students from East Asia and the Pacific studying abroad chose to study within the same region in 2007, leading to the greatest flow of student mobility being in intra-Asian study abroad within the region. On the other hand, the flow of students from Asia to North America has drastically decreased in the last decade.

Indeed, an emerging pattern of intra-Asian student mobility is now replacing the unidirectional one, and this has profound implications. These students shed a new light on centre-periphery criticisms where an emerging multi-centre is fast becoming the dominant model of student mobility. Asian universities are also being conceptualised as both global and Asian in a way that reconfigures the global in Asian terms. For example, in Singapore, the National University of Singapore approaches student life and educational practices to produce students who are 'global citizens' alongside 'perspectives from Asia'. This combination is emphasised through an increasing number of institu tional partnerships with other Asian universities and the active encouragement of students to go beyond traditional destinations for study abroad of North America and Western Europe (Collins and Chong 2012). While it may be true that 'Western academic paradigms' (Mok 2007; Deem, Mok, and Lucas 2008) do drive the global standards by

Table 1 Distribution of destinations for students from East Asia and the Pacific studying abroad, 2007

Destination	%	Change in % points relative to 1999
Arab states	0.2	-0.3
Central and Eastern Europe	1.3	-0.4
Central Asia	0.4	+0.3
East Asia and the Pacific	41.8	+6.0
Latin America and the Caribbean	0.2	+0.1
North America	33.0	-10.0
Western Europe	22.9	+4.4
South and West Asia	0.2	-0.1
Sub-Saharan Africa	0	0

Source: UNESCO Institute for Statistics (2009).

which Asian universities navigate, there is more than simply the borrowing of knowledge and institutions from the West.

Meanwhile, as international student mobility grows rapidly within Asia, competition amongst universities for student markets has become more pronounced. This is because the net flow of students in Asia is still negative—meaning that the number of outbound students from Asia still exceeds the number of inbound students to Asia. Even the four 'Tiger' countries—Hong Kong, Singapore, South Korea and Taiwan—continue to send more students to developed and high-income countries than they receive. Although China has become a major host country for the international student market, the number of outbound students from China considerably exceeds the number of inbound students to China. Only Japan is the exception in Asia, where it has a positive net flow of students. While intra-Asian student mobility has increased, it does not mean that Asia no longer sends great numbers of students to North America and Western Europe. In fact, Asian countries may even stress the importance of sending their students overseas to developed Western societies to acquire advanced knowledge and then have them return back to benefit the human capital formation in their home countries. At the same time, under the name of internationalisation, Asian countries have begun to devise incentives and mechanisms for enhancing the inflow of foreign students; however, the source of inbound students is primarily limited to other Asian countries. What has resulted is that Asian countries actually compete in the same larger pool of Asia itself for student markets (Chan 2012). And with the emergence of new players in the region such as China, Hong Kong, Singapore and South Korea, and a lack of strategies to attract students from outside Asia, the competition within Asia for Asian students will only become more fierce. In fact, competition amongst universities even within the same country has further intensified, especially in South Korea.

4 Internationalisation policies in South Korea

4.1 *Forces driving the policies*

Far from being immune to the phenomenon, South Korea is fully adopting internationalisation policies in the higher education sector in order to remain competitive in a global landscape. Beginning in the early 2000s, the Korean government introduced a series of policy initiatives to recruit more foreign students as a means of generating more income for its universities faced by a shrinking population of domestic students. The initiatives eventually led to the reconsideration of quality standards for education and research in the situation of global competition in higher education.

An understanding of the driving forces behind Korean internationalisation policies requires an examination of the socio-economic changes of the last couple of decades. In 1995, when the World Trade Organisation was established and included 'higher education services' in its list of trade negotiations, a clear shift began in the future direction of higher education reform. South Korea internalised this neoliberal turn in higher education on a domestic level with the education reform plan introduced in 1995 by the Kim Young-sam administration. The plan emphasised that universities as sources of knowledge production should become more market-oriented and closely aligned to the needs of the labour market (Park 2000). While the real workings of Korean university governance models did not change much, there was an increase in market-oriented rhetoric surrounding higher education—with symbolic keywords like higher education industry, consumer orientation, competition and marketisation—that represented a clear shift in the formal purpose of higher education in South Korea

(Byun 2008). Further pushing the neoliberal turn was the Asian financial crisis of the late 1990s. In the wake of the crisis, the Korean government has attempted to minimise the country's educational trade deficit by pursuing measures that discourage domestic students from studying abroad, while encouraging foreign students to come study in South Korea.

Behind the neoliberal swing in higher education lie the dramatic demographic shifts happening in South Korea. The driving force behind Korean internationalisation policies is the overall decline in its higher education student population that South Korea is experiencing. This trend is primarily due to a continuing growth in Korean students going abroad for their higher education (see Table 2). Increasingly, a larger proportion of Korean students are going overseas for their undergraduate degrees, whereas traditionally going abroad was undertaken by students pursuing their graduate degrees. Previously, the perception of studying abroad for an undergraduate degree was that it was for academically weak students who were trying to 'escape' the competitive education system in South Korea. However, this perception has by and large disappeared as the proportion of undergraduate-level students going overseas to study has increased dramatically since the 2000s. A large section of such students consists of those graduating from top Korean high schools. The primary reason behind this shift is the increasing demand for holders of foreign degrees and for English-language speakers in the Korean job market (Park 2011). The continuing increase in outbound undergraduate students, coupled with a falling fertility rate since the 1990s, which has resulted in an overall decline in the college-age population, has forced Korean universities to recruit from overseas; this circumstance is felt especially hard by private institutions located in smaller cities outside the Seoul metropolitan region that rely more heavily on tuition revenues. As the domestic population of students is quickly declining, and the need to increase the inflow of students has sharpened, the Korean government has adopted aggressive plans for foreign student recruitment as part of Korean internationalisation strategies.

4.2 *Specific government initiatives*

Government interest in inbound foreign students has resulted in two large-scale initiatives intended to increase substantially foreign student

Table 2 Korean students in higher education overseas, 1991–2011

Year	Number of students	% Change
1991	53,875	--
1993	84,765	57
1995	106,458	20
1997	133,249	20
1999	120,170	-10
2001	149,933	25
2003	159,903	6
2005	192,254	20
2007	217,959	13
2009	240,949	11
2011	289,288	20

Source: MEST.

enrolment. The first initiative was the Study Korea Project launched in 2004 and continuing today that actively targets foreign student enrolment in Korean universities. The second initiative was the Brain Korea 21 Project, running in two phases from 1999 to 2012, that internationalised the research capacity of Korean universities and thereby indirectly increased foreign student enrolment. More recently, the Korean government also launched a large-scale initiative for the internationalisation of research and academic staff through the World Class University Project, rolled out from 2008 to 2013.

The Study Korea Project is a drive by the Ministry of Education, Science, and Technology (MEST) to expand cooperation and exchanges between Korean and foreign universities in order to increase foreign student enrolment. In order to realise this objective, MEST has promoted government scholarships, improved the study and living conditions for foreign students, and focused on administrative support capabilities. The goal is to establish South Korea as the education hub of Northeast Asia through the following key policy tasks as indicated in the Study Korea Project 2007 report (MEST 2007): (1) improve infrastructure for foreign students; (2) foster foreign student recruitment networks abroad; (3) increase publicity on study opportunities in South Korea; and (4) establish an effective administrative and support system. In conjunction with the fast-growing Asian student market, the project has resulted in unprecedented growth in foreign student enrolment in Korean universities, as illustrated at Table 3.

Table 3 Foreign student enrolment in Korean higher education institutions, 2000–2012

Year	Enrolment	% Change	Degree programme	Language/other programme
2000	3,963	--	--	--
2001	4,682	18	--	--
2002	5,759	23	--	--
2003	12,314	114	7,962	4,352
2004	16,832	37	11,121	5,711
2005	22,526	52	15,577	6,949
2006	32,557	45	22,624	9,933
2007	49,270	51	32,056	17,214
2008	63,952	30	40,585	23,367
2009	75,850	19	50,591	25,259
2010	83,842	11	60,000	23,842
2011	89,537	7	63,653	25,884
2012	86,878	-3	60,589	26,289

Source: MEST.

The original goal of the project was to increase foreign student enrolment to 50,000 by the year 2010, but because this figure was almost attained as early as 2007, a second round of the Study Korea Project was announced in 2008 with the goal of increasing enrolment to 100,000 by the year 2012. While the objective behind the first round of the Study Korea Project was to generate income from increased foreign student enrolment, by contrast the second round has placed heavier emphasis on those aspects in human resource development that might attract foreign students by letting them develop as ambassadors for South Korea who can contribute to future international business and trade relations. Of the foreign student population in South Korea, a high percentage notably is from other Asian countries, particularly from China.[3]

---

[3] In 2011, Chinese students accounted for 66 percent of total foreign student enrolment followed by Japanese (5 percent), Mongolian (4 percent), American (3 per-

The Brain Korea 21 Project (hereafter BK21 Project) was an initiative to internationalise the research capacity of Korean universities with the aim of improving their global rankings and thereby indirectly increasing foreign student enrolment. The project was funded by the Korea Research Foundation, a government-sponsored organisation, and materialised in two phases, lasting from 1999 until 2005 and from 2006 until 2012 respectively. The project allocated resources to a selection of elite universities to nurture at least 10 of them into world-class universities on the basis of research and development capability. The overall objectives of the BK21 Project were to: (1) achieve greater worldwide visibility for Korean research through publication in international journals; (2) support globally competitive researchers through scholarship programmes; and (3) improve the overall competitiveness of the higher education system on the basis of the quality of students and academic activities (Moon and Kim 2001; Byun and Kim 2010). Phase I allocated funding totalling 1.34 trillion won to a group of 14 universities. The project measured its success primarily by the number of papers published in Science Citation Index (SCI) journals. In quantitative markers, the project proved to be a success, as the number of papers published in SCI journals nearly doubled between 1998 and 2004 (see Table 4).

Phase II allocated funding totalling 2.03 trillion won to cultivate graduate students and postgraduate researchers to become globally competitive researchers and thereby enhance the human capital capability of South Korea. This was evaluated through a basket of qualitative indicators that measured the human resource capability of Korean universities. The primary difference between the first and second phases is that Phase I developed the general research capacity of universities by targeting the science and engineering fields, whereas Phase II encouraged each university to choose the areas in which it wanted to concentrate its resources and differentiate itself from other universities (Seong et al. 2008). Since its adoption, the BK21 Project has changed the nature of Korean academic culture by instituting a results-oriented evaluative system where universities compete amongst each other in research output and where faculty members are assessed by their research performance (Shin 2009; Shin and Jang 2013).

---

cent), Vietnamese (2.5 percent), and Taiwanese (1.7 percent). See MEST, *Brief Statistics on Korean Education* 2012.

Table 4 Scientific Citation Index journal publications in South Korea, 1998–2004

Year	Number of publications	% Change	World ranking
1998	9,444	--	18
2000	12,013	27	16
2002	14,916	24	13
2004	18,497	24	13

Source: MEST (2005).

Table 5 Full-time foreign faculty in Korean higher education institutions, 2005–2012

Year	Number of foreign faculty	% Change	% Total
2005	2,131	--	3.2%
2006	2,540	19%	3.7%
2007	2,919	15%	4.1%
2008	3,433	18%	4.7%
2009	4,127	20%	5.5%
2010	4,957	20%	6.4%
2011	5,462	10%	6.6%
2012	5,964	9%	7.0%

Source: MEST, Brief Statistics on Korean Education 2005-2012.

More recently, the Korean government launched a large-scale initiative for the internationalisation of research and academic staff. The World Class University Project ran from 2008 to 2013 as a higher education subsidy programme that invited foreign scholars in possession of advanced research capacities to collaborate with Korean faculty members (see Table 5). The primary motivation of this project was to counterbalance the outflow of prominent scholars in South Korea and to increase the global rankings of Korean universities. This was the first time the government had attempted to 'import' foreign scholars on so large a scale. Foreign scholars were invited to establish new academic programmes, particularly in key growth-generating fields. They were also recruited as full-time professors to conduct research and teaching activities within existing programmes. Distinguished senior scholars were also recruited as visiting researchers and lecturers. The government invested 825 billion won during the five-year project.

The policy direction highlighted by the three programmes underscores the need for Korean universities to improve institutional quality and to create campus settings that better accommodate foreign students, a need that has become a critical component in Korean inter nationalisation strategies. In effect, the Korean government has enhanced the quality of education at domestic institutions as a way to direct resources toward incoming foreign students.

5 Contentious issues in Korean internationalisation policies

Because special funding is allocated on the basis of government evaluation, universities have responded aggressively towards government policy in a way that has spurred deep changes in their institutions. Some of the most tangible developments happening at Korean universities are the rise of English as the academic lingua franca, the establishment of institutional standards that give preference to research-intensive universities, and a shift in governance models where university administrators are emerging as powerful decision-makers.

5.1 *English as a medium of teaching*

English is certainly a contentious part of the process and consequences of Korean higher education reforms that affect a wide variety of practices in universities. The most visible component to these reforms is to convert a sizable proportion of university curricula into the medium of English to cater towards an international demographic. Following the launch of the Study Korea Project in 2004, the government began initiatives to provide Korean universities with financial support for increasing the number of English-taught courses, and as a result, the proportion of such courses has risen steeply. Today, top-tier private institutions such as Yonsei University and Korea University conduct up to a third of all their classes in English; others such as the Korea Advanced Institute for Science and Technology (KAIST) and the Pohang University of Science and Technology (POSTECH) have ambitiously pledged to adopt English as the only language of instruction.

Even Seoul National University (SNU)—a national university established by the Korean government to provide higher education in the service of South Korea's national interests—conducts over 15 percent of its classes in English.

Arising out of the rapid integration of English-taught courses is the question of whether these courses are effective settings for student learning in a context where English is not the primary language. English-taught courses naturally bring a diverse population of students into the same class, but how effective are the courses for the Korean students who are still the majority populations at Korean universities? One study conducted at Korea University found that Korean students encountered difficulty in their understanding of course content because of language when taking English-taught courses (Byun et al. 2011). Furthermore, English-taught courses are not necessarily taught by foreign faculty but are more often than not taught by Korean faculty members with the language prerequisites; however, limitations in language mean that Korean faculty may be impeded in their teaching ability when required to teach in English. In fact, the same study conducted at Korea University found that Korean students thought that Korean faculty would explain things too briefly and simply in their English-taught courses because certain concepts were too difficult to explain in a language that was not their native tongue, and that Korean faculty conceded they were to covering less material in English-taught courses because of language limitations. The rapid rise of English-taught courses has also created an 'English divide' between students who are good at English and those who are not. Another study conducted at Korea University found that English-taught courses used a fixed grading scale, while Korean-taught courses typically used a forced grading curve where receiving an 'A' was much harder to come by. Those students who were not confident in their English ability generally avoided taking English-taught courses and thus received much lower grades than those who took more English-taught courses. This difference led to a rising sense of unfairness and inequality amongst the students, because those with greater English fluency usually came from higher socio-economic backgrounds (Jon and Kim 2011). Additionally, the same study found that there was also increased resentment from students who believed that more English-taught courses did not make their campus more 'international' but instead more 'American'. Bearing in mind that Korea University now requires that all undergraduate students take a certain number of English-taught courses in order to graduate and that all faculty hired after 2003 must teach all their courses in English, the rapid integration of English instruction is certainly affecting the student learning experience in this particular institution. It is not a far stretch to surmise that the same issues raised at Korea University are prevalent in varying degrees throughout all Korean universities that have rapidly integrated English instruction.

In turn, the dramatic increase in English-taught courses also fuels a demand for faculty able to teach in English. Many Korean universities require newly hired professors to teach at least some courses in English. Furthermore, because SCI journals are predominantly English-language publications, English is quickly evolving into the primary language for publication of scholarly work as part of a reward mechanism for employment, promotion and tenure. Criteria for hiring and promoting faculty members have certainly shifted to include their ability to conduct classes in English and the number of articles that have been published in SCI journals. What this has indirectly resulted in is a preference for holders of foreign degrees, particularly from the US. Korean faculty who have completed their bachelor's and master's degrees in South Korea opt to pursue their doctoral studies in the US, even if their end goal is to return to the Korean academic environment as a faculty member (Shin 2012). Whether desirable or not, higher education trends in South Korea are pushing English as the primary language of scholarly communication, and deeply embedded within this change is the perception that Korean higher education is becoming more 'Americanised'.

5.2 *Effects of changed institutional standards*

At the same time, special funding on the basis of government evaluation has also resulted in the establishment of institutional standards that give preference to research-intensive universities and thus engenders competition amongst Korean universities. The BK21 Project has made research output the primary objective when determining a university's funding status. The way that the project measures research output is by the number of papers published in SCI journals by institution. Though the project proved to be a success as the number of papers published in SCI journals nearly doubled between 1998 and 2004, the growth rate of research publications was not different from that of the US or Japan, and even less than that of China (Shin 2009). Hence, while the project contributed to the growth in publications for Korean universities, the project did not lessen the gap between Korean universities and world-class universities. What the project did, however, was to establish a culture of research production as the primary means of evaluating a university's value. While specific universities (primarily SNU, KAIST and POSTECH) have traditionally been the strong research universities of South Korea, others such as Yonsei University, Korea University, Sungkyunkwan University, and Hanyang University have emerged as strong contenders for world-class status. These four universities did not clearly posit themselves as research universities prior to the implementation of the BK21 Project in 1999, but the four outpaced the traditional three research universities in terms of growth in research production and subsequently came to define themselves as research universities of a similar stature (Shin 2009). Thus, the effects of the BK21 Project are most apparent in the previously second-tier research universities, where they are actively reforming their systems to hire researchers and increase research output.

Encouraged by the results of the first phase, a second phase of the BK21 Project was implemented in order to cultivate graduate students and postgraduate researchers into reaching the status of globally competitive researchers and thereby enhance the human capital capability of South Korea. In particular, Phase II resulted in a clear cultural shift within Korean universities that aspire to world-class status. Since the BK21 Project, the Korean government has launched an initiative to deregulate universities in order to allow for more autonomy and thereby enhance the competitiveness of universities. This development has became particularly acute as Phase II encouraged a university to choose the areas in which it wanted to concentrate its resources and differentiate itself from other institutions. It is against this backdrop that Korean universities have adapted themselves to government policies based on special funding. For example, SNU has made its evaluation for faculty much more rigid by not allowing automatic tenure status for associate professors; instead, associate professors are now required to publish a minimum number of papers if they wish to be promoted to tenure, and must also acquire recommendation letters from distinguished scholars in the field if they wish to be promoted to full professor (Shin and Jang 2013). At POSTECH, newly hired assistant professors have seven years in which to apply for and pass their tenure review, and those who fail will have only a one-year grace period before they must leave. POSTECH is also one of the first champions of a performance-based salary system whereby the faculty salary is not determined by seniority but by a faculty member's accomplishments over the preceding three years in teaching, research and service (Rhee 2011). In effect, these processes have forced junior professors to internalise the 'publish or perish' mantra. Professors are also discouraged from doing service work, because service activities may take away time from research.

Resistance in response to the effects of the BK21 Project has occurred from multiple directions. Resistance from academics has been the most vocal, and thus a lot of policy changes implemented in research universities only affect newly hired faculty. This has led to direct conflicts between senior and junior faculty members. In a senior-based society like South Korea, senior professors assign service work to their juniors, which puts junior professors in a dilemma. On one hand, they must put more time into service activities; on the other, they are evaluated by more stringent publication requirements and are discouraged by the university to take on too much service work. In conjunction with new evaluation criteria that value meritocracy over seniority, this generational gap has become only more pronounced.

Resistance also comes from inter-departmental sources. One side effect of the BK21 Project is for universities to conform to a single set of criteria based on research output. Even within a single university, academic units (colleges and departments) have responded in conformist ways. Unfortunately, the criteria do not take into account differences by discipline, for example, the hard sciences versus the humanities and social sciences, and this has caused tension between academic units within a university. In fact, the disciplinary divide is exacerbated in the way academic units respond to the project—with the hard disciplines responding aggressively and the soft disciplines responding defensively. Those in the soft disciplines argue that humanities and social science research has been isolated from research funding, and that stringent publication demands in their respective fields do not necessarily produce better researchers. The conflict between disciplines in combination with the conflict between senior and junior faculty members is unlikely to be mediated in the changing environment of Korean higher education.

University governance models are also changing rapidly. Historically within a Korean university, professors have a strong influence on academic but not administrative affairs, while the government has a strong influence on administrative but not academic affairs. Since the implementation of the BK21 Project and more recently the World Class University Project, universities are now encouraged to handle administrative affairs on an institutional level. While the government may provide guidelines and conduct inspections within universities, procedural affairs such as management, organisation, finance and personnel are left to the universities themselves. Still, the government directs an evaluation-based budget allocation, which has a significant impact on universities. Because the evaluation-based budget allocation is determined by a report submitted by each university, most universities are realigning their institutional policies more closely to government guidelines regardless of their mission focus, regional location, and the characteristics of their faculty members and student body. These guidelines also require new funding sources to support research-intensive endeavours, and to that end universities are aggressively searching for external funding from public and private partnerships. Through this process, the influence of university presidents has increased tremendously, and shared governance is losing influence. Planning and evaluation as a result of the BK21 and World Class University Projects have empowered the university administration as the strongest actor in higher education governance. Hence, while internationalisation policies result in a decentralisation model between the government and the university, it also results in a highly centralised model within a university (Shin 2011).

6 Conclusion

By examining South Korea's place in a global context, I have revealed a local trajectory of a broader phenomenon where Asian universities respond and react to the spread of global competition in higher education. The above discussions show how global competition in higher education is certainly shaping internationalisation policies and student mobility trends in Asia. This phenomenon is clearly affecting higher education in South Korea, where universities are fully adopting internationalisation policies in order to remain competitive in a global landscape. Arising out of these policies are contentious issues in Korean higher education, specifically the rise of English as the academic lingua franca, the establishment of institutional standards that give preference to research-intensive universities, and a shift in governance models whereby university administrators are emerging as powerful decision-makers.

The case of South Korea is indicative of what is happening throughout Asia, where competition for student markets has become more pronounced as Asian universities devise incentives and mechanisms for enhancing the inflow of foreign students. By understanding how internationalisation policies arise out of the socio-economic realities of South Korea and create contentious issues in Korean higher education, we can better understand how Korean higher education connects to the larger debates surrounding globalisation.

REFERENCES

Altbach, Philip G. (2009), 'Peripheries and Centers: Research Universities in Developing Countries', in: *Asia Pacific Education Review*, 10 (1), pp. 15–27

Altbach, Philip G. (2004a), 'The Costs and Benefits of World-Class Universities', in: *Academe*, 90 (January/February), pp. 20–23

Altbach, Philip G. (2004b), 'Globalisation and the University: Myths and Realities in an Unequal World', in: *Tertiary Education and Management*, 10 (1), pp. 3–25

Altbach, Philip G. and Jane Knight (2007), 'The Internationalization of Higher Education: Motivations and Realities', in: *Journal of Studies in International Education*, 11 (3/4), pp. 290–305

ARWU (Academic Ranking of World Universities) (2003), 'Academic Ranking of World Universities 2003'. Online: www.arwu.org/ARWU2003.jsp (accessed 22 April 2013)

Byun, Kiyong (2008), 'New Public Management in Korean Higher Education: Is It Reality or Another Fad?', in: *Asia Pacific Education Review*, 9 (2), pp. 190–205

Byun, Kiyong, Huijung Chu, Minjung Kim, Inwoo Park, Suhong Kim and Juyoung Jung (2011), 'English-Medium Teaching in Korean Higher Education: Policy Debates and Reality', in: *Higher Education*, 62 (4), pp. 431–49

Byun, Kiyong and Minjung Kim (2010), 'Shifting Patterns of the Government's Policies for the Internationalization of Korean Higher Education', *Journal of Studies in International Education*, 14 (3), pp. 1-20

Chan, Sheng-Ju (2012), 'Shifting Patterns of Student Mobility in Asia', in: *Higher Education Policy*, 25 (2), pp. 207–24

Chan, Wendy W. Y. (2004), 'International Cooperation in Higher Education: Theory and Practice', in: *Journal of Studies in International Education*, 8 (1), pp. 32–55

Collins, Francis Leo and Ho Kong Chong (2012), 'Constructing a "Global University Centered in Asia": Globalizing Strategies and Experiences at the National University of Singapore', in: Deane E. Neubauer and Kazuo Kuroda (eds), *Mobility and Migration in Asian Pacific Higher Education*, New York: Palgrave Macmillan, pp. 157–74

Deem, Rosemary, Ka Ho Mok and Lisa Lucas (2008), 'Transforming Higher Education in Whose Image? Exploring the Concept of "World-Class" University in Europe and Asia', in: *Higher Education Policy*, 21 (1), pp. 83–97

Gertel, Hector R. and Alejandro D. Jacobo (2010), 'Quality-Oriented Management of Higher Education in Argentina', in: Laura M. Portnoi, Val D. Rust and Sylvia S. Bagley (eds), *Higher Education, Policy, and the Global Competition Phenomenon*, New York: Palgrave Macmillan, pp. 73–86

Hazelkorn, Ellen (2008), 'Learning to Live with League Tables and Rankings: The Experience of Institutional Leaders', in: *Higher Education Policy*, 21 (1), pp. 193–215

Jon, Jae-Eun and Eun-Young Kim (2011), 'What It Takes to Internationalize Higher Education in Korea and Japan: English-Mediated Courses and International Students', in: John D. Palmer, Amy Roberts, Young Ha Cho and Gregory S. Ching (eds), *The Internationalization of East Asian Higher Education*, New York: Palgrave Macmillan, pp. 147–71

Knight, Jane (2010), 'Internationalization: Reactor or Actor to the Competitive Imperative?' in: Laura Portnoi, Val D. Rust and Sylvia S. Bagley (eds), *Higher Education, Policy, and the Global Competition Phenomenon*, New York: Palgrave Macmillan, pp. 205–19

Knight, Jane (2004), 'Internationalization Remodeled: Definition, Approaches, and Rationales', in: *Journal of Studies in International Education*, 8 (1), pp. 5–31

Marginson, Simon (2010), 'Global Comparisons and the University Knowledge Economy', in: Laura Portnoi, Val D. Rust and Sylvia S. Bagley (eds), *Higher Education, Policy, and the Global Competition Phenomenon*, New York: Palgrave Macmillan, pp. 29-41

Marginson, Simon (2006), 'Dynamics of National and Global Competition in Higher Education', in: *Higher Education*, 52 (1), pp. 1–39

MEST (Ministry of Education, Science, and Technology), *Brief Statistics on Korean Education* 1990–2012, Seoul: Ministry of Education, Science, and Technology

MEST (2007), *Study Korea Project*, Seoul: Ministry of Education, Science, and Technology

MEST (2005), *Brain Korea 21*, Seoul: Ministry of Education, Science, and Technology

Mohrman, Kathryn, Wanhua Ma and David Baker (2008),'The Research University in Transition: The Emerging Global Model', in: *Higher Education Policy*, 21 (1), pp. 5–27

Mok, Ka Ho (2007), 'Questing for Internationalization of Universities in Asia: Critical Reflections', in: *Journal of Studies in International Education*, 11 (3/4), pp. 433–54

Mok, Ka Ho and Anthony B. L. Cheung (2011), 'Global Aspirations and Strategising for World-Class Status: New Forms of Politics in Higher Education Governance in Hong Kong', in: *Journal of Higher Education Policy and Management*, 33 (3), pp. 231–51

Moon, Mugyeong and Ki-Seok Kim (2001), 'A Case of Korean Higher Education Reform: The Brain Korea 21 Project', in: *Asia Pacific Education Review*, 2 (2), pp. 96-105

Ntshoe, Isaac and Moeketsi Letseka (2010), 'Quality Assurance and Global Competitiveness in Higher Education', in: Laura M. Portnoi, Val D. Rust and Sylvia S. Bagley (eds), *Higher Education, Policy, and the Global Competition Phenomenon*, New York: Palgrave Macmillan, pp. 59–72

Park, Joseph Sung-Yul (2011), 'The Promise of English: Linguistic Capital and the Neoliberal Worker in the South Korean Job Market', in: *International Journal of Bilingual Education and Bilingualism*, 14 (4), pp. 443–55

Park, Se-Il (2000), Managing Education Reform: Lessons from the Korean Experience: 1995 –97, Seoul: Korea Development Institute

Rhee, Byung Shik (2011), 'A World-Class Research University on the Periphery: The Pohang University of Science and Technology, the Republic of Korea', in: Philip G. Altbach and Jamil Salmi (eds), *The Road to Academic Excellence: The Making of World-Class Research Universities*, Washington, DC: The World Bank, pp. 101-127

Rust, Val D. and Stephanie Kim (2012), 'The Global Competition in Higher Education', in: *World Studies in Education*, 13 (1), pp. 5–20

Seong, Somi, Steven W. Popper, Charles A. Goldman and David K. Evans (2008), *Brain Korea 21 Phase II: A New Evaluation Model*, Santa Monica CA: RAND Corporation

Shin, Jung Cheol (2012), 'International Mobility of Faculty and Its Impacts on Korean Higher Education', in: Deane E. Neubauer and Kazuo Kuroda (eds), *Mobility and Migration in Asian Pacific Higher Education*, New York: Palgrave Macmillan, pp. 65–81

Shin, Jung Cheol (2011), 'South Korea: Decentralized Centralization—Fading Shared Governance and Rising Managerialism', in: William Locke, William K. Cummings and Donald Fisher (eds), *Changing Governance and Management in Higher Education*, New York: Springer, pp. 321–42

Shin, Jung Cheol (2009), 'Building World-Class Research University: The Brain Korea 21 Project', in: *Higher Education*, 58 (5), pp. 669–88

Shin, Jung Cheol, and Yong Suk Jang (2013), 'World-Class University in Korea: Proactive Government, Responsive University, and Procrastinating Academics', in: Jung Cheol Shin and Barbara M. Kehm (eds), *Institutionalization of World-Class University in Global Competition*, Dordrecht: Springer, pp. 147–63

Slaughter, Sheila and Gary Rhoades (2004), *Academic Capitalism and the New Economy: Markets, State, and Higher Education*, Baltimore: The Johns Hopkins University Press

UNESCO Institute for Statistics (2009), *Global Education Digest*, Montreal: UNESCO Institute for Statistics

van Vught, Frans (2008), 'Mission Diversity and Reputation in Higher Education', in: *Higher Education Policy*, 21 (2), pp. 151–74

THE MILLENARIAN DIMENSION OF UNIFICATION THOUGHT

Lukas Pokorny

ABSTRACT

The South-Korea based Unification movement is a global religious organisation energetically involved in a considerable number of peace promotion and inter-faith campaigns. The movement strives to bring to fruition the millenarian vision of its founder and self-styled 'Lord of the Second Advent', Mun Sŏn-myŏng. This study sheds light on the millenarian dimension of Unification thought that serves as the doctrinal backbone of the movement's varied activities with its worldwide peace agenda at its centre.

Key words: millenarianism, Unification Church, new religious movement, Korean religion

1 INTRODUCTION

Korea's recent history has witnessed a veritable blossoming of new religious movements (*sinjonggyo*),[1] some of which have expanded overseas in the past decades with a steadily rising global community. Of those internationally active religious organisations, the Unification movement (UM; *t'ongil undong*) has emerged as the most well-known in its world-renewing mission. Winning worldwide notoriety in the 1970s, particularly owing to fervent proselytism and (unsubstantiated) allegations of mind-control and brainwashing (Barker 1984), the UM has ever since been held in disdain by the Christian mainstream, by large sections of the media, and as a consequence thereof, to some degree by the general public. Founded by the Korean preacher Mun Sŏn-myŏng (1920–2012) in war-torn South Korea in the mid-1950s, within half a century the UM had developed into a world-spanning

[1] In lieu of *sinjonggyo*, Korean scholars predominantly tend to use the somewhat derogative term *sinhŭng chonggyo* or 'newly emerged religion'.

network of hundreds of affiliated organisations, centred on a religious master-plan that represents the motivational incentive and ideological bracket of the overall venture. It is, in fact, the millenarian dimension of Unification thought which acts as the doctrinal justification and propulsion for the movement's many activities. These activities are united in the UM's pursuit for world peace. In Unificationist terms, 'peace-building' entails rendering the world ripe for the settlement of the 'Kingdom of Heaven on earth' (*chisang ch'ŏnguk*). This utopian land of ultimate bliss under the reign of God is fully materialised and awaits humanity when a sufficient number of faithful follows Mun's sacred course, which then concludes the UM's millenarian goal.

Unification thought is inextricably linked with its creator, major subject and leading advocate Mun Sŏn-myŏng. Section 2 of this essay will, therefore, present the major stages of his life and the genesis of his movement. The third section will amplify the millenarianism of the UM, and, in a first step, the concept of millenarianism will be elucidated. Subsequently, the main tenets of the group's millenarian portfolio will be outlined and connected to the UM's Korea-centric rationale of the coming salvational transformation; then, set against the millenarian backdrop, the UM's 'agenda for peace' will be discussed. The concluding section will highlight the key issues of the discussion.

2 Historical overview: Mun Sŏn-myŏng and the Unification movement

Mun Sŏn-myŏng[2] was born Mun Yong-myŏng on 25 February 1920[3] in the village of Sangsa, in Tŏgŏn township of Chŏngju county in North P'yŏngan province, in today's North Korea. Among 13 children, of whom five died prematurely, he was the second son to Mun Kyŏng-yu (1893–1954) and Kim Kyŏng-gye (1888–1968). At about ten years of age, Mun was sent to the local village school (*kŭlbang*) where he was instructed in traditional Confucian learning before en-

[2] Mun changed the first part of his given name in the early 1950s whilst he was a war refugee in the coastal city of Pusan. For an extensive semi-authorised account of Mun's childhood and early adult life, see Breen 1997.

[3] An alternative date of birth frequently mentioned is 6 January 1920—this refers to the lunar calendar.

tering formal school education.[4] At the time, a series of misfortunes and calamities struck his family, prompting his parents to convert to Presbyterianism (*changnogyo*). Mun was consequently immersed in the Christian faith and—according to tradition—experienced a life-altering vision during Easter time of 1935.[5] In an epiphany, Jesus Christ assigned Mun the divine mission to 'save the people and realise God's peace on this earth' (Mun: 2010b: 68).[6] From an emic perspective,[7] this event marks the inception of Mun's lifelong pursuit of restoring the Kingdom of Heaven on earth. Over the following years, whilst continuing his educational training in Seoul (1938–41) and Tōkyō (1941–43), he rigorously dedicated himself to prayer and Bible studies. During his time as a student of technical engineering at a technical school affiliated with Waseda University, Mun is said to have ultimately discovered the 'secrets of the universe' (*uju'ŭi pimil*) and the cause for God's bitter grief. The introductory chapter to the present edition of the *Wŏlli kangnon* (Exposition of the Principle) reads retrospectively:

> God has already sent one person on this earth to solve the fundamental problems of human life and the universe—this person is the very Mun Sŏn-myŏng. Whilst for several decades wandering the spirit world, which is so boundless as to be beyond one's imagining, he walked a bloody path of suffering in his quest for truth only Heaven remembers. ...Being all alone, he battled and prevailed over myriads of devils of the spirit world and the physical world. Then, in an intimate spiritual communion with God, freely coming into contact with Jesus and numerous saints of the paradise, he illuminated all the secrets of heaven[8] (*WK* Preface: 18).

---

[4] Mun's recently published autobiography, *P'yonghwa'rŭl sarang hanŭn segyein'ŭro* (As a peace-loving global citizen), describes several key episodes in his youth and young adulthood. However, other than the fact that his memoirs have allegedly been ghost-written and edited on the basis of Mun's own accounts (personal conversation with UM members) and appear under-reported and circumspect, a closer look reveals discrepancies with other biographical sources. Yet the book is proudly distributed by the movement, and has become a bestseller in South Korea. An English edition was published in 2010, but the translation differs noticeably from the Korean version. Mun's classical education is considered to account for the Confucian impact (Chryssides 1991: 58-60) on Unification thought.

[5] The exact dating differs and is inconsistent in the various sources. Most UM narratives indicate—perhaps symbolically—Easter day (*puhwalchŏl*), that is, 21 April 1935 (see, for example, Mun 2010b: 62).

[6] This and all other translations into English in this essay are by the author.

[7] That is, from the believer's point of view.

[8] The version of the *Wŏlli kangnon* quoted here is the colour-coded 40th Korean edition, published in 1999 by the Family Federation for World Peace and Unification

Upon returning to Korea, Mun associated with various messianic groups, which played a significant role in shaping Unification thought (Chryssides 1991: 93–107).[9] He married and travelled to the 'Jerusalem of the East' (*tongyang'ŭi yerusallem*), that is P'yŏngyang, in 1946, furthering his mission to fulfil 'God's providence of restoration'.[10] In 1948, following years of persistent conflict with both the Japanese and the North Korean authorities, Mun was once again arrested. This time he was sentenced to five years of forced labour for displacing social order, amongst other offences.[11] Early in the Korean War, in late 1950, the advance of United Nations (UN) forces enabled Mun to escape, initially to P'yŏngyang and, in early 1951, to Pusan, where he was to erect his first 'church', a small hut made of mud and cardboard. The *Wŏlli wŏnbon* (Original text of the Principle), compiled by Mun and his disciples one year later, and containing the nucleus of Unification thought, served as a decisive instrument to spread his teachings in the years ahead.[12] Successful proselytising brought about the foundation of the Holy Spirit Association for the Unification of World Christianity (HSAUWC, S*egye kidokkyo t'ongil sillyŏng hyŏphoe*) in Seoul in 1954, but also, once again, repressive measures by the government.[13] That same year, Kim Sang-ch'ŏl (1915–2011), a central figure in the early movement, became a temporary overseas missionary to England and Wales, heralding the UM's internationali-

---

(FFWPU). The work comprises a preface and two main sections divided into seven and six chapters respectively, each with an introduction. The chapters are further divided into numerous subchapters. Essentially, the first part delineates key doctrinal concepts, whilst the second part details the providential course of humankind. The work is referenced in this paper as *WK*.

[9] Colonial suppression and the turmoil of the Korean War (1950–53) have been conducive to the emergence of messianic and millenarian movements in Korea (Choe 1993; Pak 1998).

[10] He divorced Ch'oe Sŏn-gil in 1957. According to the UM narrative, Mun was complying with his wife's wish because she would not support his divine assignment.

[11] For an insider's account on Mun's time in P'yŏngyang and Hŭngnam prison, see Kim Won Pil 1982.

[12] An extensively revised version—*Wŏlli haesŏl* (Explanation of the Principle)—was drafted in 1957. The latest version—*Wŏlli kangnon* (Exposition of the Principle)—was published in 1966. For an emic discussion of the formation of these texts, see Kim Jin-choon 1998.

[13] Mun was jailed for three months in 1955. The situation eased over the following years, in particular under the government of Pak Chŏng-hŭi (1917–79), which matched the UM's anti-Communist zeal. About twenty years later, Mun faced imprisonment yet again when he was convicted of tax fraud between 1973 and 1975 by a US federal court. The 18-months sentence (1984–85) instigated a longstanding media debate on religious liberties and, surprisingly, turned the tide of public opinion in favour of the UM.

sation, which officially started on more favourable terms in 1958.[14] Spring 1960 marked another watershed moment in the history of the UM when Mun performed the 'marriage of the lamb'[15] (*ŏrinyang* [*hon'in*] *chanch'i*) by marrying Han Hak-cha (b. 1943).[16] Together with his second wife he 'accomplished the mission received by God to become True Parents'[17] and was now in a position to work towards 'opening the gates of the Kingdom of Heaven' (Mun 2010b: 223). Accordingly, the 'True Couple' (*ch'am pubu*) embarked on conducting mass 'blessings' (*ch'ukpok*) to expedite this ambitious task. Starting in the same year, 1960, these wedding rituals, as illustrated at Figure 1, were to become a familiar feature of the UM.

Figure 1 Mun Sŏn-myŏng and Han Hak-cha give the benediction at a blessing ceremony at Sun Moon University, Asan campus, October 2009[18]

[14] The UM's international expansion began in Japan but soon extended to the United States, in 1959, and to Europe, in 1963.

[15] Cf. *WK* II.1.3.1.2.1: 291 with reference to Rev. 19.7.

[16] Han gave birth to 14 'True Children' (*ch'am chanyŏ*) between 1960 and 1982. Prior to that, his first wife delivered a son in 1946. In 1955, Mun fathered an illegitimate child with Kim Myŏng-hŭi.

[17] It was only from July 1992 that Mun revealed to the public that they were the 'True Parents of humankind' (*illyu'ŭi ch'am pumo*), the 'Saviour' (*kuseju*), the 'Lord of the Second Advent' (*chaerimju*) and the 'Messiah' (*mesia*).

[18] All photographs are reproduced with permission of the Unification Church Korea Headquarters.

In subsequent years, the UM increased fundraising, amassing substantial revenue and thus providing a sound basis for future ventures.

In 1965,[19] Mun began his first 'world tour' through 40 countries and, whilst visiting the United States (US), is said to have realised that 'the new culture that will be established in the future must rise, having set foot on the United States' (Mun 2010b: 185). Six years later, he took up residence in the US, moving the UM headquarters to Tarrytown, New York. Mun's relocation to the 'second Israel' indeed precipitated the expansion of the UM, which was gradually turning into a global business conglomerate with investments in numerous industries and countries.[20] A plethora of commercial, political, educational and cultural enterprises—which had mushroomed over the preceding decades—yielded a multibillion-euro estate and concomitant controversy.[21]

Highlighting the UM's major ideological message, Mun inaugurated the Family Federation for World Peace and Unification (FFWPU, *segye p'yŏnghwa t'ongil kajŏng yŏnhap*) in May 1994. The new organisation superseded the HSAUWC and continues to spearhead the UM's religious agenda. With the introduction of his youngest son, Mun Hyŏng-jin (b. 1979), as the international president of the FFWPU and its Korea branch in April 2008, Mun, then 88 years old, stepped

[19] One year before, in early 1964, the UM was claiming to have 32,500 or so worldwide members with the vast majority of followers living in South Korea and Japan (Choi 1967: 169). Eleven years later, in 1975, the UM reported a membership of more than one million adherents in 130 nations (HSAUWC 1975: 31).

[20] Yet the bulk of the UM's financial assets is generated on the Japanese market. Given an estimated 560,000 adherents, the Japanese branch of the UM, to date operating under the name HSAUWC (*Sekai kirisutokyō tōitsu shinrei kyōkai*), in its short form 'Unification Church' (*Tōitsu kyōkai*), would be the largest non-Japanese religious movement in the country, even surpassing Catholicism and Protestantism. However, the figure is likely to be somewhat overstated.

[21] The Korean peninsula plays a significant role in Mun's providence for humanity. See Section 3.3. Unsurprisingly, Korea has also been a focal point in the UM's variegated 'agenda for peace'. Notable ventures are the Tongil Group (*t'ongil kŭrup*, 1963), which includes a number of holdings such as 'Ilhwa' (*irhwa*, 1971), a pharmaceutical company well-known for its ginseng products, Ilshin Stone (*ilsin sŏkchae*, 1971), and the *Segye Ilbo* (1989), a major newspaper; Sun Moon University (*sŏnmun taehakkyo*, 1986) with two separate campuses in Asan and Ch'ŏnan; the prestigious K-League football club Seongnam Ilhwa Chunma (*sŏngnam irhwa ch'ŏnma*, 1989); Pyeonghwa Motors (*p'yŏnghwa chadongch'a*, 1999), a Seoul-based car manufacturer and retailer in North Korea; the CheongShim International Medical Centre (*ch'ŏngsim kukche pyŏngwŏn*, 2003); and the Family Party for Peace and Unification (*p'yŏnghwa t'ongil kajŏng tang*, 2007–08), a short-lived political spin-off, which was unsuccessful in the April 2008 legislative elections, when it received only about 181,000 votes, 1.1% of all votes cast.

down into semi-retirement. Later years saw Mun spending most of his time in South Korea, struggling with rather delicate internal conflicts that largely involved his third son Mun Hyŏn-jin (b. 1969).[22] The UM today, headquartered in Seoul at the, according to Mun, 'axis of world peace' (*segye p'yŏnghwa'ŭi ch'uk*), is a multifaceted religious organisation with a global reach, spanning over five continents and claiming three million members worldwide. Mun Sŏn-myŏng died on 3 September 2012 after having been under treatment for pneumonia for several weeks.

3 The Millenarian Dimension of Unification Thought

From the outset of its international amplification, the UM has been constantly reproached by its many adversaries for disguising its religious 'grand scheme' in the form of diverse cultural, social and political initiatives. Indeed, an enormous range of campaigns and organisations have been launched over the decades to further the spirit of Unification thought (*t'ongil sasang*) at various levels of society. The propagation of a political message in keeping with Mun's teachings, albeit usually not instantly apparent or disclosed, is part and parcel of many of the UM's initiatives, with CAUSA, and Mun's meeting with Kim Il Sung in P'yŏngyang on 1991 (illustrated at Figure 2) as prime examples.[23]

Today, the Universal Peace Federation (UPF, *ch'ŏnju p'yŏnghwa yŏnhap*), founded in 2005 as a 'global alliance…dedicated to building

---

[22] A number of unapproved decisions taken by Mun Hyŏn-jin and various other leading members, notably Kwak Chŏng-hwan (b. 1936), chairman of News World Communications and former president of the K-League, have caused tension within the highest ranks of the UM and thus serious irritation amid the global community.

[23] Founded in 1980, CAUSA, the Confederation of the Associations for the Unification of the Societies of the Americas, rigorously advocated anti-communism until the conclusion of the Cold War. This was perfectly in line with Unification thought, for it is held that the 'communist world' (*kongsanjuŭi segye*) was epitomising Satan's sovereignty (*WK* II.4.7.2.7: 473). Mun insisted that his activities, culminating in meetings with Mikhail Gorbachev (b. 1931) and Kim Il Sung (1912–94) in 1990 and 1991 respectively, led to the demise of communism. Unification theology describes the 'summit' between Kim, who was considered to embody the 'Second Advent of Satan', and Mun as the reconciliation of Cain and Abel (see Figure 2). In the aftermath of his visit, Mun voiced his intention for future close economic assistance and co-operation with North Korea as a means of expediting world peace.

a world of peace',[24] is at the forefront of a number of UM organisations exercising notable political commitment. The UM's political aspirations are not accidental but rest firmly on an elaborate millenarian foundation, which is 'inherently political because it arises from the perception of political evil' (Daniels 2005: 5). Unification thought is claimed to make for a 'political society realising the ideal of creation' (*WK* II.4.7.2.7: 474), which will be the messianic kingdom created by Mun Sŏn-myŏng.

Before a discussion of the distinct millenarian setting of Unification thought, this paper examines briefly the notion of millenarianism.

Figure 2 Mun Sŏn-myŏng meets Kim Il Sung in P'yŏngyang, December 1991

[24] See http://www.ambassadors4peace.org/about (accessed 6 June 2012). The UPF supplanted the Interreligious and International Federation for World Peace (IIFWP, *segye p'yŏnghwa ch'ojonggyo ch'ogukka yŏnhap*), founded in 1998.

3.1 *Millenarianism*

The term 'millenarianism' derives from the Latin word *mīlle* meaning 'thousand',[25] and was originally used in Christian theology to denote belief in the millennium. The millennium refers to a passage in the book of Revelations, the last book of the New Testament, and commonly signifies a thousand-year-long period of bliss and harmony following the parousia—the second coming of Christ—at the end of time.[26] In the study of religions, conventionally the theological concept of millenarianism is divested of its allegorical qualities and retains only its doctrinal substratum, that is, the idea of transformation. The works of the English historian Norman Cohn (1915–2007) were momentous in redefining millenarianism and engendering a conceptual tool that proved to be valuable for scholarship outside theology as well as for a better understanding of soteriological responses—those grounded in the doctrine of salvation—to calamities of the human condition (Clarke 2009: 354).[27] Cohn understood millenarianism as a 'particular type of salvationism' and thus characterised millenarian movements as driven by salvific fantasies which were deemed collective, terrestrial, imminent, total and accomplished by supernatural

[25] The terms 'chiliasm'—stemming from the Greek word χίλιοι ('thousand'), 'millennialism' or, though less commonly used today, 'millenarism', are largely used interchangeably in the literature, yet primarily stress a meaning perpetuated by Christian theology. Various authors tend to employ the term 'apocalypticism' in a similar fashion.

[26] 'Then I saw an angel coming down from heaven, holding in his hand the key to the bottomless pit and a great chain. He seized the dragon, that ancient serpent, who is the Devil and Satan, and bound him for a thousand years, and threw him into the pit, and locked and sealed it over him, so that he would deceive the nations no more, until the thousand years were ended. After that he must be let out for a little while' (Rev. 20.1–3). (The version of the Bible from which this passage is taken is the New Revised Standard Version, anglicised edition, of the *Holy Bible Containing the Old and New Testaments with the Apocryphal/Deuterocanonical Books* (1995), Oxford: Oxford University Press.) There are differing interpretations of this seminal paragraph based on literal or symbolic readings, particularly concerning the point of Christ's Second Advent.

[27] It is widely surmised by scholars of millenarianism that millenarian movements emerge primarily—as Barkun puts it—'as the artefacts of disaster situations' (1986: 52). Social and/or economic distress results in attempts to bring about change in society or within the moral community (Burridge 1975: 9). This assertion would be endorsed when taking into consideration the origin of the UM, which evolved in the midst of a period of social and political unrest. However, critics of theories of 'relative deprivation' argue that these do not satisfactorily explain the development of millenarian movements, as times of crisis do not necessarily call forth millenarian endeavours.

agencies (Cohn 2004: 13; Cohn 1962: 31). Aware of the limitations of Cohn's wording, the Israeli sociologist Yonina Talmon-Garber (1923–66) offered a slightly revised and more resonating description, defining millenarian groups as ones that anticipate imminent, total, ultimate, this-worldly and collective salvation (Talmon 1966: 159). Inspired by Talmon's now classical approach, I shall define millenarianism as a belief focussing upon an all-embracing salvational transformation of the current world order.[28] This change towards salvation will be

a) collective, in that the 'fruits of the transformation' will be shared at least by those who are faithful
b) this-worldly, in that it will occur on this earth or in our cosmos
c) imminent, in that it will occur soon, possibly within the believer's lifetime
d) ultimate, in that it will bring about the final state of being in history or in the current cosmic cycle (given a cyclical worldview)
e) and total, in that the whole world or cosmos will be involved.

The transformative spirit of millenarian movements echoes a 'revolutionary ideology' (Landes 2005: 20) in response to political helplessness and disfranchisement. A millenarian mindset blurs or completely ignores the boundaries between the secular and the religious, comprehending both domains as a wholly integrated system. Against this background, it is not surprising that Unification thought promotes political reform based on 'the word of God' (*hananim'ŭi malssŭm*):

> That is to say, since political parties ignore the will of God, it could be said that they are like peripheral nerves centring on the spinal cord which has become incapable of transmitting commands of the brain. ...Therefore, the purpose of the ideal of the Second Advent is to make the present political system, which resembles the structure of fallen humankind at the time of Jesus, perfectly display its original function centring on the will of God by connecting it to the perfect central nerve (*WK* II.5.3.2: 499–500).

[28] Millenarian ambitions are tightly intertwined with soteriological beliefs, for the expected transformation or the religious pursuit to bring it to pass sanctions personal salvation; that is, an alternative state, likely to be ultimate, of a *homo religiosus* who transcended his or her dianoetic, emotional, volitional and/or 'spiritual' status quo ante.

A millenarian *weltanschauung* entails the pursuit of transformation. This impending shift to a glorious new age may be impelled by the perennial development of the inner self. In other words, living pursuant to the soteriological directives set by a given doctrinal framework may bring the believer to impact on the future course of events, turning him or her into a 'vehicle of change'. In any case, the faithful will rejoice in the benefits of the transformation, irrespective of whether a person's activities and moral condition are considered to alter the tenor of being. The transition towards a millenarian state of completion—which is variously manifested, for example, as a restored golden age, a utopian society, or a world of universal peace and harmony—is designed to come about gradually ('progressive millenarianism') or cataclysmically ('catastrophic millenarianism') (Wessinger 1997), both in a varying fashion. Interestingly, early Unification thought, in principle, allowed for both options (*WK* II.5.4.4.1: 519–21); however, the 'redemptive' and political actions of Mun Sŏn-myŏng are viewed as having, eventually, averted global disaster in the form of World War III, paving the way for a 'progressive salvational transformation' of the current world order.[29]

3.2 *Unificationism*

With Mun and his wife crowned 'King and Queen of Peace' (*p'yŏnghwa'ŭi wang*) on several occasions throughout 2004 and thereafter—including a coronation ceremony in Washington attended by a number of high-ranking US politicians—the realisation of 'Cheon Il Guk' (*ch'ŏnilguk*) or the Kingdom of Heaven on earth under the banner of Unification thought was considered to be near at hand. Previous years had indeed seen a culmination of purported watershed events pertaining to the Unificationist belief of the 'perfection of restoration' (*pokkwi'ŭi wansŏng*). Being tantamount to 'global salvation' (*segye kuwŏn*), the idea of restoration—which, essentially, indicates humankind's liberation from 'Satan's bondage' (*sat'an'ŭi kulle*)—represents the guiding principle of Unification thought. His adherents

[29] Applying Catherine Wessinger's typology (2011), early Unification thought expresses the idea of 'avertive' millenarianism, espousing a catastrophic millenarian scenario which factors in the transition to progressive millenarian expectations, provided that specific action is taken in concert with pertinent soteriological beliefs. See also Wojcik 2011.

believe that, commissioned to fulfil God's providence, Mun ultimately descended on earth as God's ambassador to 'lead the 6.5 billion people of the world and tread the path of establishing the Kingdom of Heaven on earth' (Mun 2010a). Imbued with the moral 'spirit of the Korean peninsula',[30] Mun was to become the 'True Parent of humankind' and the 'King of Kings' (*manwang'ŭi wang*), for he is said to have revealed the mystery of God's poignant sadness and the means to cope with it. Mun's deep insights into the principle of creation, the biblical Fall, its impact on humanity and its redemption, comprise the nucleus of Unification thought. Unificationists treat Mun's teachings as the providential exposition of and response to God's innermost feeling of sorrow (*han*) and, accordingly, the key to resolving universal suffering in a world of chaos and contingency.

At its heart, Unification theology (*t'ongil sinhak*) provides an alternative reading of the Bible; however, it markedly deviates from mainstream Christian doctrines and thus ordinarily is not accepted as part of the ecumenical movement—this in spite of the UM's assiduous involvement in initiatives aimed at inter-religious dialogue. Mun's allegedly divinely endorsed interpretation of the biblical narrative weaves together a number of doctrinal strands, which clearly display a particular intellectual socialisation. 'The Korean religious heritage', as Kim Young Oon puts it (1980), is strikingly evident not only in Unification thought per se but in ritual practice and various elements of material culture.[31] Notwithstanding the bold influence of the pluralistic Korean religious environment,[32] Unification thought has evolved from a mindscape largely incorporating major Christian themes. Small wonder Unificationist teachings utilise a theological nomenclature and draw upon central biblical themes in constituting their exclusivist message of salvation.[33]

With the story of the Fall of Man (*ingan t'arak*, Gen. 3.1–3.24) at its very centre, Unification thought bridges creation and eschatological[34] theory to rationalise its millenarian agenda: '...God's purpose of creation in all respects has been to establish the Kingdom of Heaven

[30] Cf. also *WK* II.6.3.3.4: 559–60 in reference to Acts 2.17.

[31] The True Parents' liturgical garments and headgear, mimicking to some extent, for example, shamanistic regalia, or the emphasis on spiritism, are among the most salient syncretistic features of the UM.

[32] A number of scholars have associated elements of Unification thought with varied East Asian religions. See, amongst others, Chryssides (1991: 46-68).

[33] Hence the informal name 'Unification Church' (*t'ongil kyohoe*).

[34] Dealing with the final events in the history of the world or of humankind.

on earth' (*WK* I.3.1.1: 112). Unificationists cherish the idea that God (*hananim*) is the 'eternally self-existent absolute transcending time and space' (*WK* I.1.2.1: 29) and inhering the 'original force of all beings' (*manyu wŏnnyŏk*). This all-underlying prime power facilitates a system of universal reciprocity based on the principle of 'give and receive action' (*susu chagyong*). Originating from God, the ubiquitous intrinsic relationality of *ŭm* and *yang*[35] furnishes the universe, which, at large, becomes God's 'substantial object' (*silch'e taesang*). At this point, Unification thought attaches utmost importance to the role of humankind. Created to oversee, harmonise and encapsulate the whole cosmos (*WK* I.1.6.2: 63–64), humans were to fulfil God's 'purpose of creation' (*ch'angjo mokchŏk*) by realising the 'Kingdom of Heaven' (*ch'ŏnguk*) and thus turning into God's 'good object partner capable of bringing Him joy' (*WK* I.1.3.2: 46). The Kingdom of Heaven on earth can only be installed on the grounds of the 'four position foundation' (*sawi kidae*), which is in turn the indispensable condition for the completion of the 'three great blessings' (*samdae ch'ukpok*).[36] The four position foundation, founded upon the symbiotic relationship of God, husband, wife and children, unifies in God, who bestows 'eternal love' on His object partners and conversely receives 'beauty' whilst being stimulated with eternal joy. A family centred on God and being mindful of the 'ideal of creation' (*ch'angjo isang*) becomes a place of absolute goodness and peace, and the nucleus of the UM's millenarian project; in other words, the Kingdom of Heaven on earth. This 'ideal world in which not even a shadow of sin could be found' (*WK* I.1.3.2: 49) is populated by perfected individuals who apprehend their own divinity (*WK* I.3.2.1: 115), becoming 'God's temple' (*hananim'ŭi sŏngjŏn*).[37] By living in concord with nature and partaking in harmonious family relations, personal enlightenment and world peace will be achieved, all along shepherded by the 'True Parents of humankind', who have been charged with conveying God's mandate. Once the millenarian dream has been accomplished, those entering the 'spirit world' (*yŏnggye*) will be entitled to establish the 'Kingdom of Heaven in heaven' (*ch'ŏnsang ch'ŏnguk*).

---

[35] Chinese: *yin* and *yang*.

[36] The *WK* references God's command in Gen. 1.28: 'Be fruitful and multiply, and fill the earth and subdue it; and have dominion over the fish of the sea and over the birds of the air and over every living thing that moves upon the earth.'

[37] See *WK* I.1.3.2: 46 in reference to John 14.20 and I Cor. 3.16.

However, the implementation of God's grand design has been deferred and humankind has been put under the 'sovereignty of Satan' (*sat'an chugwŏn*). The first ancestors, Adam (*adam*) and Eve (*haewa*), by divine will were intended to complete the four position foundation and thus attain perfection in a conjugal relationship centred on God. Much to God's regret, His loving intent was undermined, resulting in the Fall of Man. Envious of God's affection for humans, the Archangel Nusiel[38] (*ch'ŏnsajang nusiel*) seduced Eve and consummated a sexual relationship on a spiritual level. The illicit intercourse tainted Eve, who imbibed Satan's disposition (*WK* I.2.4.6: 100–101) and hence elicited the 'spiritual Fall' (*yŏngjŏk t'arak*). Struck by overwhelming feelings of compunction, Eve turned to Adam and both entered into an untimely carnal relationship. Antagonising God's purpose of creation, they built a four position foundation centred on Satan, which entailed the 'physical Fall' (*yukchŏk t'arak*). Their offspring became 'sons and daughters of Satan' (*sat'an'ŭi chanyŏ*), inheriting 'an original nature that corresponds to the nature of the Fall' (*t'araksŏng ponsŏng*) and, consequently, inaugurating Satan as the 'god of this world' (*sesang'ŭi sin*).[39] Having become part of the 'lineage of Satan' (*sat'an'ŭi hyŏlt'ong*), humankind created 'hell on earth' (*chisang chiok*), a place of universal suffering, social strife and dawning ecological chaos. At this juncture, Unificationist soteriology tries to console and inspire the faithful with confidence in God's providence to restore humankind's original state and conclude the age of Satan's dominion.

Mun Sŏn-myŏng is stated to have heralded the 'Last days' (*malse*), a period when a world of evil will be gradually transformed into the 'Garden of Eden' (*eden tongsan*), thereby fulfilling God's providence of restoration (*WK* I.3.3.1: 122–23). In fact, Mun is not seen as the first human empowered by divine intervention to resolve man's 'original sin' (*wŏnjoe*) and release humankind from the tutelage of Satan. After Noah (*noa*), whose family survived the great Deluge, failed to carry out God's millenarian vision because of his son's transgression,[40] God delegated Jesus (*yesunim*) to accomplish the ideal of creation. He was to bring redemption upon the people by spiritually and physically engrafting (*chŏpput'im*) humanity,[41] and thus reinstating a

---

[38] Referencing Isa. 14.12; the *WK* refers to Lucifer as 'Nusiel'.
[39] Cf. II Cor. 4.4.
[40] Cf. Gen. 9.22.
[41] Cf. Rom. 11.17.

four position foundation centring on God. But Jesus, who prolonged Adam's existential task, eventually failed because he could not fully 'subdue' Satan (*WK* I.4.1.4: 162; *WK* II.2.3.2.3: 384–85) and therefore died prematurely on the cross, having been persecuted and abandoned by the people. He could not procreate sinless children in order to raise a 'True Family' (*ch'am kajŏng*), the kernel of the Kingdom of Heaven on earth, and accordingly has not 'perfectly liquidated our original sin' and 'leaves humankind's original nature [at the time] of creation not perfectly restored' (*WK* I.4.2: 154). Having said this, Unificationists reason that Jesus' crucifixion was not futile because it entailed spiritual salvation. By spiritually engrafting fallen men, the resurrected Jesus rose as the 'spiritual Messiah' (*yŏngjŏg'in mesia*), but knowing that humankind was not yet recaptured as the 'children of God's direct lineage' (*hananim'ŭi hyŏlt'ongjŏk chikkye'ŭi chanyŏ*), he promised to return and complete his providential objective (*WK* II.6.2.2: 540):

> He who is coming at the Second Advent also restores the 'Foundation for the Messiah' substantially, starting from the family level, and if he then does proceed to clan, racial, national, worldly, and cosmic level, and on that foundation realise the Kingdom of Heaven, [his mission] is not fulfilled (*WK* II.2.3.3.2: 397).

According to Unification thought, Christ at the Second Advent will finally purify men's satanically stained bodies, redeeming the original sin and leading humankind to eternal salvation as God's object of love and joy. The 'third Adam' lays the foundation of the Kingdom of Heaven by entering into matrimony with the 'restored Eve', siring unsullied children and attaining True Parenthood. Unificationists have faith in Mun Sŏn-myŏng as the Second Coming of the Messiah who brought to fruition the spirit of the *Wŏlli kangnon*. Other than Jesus, only Mun has gained a sweeping victory over Satan. He married and fathered children free from sin and thus created an 'archetypal family', which unites in God. The UM's well-known blessing ritual is considered to emulate Mun's union with Han Hak-cha, engrafting the brides and grooms to him, making them perfect in spirit and flesh; in short, recovering their divine lineage as children of God. The newly blessed couples join forces with the True Family to free enslaved humankind and eventually turn hell on earth into the Kingdom of Heaven on earth.

The blessing ceremony is the decisive initiation rite in the pursuit of transformation. Through re-connecting to 'God's lineage' (*hananim'ŭi p'itchul*) the 'initiates' are capacitated to create 'God's homeland' (*hananim'ŭi choguk*), an 'ideal nation' as the basis for the 'kingdom of the peaceful and ideal world' (Mun 2005). The UM's millenarian zeal, as devoutly sustained by its adherents, is on a trajectory towards world peace, the most apparent consequence of the expected change. Promulgation of the Unificationist creed is indeed the only means by which to counteract social dissonance and moral decay whilst reviving cosmic harmony. The UM's missionary fervour stems from the very idea that only the 'cosmic ideology' (*ch'ŏnjujŏg'in inyŏm*) or Unification thought, may bind together humanity under the loving care of the True Parents (see Figure 3 below), enabling men to live in happiness within 'one great family' (*hana'ŭi taegajok*) (*WK* I.3.4.3: 141). Unification thought exhorts people to internalise the basic doctrinal tenets and to establish independently a four position foundation centring on God, for 'since the Fall occurred amid the family, restoration must occur amid the family', and through the family 'the Kingdom of Heaven on earth and the Kingdom of Heaven in heaven, being the original ideal of creation', must be built (Mun 2007b). Unificationists call for the need to live for the sake of others, holding fast to 'true love' (*ch'am sarang*) and realising utmost virtue. In so doing, whilst in addition receiving the True Parents' blessing, which ritually affirms one's sincere will and dedication to Mun's cause, the millenarian goal will be at hand, which is to say that humankind will at some point enter an eternal era of universal peace, prosperity and felicity, first on earth and subsequently, after death, in the spirit world. To succeed in its global aspirations to bring about the Kingdom of Heaven, the UM is keen to spread its word on an equally global scale. Various UM initiatives and campaigns serve this aim to deliver Mun's divinely validated scheme in these final Last days with the UPF being 'in the vanguard of accomplishing the great revolution of restoring the conversion of the lineage of humankind' (Mun 2007a).

In spite of the UM's international claim and the fact that its activities assume a worldwide reach, the anticipated change is rooted in a single region. The Korean peninsula, being divided along the 'line of confrontation' (*taech'isŏn*) between God and Satan, is allotted the fate of acting as a beacon to guide humanity towards its salvational fulfilment. Mun repeatedly emphasised that Korea, by virtue of the Korean

Figure 3 'True Parents' greet the assembled couples and well-wishers at a blessing ceremony at Seoul Olympic Stadium, February 2000

people, is indeed the fulcrum of God's providence and the springboard of the Kingdom of Heaven.

3.3 *Koreacentrism*

The UM's ethnocentric stance is not conspicuous among Korean new religious movements.[42] Rather, it reflects the frequent case that millenarian conation is closely connected with the notion of ethnic superiority or distinctiveness in terms of salvific efficacy. For Mun, Korea has become the place of God's dearest love and the chosen land in

[42] Cf., inter alia, Ch'ŏndogyo, Dahn World (*tan wŏltŭ*), Taejonggyo, Wŏnbulgyo, Chŭnsangyo-derived groups such as Chŭngsando or Taesun Chillihoe, or movements that have emerged from a Protestant environment, such as Hananim'ŭi kyohoe segye pogŭm sŏngyo hyŏphoe or Yŏŭido sunbogum kyohoe.

which all civilisations culminate (*WK* II.6.3.3.5: 561–63). The Unificationist exegesis of the Book of Revelation indicates correspondingly that the Messiah will return in the East and that it is beyond question that this 'nation of the East' is Korea:[43]

> From olden times, the nations of the East are said to be the three Eastern countries of Korea, Japan and China. However, among them, Japan is the nation that from generation to generation has continued to worship *Ch'ŏnjotaesin* [i.e., *Amaterasu Ōmikami*]. Moreover, it has met the age of the Second Advent as a totalitarian nation, and…at that time it has been the nation which has severely persecuted Korean Christianity… Furthermore, China is the nation that turned Communist. Thus, these two nations are both countries at Satan's side (*WK* II.6.3.3: 550–551).

In marked contrast, Korea possesses the qualifications to 'receive the Messiah', being a pious and God-revering people since time immemorial. Even at the height of power, the Korean people have always been peaceable and virtuous, never threatening other countries. Instead, Koreans have been subjugated and ill-treated throughout the centuries, whilst retaining their resignation to God's will. Korea's supposedly tragic yet indomitable role in world history, which, incidentally, nicely demonstrates the reoccurring topos of *han* as a persistent theme in Korean culture, elevates Koreans to—what Mun called—the 'third Israel' (*che3 isŭrael*), a people entrusted by God to foster His plan to reconcile humankind with its Creator. Hence, the Korean historical heritage and 'ethnic qualities' render the Korean people 'God's elect' (*sŏnmin*). With the circulation of the *Chŏnggamnok*[44] in the Chosŏn dynasty (1392–1910), God unfolded the Coming of the Messiah, preceding the arrival of Christianity. Thenceforth, Koreans purportedly started to nurture a messianic creed (*WK* II.6.3.3.4: 558–59). Infused by a spirit of utmost virtue, Koreans created a foundation for the saviour (Mun 2010a). Given Korea's providential importance and the Korean people's moral grandeur, it is only natural that the Messiah was to incarnate as a Korean on Korean soil, which came true, as Unificationists assert, with Mun Sŏn-myŏng. With that said, it is not surprising that Mun called for the unification of all the languages of the world. In the Kingdom of Heaven on earth, the mother tongue of the True Parents, Korean, will become the universal language, avoiding

---

[43] The *WK* references Rev 7.2.

[44] An influential prophetic book, probably written in the 18th century and targeting the demise of the dynasty.

Babel and conciliating humanity. 'The whole of humankind will become one people using one national language and thus establishing one nation' (*WK* II.6.5: 568) under the direct dominion of God. To inhale the spirit of the future Kingdom of Heaven on earth people shall learn the Korean language. Only then may the believer fully grasp the teachings of Mun, who preached exclusively in Korean.

3.4 *Agenda for peace*

The UM's millenarian dream is envisioned as having commenced on the Korean peninsula through the millennia-long spiritual and virtuous dignity of the Korean people and been put into force by the ministry of the Lord of the Second Advent, namely Mun Sŏn-myŏng.

However, to promote a religious programme, destined to change imminently and radically the stream of history by winning over a 'critical mass' of faithful supporters who will turn the tables in favour of those enfranchised from and directed against 'Satan's sovereignty', it is imperative to convey the message internationally, using different forums to address as many people as possible, or—and the UM pursues this strategy to great lengths—to affect decision-makers, and policymakers in particular, at various levels. Complying with Mun's universal claim, the UM's millenarian efforts run on a global stage in the shape of a wide range of organisations and charities, which, inspired by and partly focusing on varied aspects of Unification thought, work towards a shared aim—the establishment of 'one family under God' (*hana'ŭi hananim arae han kajŏng*) or, more explicitly, world peace. Early on, the UM recognised the UN, specifically as a useful platform to disseminate its core political and social ideas.[45] Since the 1990, several groups gained the status of non-governmental organisation at the UN, including the International Relief and Friendship Foundation (*kukche kuho ch'insŏn chaedan*), the International Religious Foundation (*kukche chonggyo chaedan*), the Women's Federation for World Peace (*segye p'yŏnghwa yŏsŏng yŏnhap*), FFWPU, and IIFWP, which was superseded by UPF. Pointing continuously to the dysfunctionality of the UN as it sought to impel world peace and meet the multifarious challenges of a modern world (Mun 2003), Mun ad-

[45] For an insider's evaluation of the UM's relationship with the United Nations, see Mickler 2008.

vocated an inner renewal of the UN. His proposals appealed for a religiously motivated reform, centring on the creation of UN-governed 'peace zones' (*p'yŏnghwa chigu*), the appointment of influential 'inter-religious ambassadors' (*ch'ojonggyo taesa*) in a newly designed bicameral system, and the proclamation of a worldwide celebratory 'True Parents Day' (*ch'am pumo'ŭi nal*) (Mun 2000). These first steps, if applied, should have brought the UN in line with Unificationist ideals, which have been strenuously upheld in the movement's millenarian pursuit. However, the UM's reformist activities were not crowned with success. As a result, in recent years, the UM's deliberations have shifted from systemically transforming a 'malfunctioning' UN or 'Cain UN' (*kain yuen*) to initiating a novel alternative network of organisations termed 'Abel UN' (*abel yuen*), with which to replace the former.[46] The Abel UN, with the UPF its current flagship, aims at the realisation of 'the kingdom of the peaceful, ideal world'. Mun not only gave assurances that the Abel UN will 'guarantee world peace' but conceded that its settlement is 'the most revolutionary and wondrous event since God's creation of humankind' (Mun 2003). The UPF in particular embodies 'God's victory' and the 'fruition of True Parents' blood, sweat and tears' (Mun 2005), representing the UM's organisational device to execute its millenarian agenda on a political level.

To keep its salvational enterprise going, countless initiatives and events have been launched in the past years: global peace tours, joined by a number of prominent guest speakers, or peace-building and interfaith conferences hosted on all continents, to name just a few. The UM's 'ambassadors for peace' (*p'yŏnghwa taesa*) programme is regarded as another cornerstone of the future 'Peace Kingdom' (*p'yŏnghwa'ŭi ch'ŏnguk*). Established in 2001 and arising from Mun's proposal to deploy inter-religious ambassadors within the UN structure, this worldwide peace initiative embarked on appointing tens of thousands of 'peace leaders', who were to serve as promoters and guardians of peace to help secure the foundation of the impending Kingdom of Heaven on earth. Their quest for peace equals, at a micro-level, Mun's cosmic mission, driven by the 'mandate of heaven' (*ch'ŏnmyŏng*). With the aid of the manifold UM campaigns fed into

---

[46] Unification thought regularly applies this evaluative dichotomy, signifying the contrast between something good and bad, positive and negative. It relates here to the Old Testament narrative in which Cain slew his younger brother Abel.

the Abel UN, 'True Parents' will be capable of ushering 'the Kingdom of Heaven of freedom, peace, unification and happiness centring on true love, on earth and in heaven' (Mun 2003). In fact, a 'new age' (*saeroun sidae*) has just begun. According to Mun's reckoning, 22 February 2013 was to mark 'Foundation Day' (*kiwŏnjŏl*) or 'D-Day' (*tidei*),[47] the alleged beginning of the Kingdom of Heaven on earth and the completion of God's providential course for mankind. Even though Mun expected 'Foundation Day' to be *the* soteriological caesura in the history of humankind, he remained reticent about its actual manifestation. Hence, in particular prior to Mun's demise, interpretations among followers differed greatly, ranging from the belief in an instant all-encompassing salvational change to a beginning and finally inexorable gradual metamorphosis in the form of a constantly 'growing' Kingdom of Heaven[48]—ineradicable world peace that is, so to speak, nascent. The latter view, notwithstanding doctrinal inconsistencies concerning Mun's original teachings, has now become the officially sanctioned reading of the meaning of Foundation Day; still, considerable confusion persists such as on the exact impact and outreach of this anticipated 'historic change'. However that may be, the profession of faith is that by Foundation Day (at least) the conditions for world peace will be lastingly secured owing to the True Parents' unremitting efforts (see Figure 4).

Mun's death and the ensuing loss of absolute interpretive authority will render Unification thought more than ever subject to on-going adaptation, a fact that grows conspicuously apparent in the face of this recent (re-)interpretation by UM dignitaries, identifying Foundation Day as the mere kick-off for some sort of 'embryonic' Cheon Il Guk, which is more akin to a Cheon Il Guk *in the making* than Mun's initial vision of an unmitigated heavenly paradise on earth. Suffice it to say that as a religious movement based on and, in fact, defined by millenarianism, the UM will not get around to preserving its millenarian trajectory, *unless* world peace has been effectively achieved; an ambitious target which, 'realistically speaking, would be very difficult (yet according to some not impossible!) to attain overnight'.[49] With that said, in order to keep the millenarian pattern intact, Han Hak-cha has already presaged another salvational objective to be accomplished by

[47] 13 January 2013 according to the lunar calendar.
[48] Author's conversation with UM members.
[49] Author's conversation with UM members.

the time of Mun's centenary in 2020. From this one can infer that the Kingdom of Heaven on earth as adumbrated by Mun, that is, involving every single human being and bringing about world peace, will naturally be deemed in constant need of more time for the UM leadership to render it concrete. Otherwise, the UM would forfeit doctrinal cohesion and, thus, relinquish its key ideological momentum.

Figure 4 Ch'ŏnjŏnggung (Palace of Heavenly Righteousness, commonly called Cheon Jeong Gung or Peace Palace) in Ch'ŏngp'yŏng: the major UM landmark and 'eternal' symbol for the 'True Parents' and the 'cosmic accomplishments' of their peace movement

4 Concluding remarks

Under the auspices of its religious genitor, mastermind and redeemer, Mun Sŏn-myŏng, the UM has become one of the most strident proponents for world peace. A largely self-proclaimed champion of peacebuilding and inter-religious dialogue, the UM sees itself as walking on a divinely commissioned path to repatriate God's foremost creation after ages under the regimen of Satan. Guided by the 'perfect Adam' (*wansŏng han adam*), who was Mun, Unificationists aspire to restore the primordial bond with God which original sin shattered in the Garden of Eden. It is this underlying millenarian thinking which serves as the driving force for the UM's widespread and sedulously pursued peace agenda.

The UM's set of teachings can be said to meet the criteria determined by the definition of millenarianism applied in this study (see Section 3.1, above). Unificationists cherish a belief in the Kingdom of Heaven on earth, which, when actualised, designates a blissful world of peace, affluence, equality and liberty under the tender care and patronage of God. This eternal paradise will progressively manifest itself on this earth ('this-worldly') and hereafter extend to the spirit world. The great salvational transformation driven forward by the faithful was at the brink of dawn ('imminent'), or more precisely, it was said to irreversibly 'unfold' by 22 February 2013, the day God's irrevocable providence would be completed. Foundation Day is supposed to grant humankind the potential to discern its divinity, re-enter into the divine 'blood bond' and form a communion with God in Heaven ('collective'). This change will enable the faithful to live in utmost happiness in the physical world, and eternally in the spiritual realm thereafter. God's beneficial dominion, with the True Parents as His governors, will not cease but will last forever ('ultimate') and embrace the whole cosmos ('total'). The Unificationist millennium, burgeoning on the Korean peninsula, is being brought to fruition by Mun and his spouse, who both are sited on a providential course prescribed by God.[50] For this reason, it is asserted that the True Parents' redemptive power pervades all action carried out by the UM. In other words, the UM's numerous undertakings are viewed as having a providential cause for the pursuit of building the Kingdom of Heaven on earth.[51] Ultimately, it is this very millenarian idea which acts as *the* doctrinal impetus or motivational agent for the wide array of the UM's activities with its global peace agenda leading the way.

[50] Despite his passing, for the time being, Mun is held to retain the central function within Unification soteriology, continuing his messianic role from the 'spirit world'. Accordingly, it has been announced by leading members of the UM that Foundation Day will see the (third) perfection blessing of the 'True Parents of Heaven, Earth and Humankind' (*ch'ŏnjiin ch'am pumo*) with Mun, *now* as a spiritual being, and his physical Eve, Han Hak-cha. This ceremony shall signify the wedding of God—who is joining the bodies of 'True Parents'—and the restoration of the state before the Fall.

[51] Even if God's providence is to be finally concluded, the Unificationist enterprise must not grind to a halt, for it is an essential part of the foundation and promotion of the new age.

REFERENCES

Barker, Eileen (1984), *The Making of a Moonie: Choice or Brainwashing*? Oxford and New York: Basil Blackwell

Barkun, Michael (1986 [1974]), *Disaster and the Millennium*, Syracuse NY: Syracuse University Press

Breen, Michael (1997), *Sun Myung Moon: The Early Years, 1920–1953*, Hurstpierpoint, UK: Refuge Books

Burridge, Kenelm (1975), *New Heaven. New Earth: A Study of Millenarian Activities*, 2nd edition, New York: Schocken Books

Choe, Joong-Hyun (1993), 'The Korean War and Messianic Groups: Two Cases in Contrast', PhD dissertation, Syracuse University

Choi, Syn-duk (1967), 'Korea's Tong-il Movement', in: *Transactions of the Korea Branch of the Royal Asiatic Society*, 43, pp. 167–80

Chryssides, George D. (1991), The Advent of Sun Myung Moon: the Origins, Beliefs and Practices of the Unification Church, Basingstoke, UK; London: Macmillan

Clarke, Peter B. (2009), 'Millenarianism: Historical and Social Roots', in: Peter B. Clarke and Peter Beyer (eds), *The World's Religions: Continuities and Transformations*, Abingdon, UK; New York: Routledge, pp. 353–65

Cohn, Norman (2004 [1957]), The Pursuit of the Millennium: Revolutionary Millenarians and Mystical Anarchists of the Middle Ages, London: Pimlico

Cohn, Norman (1962), 'Medieval Millenarism: Its Bearing on the Comparative Study of Millenarian Movements', in: Sylvia L. Thrupp (ed.), *Millennial Dreams in Action: Essays in Comparative Study*, The Hague: Mouton & Co, pp. 31–43

Daniels, Ted (2005), 'Charters of Righteousness: Politics, Prophets and the Drama of Conversion', in: Stephen D. O'Leary and Glen S. McGhee (eds), *War in Heaven/Heaven on Earth: Theories of the Apocalyptic*, London; Oakville CT: Equinox, pp. 3–17

FFWPU (Family Federation for World Peace and Unification) [Segye p'yŏnghwa t'ongil kajŏng yŏnhap] (1999), *Wŏlli kangnon* [Exposition of the Principle], 40th edition, Sŏul: Sŏnghwa ch'ulp'ansa

HSAUWC (Holy Spirit Association for the Unification of World Christianity) (ed.) (1975), *Day of Hope in Review: Part 2, 1974–1975*, Sun Myung Moon, Tarrytown: n.p.

Kim, Jin-choon (1998), 'A Study of the Formation and History of the Unification Principle', in: *Journal of Unification Studies*, 2, pp. 49–69

Kim, Won Pil (1982), *Father's Course and Our Life of Faith*, London: HSA-UWC Publications

Kim, Young Oon (1980), *Unification Theology*, New York: Holy Spirit Association for the Unification of World Christianity

Landes, Richard (2005), 'Roosters Crow, Owls Hoot: On the Dynamics of Apocalyptic Millennialism', in: Stephen D. O'Leary and Glen S. McGhee (eds), *War in Heaven/Heaven on Earth: Theories of the Apocalyptic*, London; Oakville CT: Equinox, pp. 19–46

Mickler, Michael L. (2008), 'Toward an "Abel" UN? The Unification Movement and the United Nations', in: *Journal of Unification Studies*, 9, pp. 49–83

Mun, Sŏn-myŏng (2010a), *Aberyuen anch'ak'kwa ch'ŏnilguk wansŏng'ŭn hanguk* (The safe arrival of the Abel UN and Korea at the completion of Cheon Il Guk). Online: www.cheonilguk.org/Malsm//2008-2010/201 00429.htm (accessed 2 August 2012)

Mun, Sŏn-myŏng (2010b), *P'yŏnghwa'rŭl sarang hanŭn segyein'ŭro* [As a peace-loving global citizen], 92nd edition, P'aju: Kimyŏngsa

Mun, Sŏn-myŏng (2007a), P'yŏnghwa mesiji 13: hananim'ŭi ttŭs'ŭro pon hwant'ae p'yŏngyang sidae'ŭi sagwan – migug'ŭl chungsim han yuen'gwa chayusegye'ŭi panghyang [Peace message 13: a historical view of the Pacific Rim Era seen through God's will—the direction of the UN and the free world centred on the United States]. Online: www.tongil.org/2009-PMKorean/pm13Korean.html (accessed 31 July 2012)

Mun, Sŏn-myŏng (2007b), *P'yŏnghwa mesiji 14: kajŏng maengse'ŭi kach'i'wa kŭ ŭiŭi* [Peace message 14: the value and significance of the family pledge]. Online: www.tongil.org/2009-PMKorean/pm14Ko rean.html (accessed 27 July 2012)

Mun, Sŏn-myŏng (2005), *P'yŏnghwa mesiji 1: hananim'ŭi isang kajŏng'gwa p'yŏnghwa isang segye wangguk* [Peace message 1: God's ideal family and the kingdom of the peaceful, ideal world]. Online: www.tongil.org/2009-PMKorean/pm1Korean.html (accessed 27 July 2012)

Mun, Sŏn-myŏng (2003), *P'yŏnghwa UN t'onghae p'yŏnghwa ch'ŏnguk wansŏngha-ja* [Let us perfect the peace kingdom of heaven through the peace UN]. Online: www.cheonilguk.org/Malsm//2003-1015.htm (accessed 1 August 2012)

Mun, Sŏn-myŏng (2000), *Yuen yangwŏnje mit segyejŏg'in kinyŏmil chejŏng chean* [Proposal to establish a UN bicameral system and a worldwide memorial day]. Online: www.cheonilguk.org/Malsm//20000818.htm (accessed 2 August 2012)

Pak, Ung Kyu (2005), *Millennialism in the Korean Protestant Church*, New York: Peter Lang Publishing

Talmon, Yonina (1966), 'Millenarian Movements', in: *Archives Européennes de Sociologie*, 7, pp. 159–200

The Holy Bible Containing the Old and New Testaments with the Apocryphal/Deuterocanonical Books (1995), New Revised Standard Version. anglicised edition, Oxford: Oxford University Press

Wessinger, Catherine (2011), 'Millennialism in Cross-Cultural Perspective', in: Catherine Wessinger (ed.), *The Oxford Handbook of Millennialism*, New York: Oxford University Press, pp. 3–24

Wessinger, Catherine (1997), 'Millennialism With and Without the Mayhem', in: Thomas Robbins and Susan J. Palmer (eds), *Millennium, Messiahs, and Mayhem: Contemporary Apocalyptic Movements*, New York; London: Routledge, pp. 47–59

Wojcik, Daniel (2011), 'Avertive Apocalypticism', in: Catherine Wessinger (ed.), *The Oxford Handbook of Millennialism*, New York: Oxford University Press, pp. 66–88

http://www.ambassadors4peace.org/about (accessed: 6 June 2012)

List of Abbreviations

CAUSA	Confederation of the Associations for the Unification of the Societies of the Americas
FFWPU	Family Federation for World Peace and Unification
HSAUWC	Holy Spirit Association for the Unification of World Christianity
IIFWP	Interreligious and International Federation for World Peace
UM	Unification Movement
UN	United Nations

UPF	Universal Peace Federation
US	United States
WK	*Wŏlli kangnon* (Exposition of the Principle)

GLOSSARY

Ch'oe Sŏn-gil 최선길 崔先吉 (Sun Gil Choi)
Han Hak-cha 한학자 韓鶴子 (Hak Ja Han)
Kim Il Sung 김일성 金日成 (Kim Il-sŏng)
Kim Kyŏng-gye 김경계 金慶繼
Kim Myŏng-hŭi김명희 金明姬
Kim Sang-ch'ŏl 김상철 金相哲 (Sang Chul David Kim)
Kwak Chŏng-hwan 곽정환 郭錠煥 (Chung Hwan Kwak)
Mun Hyŏn-jin 문현진文顯進 (Hyun Jin Preston Moon)
Mun Hyŏng-jin 문형진 文亨進 (Hyung Jin Sean Moon)
Mun Kyŏng-yu 문경유 文慶裕
Mun Sŏn-myŏng 문선명 文鮮明 (Sun Myung Moon)
Mun Yong-myŏng 문용명 文龍明
Pak Chŏng-hŭi 박정희 朴正熙 (Park Chung-hee)

Abel yuen 아벨유엔 'Abel UN'
Adam 아담 Adam
Chaerimju 재림주 Lord of the Second Advent
Changnogyo 장로교 Presbyterianism
Che3 isŭrael 제3 이스라엘 'third Israel'
Chisang chiok 지상지옥 hell on earth
Chisang ch'ŏnguk 지상천국 Kingdom of Heaven on earth
Chŏnggamnok 정감록 prophetic book, probably written in the 18th century by an unknown author
Chŏpput'im 접붙임 engrafting
Chŭngsando 증산도, most internationally active group within the Chŭngsan family of religions, founded in 1974
Chŭngsangyo 증산교 religious teachings of Kang Il-sun [Chŭngsan] (1871–1909), on which more than a hundred movements have centred their faith since the early 20th century
Ch'am chanyŏ 참자녀 True Children
Ch'am kajŏng 참가정 True Family
Ch'am pubu 참부부 True Parents
Ch'am pumo'ŭi nal 참부모의 날 True Parents Day
Ch'am sarang 참사랑 true love
Ch'angjo isang 창조이상 ideal of creation
Ch'angjo mokchŏk 창조목적 purpose of creation
Ch'ojonggyo taesa 초종교 대사 inter-religious ambassadors

Ch'ŏndogyo 천도교 historically influential religious movement, formerly known as Tonghak (1860–1905)
Ch'ŏngsim kukche pyŏngwŏn 청심 국제 병원 CheongShim International Medical Centre
Ch'ŏnguk 천국 Kingdom of Heaven
Ch'ŏnilguk 천일국 Cheon Il Guk
Ch'ŏnjiin ch'am pumo 천지인 참부모 True Parents of Heaven, Earth and Humankind
Ch'ŏnjŏnggung 천정궁 Palace of Heavenly Righteousness, Cheon Jeong Gung
Ch'ŏnjotaesin 천조대신 Amaterasu Ōmikami
Ch'ŏnju p'yŏnghwa yŏnhap 천주평화연합 Universal Peace Federation
Ch'ŏnjujŏg'in inyŏm 천주적인 이념 cosmic ideology
Ch'ŏnmyŏng 천명 mandate of heaven
Ch'ŏnsajang nusiel 천사장 누시엘 Archangel Nusiel
Ch'ŏnsang ch'ŏnguk 천상천국 Kingdom of Heaven in heaven
Ch'ukpok 축복 blessing
Eden tongsan 에덴동산 Garden of Eden
Haewa 해와 Eve
Han 한 恨 innermost feeling of sorrow
Hana'ŭi hananim arae han kajŏng 하나의 하나님 아래 한 가정 one family under God
Hana'ŭi taegajok 하나의 대가족 one great family
Hananim 하나님 God
Hananim'ŭi choguk 하나님의 조국 God's homeland
Hananim'ŭi hyŏlt'ongjŏk chikkye'ŭi chanyŏ 하나님의 혈통적 직계의 자녀 children of God's direct lineage
Hananim'ŭi kyohoe segye pogŭm sŏngyo hyŏphoe 하나님의교회 세계복음선교협회 World Mission Society Church of God
Hananim'ŭi malssŭm 하나님의 말씀 the word of God
Hananim'ŭi p'itchul 하나님의 핏줄 God's lineage
Hananim'ŭi sŏngjŏn 하나님의 성전 God's temple
Illyu'ŭi ch'am pumo 인류의 참부모 True Parents of humankind
Ilsin sŏkchae 일신석재 Ilshin Stone
Ingan t'arak 인간타락 Fall of Man
Irhwa 일화 Ilhwa pharmaceutical company
Kain yuen 가인유엔 'Cain UN'
Kiwŏnjŏl 기원절 Foundation Day
Kongsanjuŭi segye 공산주의세계 communist world
Kukche chonggyo chaedan 국제종교재단 International Religious Foundation
Kukche kuho ch'insŏn chaedan 국제구호친선재단 International Relief and Friendship Foundation
Kuseju 구세주 Saviour
Kŭlbang 글방 village school
Malse 말세 Last days
Manwang'ŭi wang 만왕의 왕 King of Kings

Manyu wŏnnyŏk 만유원력 original force of all beings
Mesia 메시아 Messiah
Noa 노아 Noah
Ŏrinyang [hon'in] chanch'i 어린양 [혼인] 잔치 marriage of the lamb
Pokkwi'ŭi wansŏng 복귀의 완성 perfection of restoration
Puhwalchŏl 부활절 Easter
P'yŏnghwa chadongch'a 평화자동차 Pyeonghwa Motors
P'yŏnghwa chigu 평화 지구 peace zones
P'yŏnghwa taesa 평화 대사 ambassadors for peace
P'yŏnghwa t'ongil kajŏng tang 평화통일가정당 Family Party for Peace and Unification
P'yŏnghwa'ŭi ch'ŏnguk 평화의 천국 Peace Kingdom
P'yŏnghwa'ŭi wang 평화의왕 King and Queen of Peace
Saeroun sidae 새로운 시대 new age
Samdae ch'ukpok 삼대축복 three great blessings
Sat'an chugwŏn 사탄 주권 sovereignty of Satan
Sat'an'ŭi chanyŏ 사탄의 자녀 sons and daughters of Satan
Sat'an'ŭi hyŏlt'ong 사탄의 혈통 lineage of Satan
Sat'an'ŭi kulle 사탄의 굴레 Satan's bondage
Sawi kidae 사위기대 four position foundation
Segye ilbo 세계일보 *Segye Ilbo* (South Korean newspaper)
Segye kidokkyo t'ongil sillyŏng hyŏphoe 세계기독교통일신령협회 Holy Spirit Association for the Unification of World Christianity
Segye kuwŏn 세계구원 global salvation
Segye p'yŏnghwa ch'ojonggyo ch'ogukka yŏnhap 세계평화초종교초국가연합 Interreligious and International Federation for World Peace
Segye p'yŏnghwa t'ongil kajŏng yŏnhap 세계평화통일가정연합 Family Federation for World Peace and Unification
Segye p'yŏnghwa yŏsŏng yŏnhap 세계평화여성연합 Women's Federation for World Peace
Segye p'yŏnghwa'ŭi ch'uk 세계 평화의축 axis of world peace
Sekai kirisutokyō tōitsu shinrei kyōkai 世界基督教統一神霊協会 Holy Spirit Association for the Unification of World Christianity
Sesang'ŭi sin 세상의 신 god of this world
Silch'e taesang 실체대상 substantial object
Sinhŭng chonggyo 신흥 종교 newly emerged religion
Sinjonggyo 신종교 new religious movement
Sŏngnam irhwa ch'ŏnma 성남일화천마 Seongnam Ilhwa Chunma
Sŏnmin 선민 God's elect
Sŏnmun taehakkyo 선문대학교 Sun Moon University
Susu chagyong 수수작용 give and receive action
Taech'isŏn 대치선 line of confrontation
Taejonggyo 대종교 historically influential nativist religious movement, founded in 1909

Taesun Chillihoe 대순 진리회 largest group within the Chŭngsan family of religions, founded in 1969
Tan wŏltŭ 단월드 Dahn World
Tidei 디데이 D-Day
Tōitsu kyōkai 統一教会 Unification Church
Tongyang'ŭi yerusallem 동양의 예루살렘 Jerusalem of the East
T'ongil kŭrup 통일그룹 Tongil Group
T'ongil kyohoe 통일교회 Unification Church
T'ongil sasang 통일사상 Unification thought
T'ongil sinhak 통일신학 Unification theology
T'ongil undong 통일운동 Unification movement
Uju'ŭi pimil 우주의 비밀 secret of the universe
Ŭm 음 陰 yin
Wansŏng han adam 완성한 아담 perfect Adam
Wŏlli haesŏl 원리해설 Explanation of the Principle
Wŏlli kangnon 원리강론 Exposition of the Principle
Wŏlli wŏnbon 원리원본 Original Text of the Principle
Wŏnbulygo 원불교 Wŏn Buddhism
Wŏnjoe 원죄 original sin
Yang 양 陽 yang
Yesunim 예수님 Jesus
Yŏŭido sunbogum kyohoe 여의도 순복음 교회 Yoido Full Gospel Church
Yŏnggye 영계 spirit world
Yŏngjŏg'in mesia 영적인 메시아 spiritual Messiah
Yŏngjŏk t'arak 영적 타락 spiritual Fall
Yukchŏk t'arak 육적 타락 physical Fall

POLITICS AND ENVIRONMENTAL DEVELOPMENT: FROM IMPOSITION AND TRANSFORMATION TO CONSERVATION AND MITIGATION IN THE DPRK

Robert Winstanley-Chesters

ABSTRACT

Examining institutional and political narratives connected to the environment from a developmental perspective, this paper reviews the evolution in environmental theory and practice within the DPRK from the close of the Korean War in 1953 to the early years of the 21st century. Within this narrative the author analyses the theoretical and practical movement of the DPRK and its institutions from a space of environmental imposition and transformation to one, in presentation at least, of conservation and mitigation.

Key words: Kim Il Sung, Kim Jong Il, developmental and environmental policy, agriculture, ideology, *chuch'e*

1 INTRODUCTION

This paper seeks to offer an analysis of those elements within the political and theoretical framework of the Democratic People's Republic of Korea (DPRK—North Korea) that relate to the development of the environment and are supportive of the construction and presentation of the DPRK as a 'lived' utopian geographic and economic space. My article concerns the movement and reconfiguration of the theoretical approaches and institutional practices within the country, the focus of which was the environmental or developmental during the years of Kim Il Sung's and Kim Jong Il's leadership, the usage and utilisation of such practices and their theoretical underpinning. In its approach, the paper will firstly undertake an analysis of the theoretical ground for political interaction with the environmental, both historically and at the turn of the 21st century. Secondly, it will identify and describe patterns of practical political policy derived from this analysis, utilising particular examples from the field of environmental management and industrial development.

In pursuing such an approach, I will often make reference to *chuch'e* (Juche) or *chuch'e* thinking. I do not accord any great level of content, coherence or cohesion to the term, but simply use it as a signifier of ideological or institutional intent. For the purposes of analysis of the DPRK's developmental and environmental approach, I find that the simple outline provided by Han S. Park (2002: 31) of the basic tenets of *chuch'e* have a particular resonance and usefulness as they connect deeply in environmental and developmental terms with the demonstrative historical narratives of the DPRK.[1] The first of these tenets is the governance of all thought, action and understanding through a sense of metaphysical nationalism. For the DPRK and its political and ideological conception, utopian possibility has been fulfilled, and in a sense living within an ideologically oriented DPRK and its environmental realm is to live within 'a paradise'. The second is the presence of a radically anthropocentric impulse which sees humanity as having dominion over all things, and capable of achieving any change or resolving any problem. Thirdly, the DPRK's ideology has an inbuilt sense of what is termed within its literature *ŭisiksŏng* or 'radical creativity'. This could be said to fuel this anthropocentric sense of dominion, in that it is through the expression of this creativity that these changes and resolutions can be achieved. The fourth theme is closely related to the third and is a sense of 'radical collectivity'. Through this collectivisation of national will and thought, radical creativity is amplified so as to make even greater the possibility of achievement. The fifth and final theme relates to *chuch'e* and other ideological elements within the DPRK's 'transcendentalism', through which nationalistic impulse, anthropocentricism, creativity and collectivity combine to incorporate the personhood of the individual (or individual action) into a sort of permanent collective national consciousness and will.

Park's summarisation of these key ideological themes, however, must be regarded as an analysis only of the formulation of the DPRK's political superstructure current at the time of his writing. Ideological construction within the DPRK does and has already

---

[1] In saying this, I am aware of the criticism levelled by Brian Myers (2010) against Park's analysis of the interior life and thematic construction of DPRK ideology and by the same author against *chuch'e's* foundational and formative moments (Myers 2006 and 2008)

changed, the shift in emphasis from *chuch'e* to *sŏn'gun* ('army first' policy) during the era of Kim Jong Il's leadership being a case in point. It is necessary to bear these shifts and revisions in mind as coming within the narratives of historical development relevant to the DPRK's environmental approach as well as of ideological developments among the DPRK's political and trading partners. Given that the DPRK appears to be predisposed towards a reflexive, adaptive level of political, philosophical and policy triangulation, which can be seen within narratives pertaining to its diplomatic and political activity, it would not be surprising if such a triangulation were also to be found in the realm of environmental thought and policy.

2 Transformation or Imposition: The Environmental and Developmental Approach in the DPRK

2.1 *Early stages*

In approaching the developmental and environmental approach of the 'infant' DPRK, the historical context of the state immediately following the Korean War (1950–53) must be borne in mind. Within Pyongyang some 75 percent of all buildings had been destroyed and there had been an enormous level of damage and destruction done to the environment (Cumings 2010: 160). Much of the industrial and agricultural infrastructure that had been put in place by the colonial Japanese administration had been destroyed, and the DPRK found itself with something of an infrastructural blank slate. The political impetus behind the need to rebuild much of the country's industrial and agricultural base provides ample opportunity for an introduction to early approaches within the DPRK towards industrial and environmental policy, which in turn provides a definite and early demonstration of the ideological influence and practical technical support from the Soviet Union and the People's Republic of China (PRC—China).

Once the war was over, the institutions of the DPRK spent quite a short period reorganising and assessing the damage done during hostilities. By September 1953 the DPRK had formulated a Three Year Plan for the reconstruction of the country, and entered into negotiations with the Soviet Union for an extension of its credit lines. The

Soviet Union ended up giving some 275 million roubles[2] worth of grant credit (Prybyla 1964), while in November the DPRK signed an agreement with China granting it some 800 million yuan worth of credit. The industrial and environmental policy this credit paid for focused primarily upon what I would term an 'impositional' approach to the natural environment. Prybyla (1964: 469) wrote that DPRK policy here followed 'the Soviet strategy of economic development', and that 'one-third of Soviet grants and credits were used to buy complete industrial installations in the USSR'. In the industrial sector the DPRK built or reconstructed iron and steel works at Hwanghae, Kimch'aek and Sungjin, an oil refinery at Namp'o, power stations at Sup'ung and Pyongyang, new mills at Sinŭiju and Pyongyang, a fertiliser plant at Hŭngnam and a seafood cannery at Sinp'o. At the same time the DPRK obtained a large number of tractors and harvesters as well as vast tonnages of fertiliser.

Kuark holds that the DPRK's agriculture policy revolved around two primary goals at the time, describing them as, firstly, 'the swift reconstruction and rehabilitation of the war-shattered factories making agricultural implements, and of farms and irrigation systems so as to increase grain production and meet the pent-up demand for food' and secondly, 'the rapid socialisation of agriculture by means of collectivisation' (Kuark 1963: 83). There is no overt claim to be creating a utopian space. However, there are many examples from this period of environmental improvements being undertaken, mainly following an impositional model. Prybyla (1964: 469), for example, reported that 'in 1956 alone, the Chinese army gave 740,000 man-days to the building of irrigation ditches and dams, including the Pyong Nam reservoir'. Very little consideration was given to the environment during this period other than that it should be productive, but wide-scale reclamation of virgin land or destruction of forests appears not to have been taking place during this period, merely improvements in already industrialised agricultural land, which led to the overall increase in industrial production. It is, therefore, difficult during this initial period to see a distinctly North Korean or ideologically indigenous approach to the environment or to agricultural development. This first decade following the end of the Korean War might therefore be categorised as

[2] Prybyla (1964) gives this figure in US dollars as measured contemporaneously. I have translated this into its Soviet rouble equivalent utilising the historical exchange record held by the Central Bank of the Russian Federation (http://cbr.ru/currency_base/OldDataFiles/USD.xls).

reflecting the initial ideological period of the DPRK in which the technocratic and impositional approach derived from Stalinist central planning doctrine held sway and in which a simple increase in productive capacity was the aim. As Kim Il Sung remarked: 'Rice is immediately socialism. We cannot build socialism without rice. I want everyone to strive to increase grain production in response to the call of the Party centre" (Kim 1956: 25).

Following this first post-war decade, however, as the DPRK's ideology and political organisation develops, it is possible to see the focus of practical environmental policy shifting accordingly. In line with Maoist influences deriving from the Great Leap Forward (1958–60), the 'Ch'ŏllima speed' movement and method uncoupled environmental and agricultural policy from productive need and connected practical policy with ideological goals. (See Section 3.1 below for a more detailed discussion of Ch'ŏllima and other incorporations into *chuch'e* thinking of Maoist revolutionary models and revolutionary speeds.) Unlike in Maoist China during the period of revolutionary models and mass action, the DPRK did not undertake such enormous acts of environmental transformation as the destruction of Lake Dian in China, which aimed to bring into being a practically utopian landscape.

2.2 *Kim Il Sung's 'Theses' and their effects*

Within the DPRK post 1964, an environmental and developmental approach is to be found connected to the rapid collectivisation of agricultural practice and ownership away from the earlier co-operative agricultural model, and the establishing of the first environmental and agricultural policy with a truly indigenous or local, ideological orientation. The framework for this approach is found in Kim Il Sung's 'Theses on the Socialist Rural Question in Our Country' (Kim 1964a). Within the theses Kim laid out a fully ideologically inspired approach to agricultural and environmental development, one which in most senses has changed little in the intervening years. It was to be achieved through the application of the 'Three Revolutions Movement'.[3] An ideological approach was to be applied to environmental

[3] The 'Three Revolutions Movement' was a key element of Kim Il Sung's 'Theses on the Socialist Rural Question in Our Country' (1964a). Initially it was essentially a structural and institutional strategy to embed party politicisation within all aspects of agricultural and rural life and to '...abolish the backwardness of the rural areas' (Kim

and agricultural practice through a change in the concepts and strategies relating to the technical, cultural and ideological aspects of environmental development. The 'Theses' also called for a hierarchical organisation of agricultural production according to the following pattern: peasantry over the urban working class, agriculture over industry, and the rural over the urban. The full incorporation of industrial management practices into the agricultural and rural economy was also called for, as well as the final stage in the collectivisation of rural ownership. The 'Theses' require agricultural and natural landscapes to be developed according to the same strategic system as the urbanised industrial areas, not just to achieve the goals of the three revolutions movement, but also to further the wider revolutionary aims of the DPRK's ideological approach. In Kim Il Sung's words, '[i]n order to eliminate the distinctions between the working class and the peasantry, it is necessary to rid the countryside of its backward state in technology, culture and ideology' (Kim 1964a: 167) Here may be seen perhaps for the first time the beginning of a real systemisation of political ideology. Atkins (1985: 328) presents the result as leading to 'the landscape of the DPRK [becoming] an outcome or a by-product of socialism but also a key medium through which society is transformed'. Yu (2005: 10) describes the strategic direction of the Seven Year Plan (1961–67) and the 'Rural Theses' as being 'not only to "upgrade" agricultural technology on the production side but also to socialize the peasantry into becoming socialist farmers.' 'The technical evolution', she adds, 'was indeed a social and political project, not just an economic and technological solution to develop rural productive forces.'

The apparent technological revolution called for in the 'Theses' led to a rapid and wide-scale revision of agricultural practice around five keys areas regarded by Kim (1965: 266) as being, in general, 'especially unrealistic'. These areas were expansion of irrigative capacity and water supply, the supply of electric power to the countryside and rural areas, the 'realignment' of agricultural land so as to incorporate mechanised agricultural processes, an increase in the use of chemical

1964a: 167). Party theorists and representatives were to form part of all agricultural and rural work teams, so that agricultural labourers considered all aspects of the Korean Workers' Party agenda at all times. The structures and concepts of the 'Three Revolutions' were later extended to feature in all aspects of productive and political life, such as in heavy industry: 'The ideological, technical and cultural revolutions are the most important tasks in the building of socialism and communism' (Kim 1973) fertiliser, and the reclamation of tidal lands and swamps to create more land for agricultural production. It is possible to examine the actual environmental impacts of the 'Theses' from a multiplicity of perspectives and directions. However, an examination of the impact of these policies on three of the areas identified as having been exposed to the practical implications of ideologically inspired action after the publication of the 'Theses' might be the most useful and revealing for this analysis

Firstly there is the practical manifestation of outcomes from the politicisation of irrigation policy. Agriculture on the Korean peninsula, and especially in the north, had always required some level of locally organised gravity-fed irrigation to support production. This irrigation system had been extended during the colonial Japanese period. However, after the publication of the 'Theses', the DPRK adopted a radically industrialised approach, disregarding almost completely the historical gravity-fed systems. Kim Il Sung in the 'Theses' declared that: 'The introduction of irrigation is a basic guarantee for preventing flood and drought damage, for gathering large, dependable harvests in farming and for assuring a steady increase in agricultural production' (Kim 1964a: 178). What followed, inspired by the 'Theses', was the building of an extensive and elaborate system of pumping stations and reservoirs—3,505 pumping stations for the main trunk network alone by 1998 (UNDP 1998)—to spread water throughout upland and lowland areas. Between 1954 and 1998, irrigated areas increased from some 227,000 hectares to 1.2 million hectares. As of 1990 there were apparently '1,700 reservoirs throughout the country, watering 1.4 million hectares of fields with a ramified irrigation network of 40,000 kilometres, which irrigated about 70 percent of the country's arable land' (Library of Congress, 'Country Profile North Korea' 2004, quoted by Yu 2005: 11). According to these two sources, the DPRK built a field-based system whereby 400,000 hectares of upland land were irrigated by 'mobile water guns, sprinkler, furrow and other drip methods for fruit trees' (Yu 2005: 12). Perhaps unsurprisingly, these developments and the completely irrigated furrow system transformed upland agriculture, massively increasing productive capacity, and transferred enormous spaces that were previously wild to agricultural exploitation. Hazel Smith recounts the relative success of this approach, which determined that 'the DPRK achieved sufficient grain production to meet the basic needs of its population beginning in at least 1973, with harvests in the late 1980s achieving record levels' (Smith 2005: 61).

Secondly, taking into account the two themes of the 'Theses'—revolutionary action required of a technical or cultural nature—changes focused on the collectivisation of agriculture were evidenced. These were partly to reflect levels of population transfer which occurred during the period of heavy industrial development from the rural to the urban environments. Just before publication of the 'Theses', policy had focused on the consolidation of agricultural co-operatives, which between 1957 and 1958 fell in number from more than 16,000 to fewer than 4,000, while the average size of each co-operative's land expanded to some 500 hectares (Noumoff 1979). Smith here is more circumspect, noting that "[d]ebate continues as to whether the social organization of agricultural production provided disincentives to increases in productivity' (Smith 2005: 61). So far as technical matters were concerned, this change in the rural landscape led to ideological developments focused on the mechanisation and 'chemicalisation' of agricultural land. The 'Theses' declared that 'the use of chemicals is an important means of increasing per-unit area yields of crops. The application of chemistry to agriculture will make it possible to improve the soil, increase land fertility, promote the growth and ripening of crops, and eliminate blights and harmful insects and weeds' (Kim 1964a: 180). A desire on the part of Kim Il Sung to 'ease the workload of the peasants' (Kim 1981: 276) was apparently one driver of this focus on the mechanisation of agricultural practice. As Yu (2005: 12) states: 'Relief from hard labor is evidenced by the priority given to the most difficult tasks in fieldwork. Ploughing, transplanting, and transporting operations were the first to be fully mechanized.' Perhaps more importantly, there was also an impetus to generate advances in productivity derived from economies of scale, which the much larger land areas held by the collective farms made possible. Supply of equipment such as tractors mirrors the growth in size of these farms, production of tractors growing from 764 per year in 1953 to some 20,000 per year by 1970 (Ministry of Unification 1992), with a concomitant increase in supply from 1.22 tractors per hectare in 1970 to some six or seven tractors per hectare by 1980. Such a change in agricultural equipment perhaps also suggests changes in the use of land as well as of general field shape, as these rural landscapes were reconfigured for the needs of an industrialised and irrigated landscape. Kim Il Sung also revisited a slogan of 1965 to demand a development that would further push ahead *chuch'e* thinking's environmental policy: 'Fertilizer is rice, and rice is socialism!' (Kim 1965: 141). This statement presages the development of a heavy focus on the use of chemical fertiliser in the agricultural process. The DPRK enormously expanded the use of fertilisers during this period, from a local production total of 259,800 tonnes in 1954 to some 4.7 million tonnes by 1984 (Kim 2008). Such production levels led to one of the highest concentrations of chemical application in agriculture anywhere in the world. Along with this massive input of chemicals into the agricultural environment there were new agricultural techniques such as double cropping and triple spacing of seedlings, contributing further to the perception of an improving environment and also determinedly ideological. In a sense these developments might form a utopian space in which the utopian element of landscape or geographic space is marked by its productivity and generative potential.

The third thematic area surrounds reclamation. Here the focus is on the ambitious attempts at the reclamation of tidal mudflats and other coastal regions demanded by Kim Il Sung in his work 'For The Large Scale Reclamation of Tidelands' (1968), to increase the availability of productive agricultural land. Kim stated within this work that '[i]n order to increase grain output and mechanize farm work in our country, it is imperative to bring tidelands under cultivation' (Kim 1968: 82). Not only did these attempts at tideland reclamation focus on the need for the creation of cultivable and productive land, they also connected to themes within the 'Theses' for the furthering of technical and ideological revolution: 'Reclaimed lands are vast plains where machines can be used for every kind of farm work. Therefore a small amount of manpower is needed to tend them' (Kim 1968: 85). As well as serving ideological aims, these projects demonstrated the reflexivity and practicality of a philosophical approach apparently inspired by *chuch'e* principles. Within such large projects problems were presented as the source of their own solution, such as the South Hwanghae province iron ore mine, which, faced with a problem related to the disposal of spoil, was instructed by Kim Il Sung to 'begin dumping this in the sea from a long conveyor belt to create a causeway linking several islands to the mainland' (Kim 1985: 89). Atkins (1985: 326) describes three such projects: 'the damming of the sea at the Amnok river to create 110,000 hectares', 'in South Pyongan province damming a stretch of land out to sea up to 16 kilometres', and 'in South

Hwanghae all the deeply indented bays were to be dammed'. These projects were to be directed by a new General Bureau of Tideland Reclamation, which in 1985 received a target from Kim Il Sung of some 500,000 hectares for reclamation. Such vast projects such as those within the Taegye, Sin and Tasada areas have dramatically changed the landscape and coastal map of the West Sea side of the DPRK. Coupled with the enormous West Sea Barrage project on the Taedong river we can see in these initiatives a shift to more practical and transformational projects within the framework of DPRK environmental thought. This practical, transformational approach to policy outcomes mirrors the demand in Kim Il Sung's 'Theses' for an agricultural environmental approach governed by the three revolutions.

3 Historical Developmental and Environmental Strategies of the DPRK

Before the Korean War, the DPRK's developmental and environmental strategy was expressed through short-term National Economic Plans in 1947, 1948 and for 1949–50 (Kuark 1963). After 1953, the country's national economic planning stretched into five- and seven-year plans. However, the influence of its ideology upon this type of co-ordinated central planning and its impact on environmental development engendered a later, radical shift in planning strategy. The DPRK's early focus on centralised industrial and developmental planning was very much a product of the influence of the Soviet Union under Stalin's leadership. However, on the death of Stalin and the solidification of the power of Nikita Khrushchev as Soviet premier, a process of radical and abrupt political change began that would have a direct impact upon environmental policy. Khrushchev's 1956 'secret speech' denouncing Stalin and a subsidiary report from April of that year entitled 'On the Personality Cult in the DPRK'[4] (Person 2007/2008; Shimotomai 2007/2008), which heavily criticised the political strategy of Kim Il Sung, created the political and ideological space for a revision of North Korean policy and strategy. The DPRK's developmental approach began to take inspiration from Mao's Great

[4] The Woodrow Wilson Centre's Cold War International History Project provided a set of documents in translation within its 16th Bulletin in 2008, giving extensive coverage of the diplomatic and political interplay between the authorities of the Soviet Union and the DPRK following this report's publication.

Leap Forward and the approach of the PRC's Second Five Year Plan (1958–62). The latter included policies such as the complete collectivisation of agricultural communes and the introduction of revolutionary speeds and models such as 'Dazhai Speed'.

3.1 *Movements to promote 'revolutionary urgency'*

It may have been the revolutionary urgency and narrative possibilities presented by this approach that most inspired Kim Il Sung, because by September 1958 in the DPRK the Ch'ŏllima movement had been launched as a theoretical movement designed to introduce revolutionary speeds and methods into conventional workplaces. This campaign utilised an approach that proved to be the first of a number demonstrating 'revolutionary urgent' tendencies within the DPRK. However, in the North Korean context the revolutionary urgency and transformational inclinations of the Great Leap Forward appear to have been blunted, at least so far as the environment and agriculture were concerned. Kim Il Sung, perhaps aware of the DPRK's labour supply issues and the general size of the population, as well as the dangers of allowing large groupings of people to form, spurned mega projects such as the draining of lakes or the wide-scale demolition and terracing of mountains. Kuark (1963: 91) saw the focus of the Ch'ŏllima movement as having been on a much smaller scale. 'Some Chinese farming techniques', she wrote, 'notably in rice cultivation (such as seeding on cold beds and dry fields, wide row and criss-cross sowing etc) were adopted', and noted that this effort did succeed in increasing production. However, at the time the radical Chinese model was quickly abandoned or not even developed as practical policy on the ground by local agencies (Kuark 1963).

Although nothing on the scale of the Great Leap Forward was attempted in the DPRK, this is not to say that transformational projects were not undertaken and their place within the developmental narrative not exploited. The impetus towards the transformative potential of developmental action and policy remains a part of the DPRK's ideological repertoire. Kim Il Sung's 1964 'Let's Make Effective Use of Mountains and Rivers' speech, for example, sees wilderness and non-utilised land as ripe for revision and reconstruction: 'Using mountains does not mean only living by them. In order to use them fully it is necessary to create good forests of economic value before anything else' (Kim 1964b: 256). At the same time, however, it is apparent that Kim Il Sung and the DPRK quickly drew away from the aspects of the 'revolutionary urgent' Great Leap Forward that directly impacted on agricultural and environmental development, and focused instead for a period on heavy industrial processes and the mechanisation of agricultural production. What Kim, the DPRK and its developing ideological construction found most useful from this reconfiguration after the Great Leap Forward and the Ch'ŏllima method itself was the concept of 'revolutionary urgency'. The DPRK to this day re-imagines and utilises this conception, reconfiguring it to suit particular new situations. Ch'ŏllima became 'Three Revolutions Speed' and then 'Pyongyang Speed', and in its most recent incarnation on 1 February 2010, it was announced that 'Korean service personnel and people are accelerating the building of a great, prosperous and powerful nation at the "Hŭich'ŏn speed", a new Ch'ŏllima speed' (KCNA 2010a).

3.2 *Taean Work Team method*

Another development in theoretical approach from this period that was deeply influential upon the DPRK's development strategy and its impact on environmental issues was the Taean Work Team method. This method also demonstrated the differing ideological approach of the DPRK in the developmental field when compared to the PRC. The Taean method revolved around an ideologically oriented system of workplace and work team organisation devised by Kim Il Sung, initially in 1961 to embed current political practice within workplaces by means of collective criticism and learning sessions. It was quickly reorganised following the publication of the 'Theses' to support the incorporation of the three revolutions movement, in a drive to connect all economic sectors with the current direction of ideological approach. Kim wrote that the

> Taean work system is the best system of economic management. It enables the producer masses to fulfil their responsibility and role as masters and to manage the economy in a scientific and rational manner by implementing the mass line in economic management, and by combining party leadership organically with administrative, economic, and technical guidance (Kim 1961: 48).

Taean working aimed to incorporate both revolutionarily enlightened workers and their political managers in a series of sub-committees that would form the heart of every company or work place. Chay (1976: 122) described it as an attempt by 'the North Korean communist leaders, aware of the growing need for managerial-technical capability, to achieve simultaneously technical capability and communist revolutionary zeal.' This is a very different system to the wider industrial and agricultural system of Maoist China. Lu (2001), for example, describes a situation in Chinese production units in which the workers barely had time to eat let alone help manage their own production. The DPRK's approach enabled some degree of moderating influence to be brought to bear on industrial and agricultural projects, especially in terms of local knowledge, knowledge that, as Lu (2001) recounts, was destroyed in the Chinese context by the sudden and urgent movement of massive numbers of workers into areas undergoing transformational development during the Great Leap Forward.

3.3 *On the spot guidance*

While it is true that the DPRK appropriated Mao's theoretical conception of 'revolutionary models', typified by Dazhai, it adopted a model of practice more local and useful to its needs. DPRK ideology and practice incorporated the notion of revolutionary modelling into the idealised personhood of the father of the nation, represented by the head of the Kim family. Both Kim Il Sung and Kim Jong Il engaged in what is referred to as 'on the spot guidance'. (Kim Jong Un in turn has taken up the practice.) On the spot guidance visits serve as set pieces when the leader of the DPRK appears at a particular industrial or agricultural project which has been or may be about to face a problem. The Leader will be shown around the project, witnessing and experiencing the problem before apparently spontaneously arriving at an ingenious or practical solution, which the project or organisation will be encouraged strongly to follow as the answer to their problems. The event will then be disseminated widely within DPRK media such as the newspaper *Rodong Sinmun*, on the Korean Central News Agency (KCNA) website, and perhaps through a book series. The guidance will also be utilised during group criticism and practical information sessions, which occur as part of the weekly routine of nearly every work place and educational institution. Thus the guidance and any element of policy development within it will become incorporated into the DPRK's ideological framework as well as into popular culture and narratives. The method can be applied to virtually every eventuality, and indeed many examples can be found nearly every day of the year as, even when there is no contemporary news or event, older examples of on the spot guidance can be used instead. This disseminative process has received some level of academic interest in the past, especially in comparison with Maoist revolutionary models. Medlicott (2005: 77), for example, declared that this is the means by which 'the state was transformed from a distant impersonal dictatorial authority to a parental figure, whose authority is often distant but just as often interceding into daily life.'

This theme also demands analysis of popular response to environmental strategy and outcome and its place within the DPRK's ideological and narrative frameworks. Discerning what we might determine to be a popular response within the DPRK is a virtually impossible exercise, especially when compared to popular responses within Western social-democratic states. What it is possible to determine is that the DPRK's strategy of response to and management of popular concepts relating to the environment and environmental development is one of incorporation. That is to say that developmental strategies of the DPRK incorporate those who will be part of their practical functioning, especially through the Taean system (Rhee 1987). The ideology of the DPRK places those involved in the strategy within the constraints of ideologically driven periods of revolutionary urgency (Shinn 1987). More than anything, as Medlicott (2005) asserts, both Kim Il Sung and Kim Jong Il assumed the position of 'revolutionary model' in such a way as to internalise the filial within the system through developmental strategies, and outcomes are demonstrated or described. This in a sense incorporates such strategies and outcomes within the popular realm and response in a way which can neither be objected to nor opposed. By doing so *chuch'e*'s approach denies the possibility of a negative response to its developmental or environmental strategy from the population, as ideology itself assumes the place and position of popular will—as Park (2002: 32) puts it, 'the self in this case is the nation as an indivisible and sacred entity'.

4 Mitigation of Environmental Failures in the DPRK Post-Warsaw Pact

The DPRK's agricultural and environmental policies and strategies have had their share of failures, although arguably not on the scale of the Soviet Union (Kormarov 1980) or the PRC (Smil 1982; Shapiro 2001). The political and academic narrative surrounding the DPRK today generally sites failures of its policies towards environmental and agricultural development within a post-1992 and post-Warsaw Pact context (Eberstadt 1994). There is a great deal of research and comment focused on the food crisis of the early to mid 1990s. Much of this research connects with the developing field of academic work on transitions from communism at the end of the Cold War period and the place of the DPRK within the new post-Cold War political world (see, for example, Eberstadt 1994 and 1999). This crisis is seen by many as evidence of both ideological and systemic failure and the ineptitude of the DPRK's economic, agricultural and industrial policy throughout its history. The famine conditions that resulted between 1992 and 1997 were in many ways an indictment of its ideological approach. However, perhaps there is a case for asserting that they might have been partly generated by a number of contributing factors including unrelated environmental impacts, such as serious droughts in the early 1990s which cut harvest levels and the intense rains in 1994 that further reduced capacity and damaged agricultural land (Noland 2004). Additional contributory factors included the collapse of the Soviet Union and the Warsaw Pact and the economic realm that the DPRK depended on for much of its trade and economic support, as well as the coming together of the cumulative technical inefficiencies and discrepancies within the DPRK's industrial and agricultural sector (Eberstadt 1994). However, in the midst of this disastrous period it is perhaps possible to determine the development of new ideological, institutional responses to environmental failures and a developing ability of bureaucratic and theoretical forces to mitigate such failures.

4.1 *Causes of environmental failures*

It is important first, before analysing the development of a strategy of environmental mitigation, to identify the roots of such environmental failures and to examine any previous politically oriented responses to them. The projects and schemes that the 'Theses on the Socialist Rural Question' inspired have been described above (in section 2.2), and in many ways it is within this environmental development strategy that many of the roots of eventual crisis are to be found. I have described the elaborate and heavily industrial transformative strategy by which the DPRK developed its agricultural irrigation system. This system, although in a sense technically advanced, functioned at great environmental expense as its use at high altitude created the conditions for high levels of soil erosion and forest degradation. Research from the Food and Agriculture Organisation (FAO) of the United Nations (UN), for example, asserts that the DPRK experiences a year on year reduction in forest cover of 1.68 percent and since 1990 has lost some 24 percent of its forest cover, equating to some 2,014,000 hectares. It also classifies 13 percent of its forests as conservation areas, the remaining 87 percent being classed as 'productive' (FAO 2005).

The industrial system of irrigation was also highly reliant on a stable and reliable electricity supply. In the years after the end of the Cold War, i.e. from around 1990, such a supply proved not to be available because of the collapse in coal and oil supplies from the former Soviet Union. This failure led to a shortage of some one billion kilowatt hours (kWh) in general electricity supply and more specifically of 300 million kWh that were required for irrigation pumping and water transfer (Williams, Von Hippel and Hayes 2000). The shortage of electricity supply created innumerable environmental problems, which in themselves have bred further problems. A 1998 report produced by the United Nations Development Programme (UNDP) pointed out that the 32,000 pumping stations which supported the irrigation system needed to be replaced at a rate of 20 percent a year to provide a normal level of efficiency; their inefficiency and failure resulted in the collapse of many terracing systems and flooding from some 102 reservoirs, leading to flooding, further soil erosion, silting up of river beds and the failure of pumping stations and hydroelectric plants, and bringing about a further diminution of electricity supply (UNDP 1998).

Another useful example is the developmental focus on the 'chemicalisation' of agriculture envisaged by the 'Theses'. This led to a rapid increase in fertiliser and chemical usage following 1964 and the implementation of the policies derived from the 'Theses', which generated a relatively rapid collapse in soil fertility. Yu (2005) asserts that 'as a result of increasing chemical inputs, the soil became acidified'. This acidification and decline in soil quality resulted in still further chemical usage, as crop management through multiple cropping and monoculture required wide-scale pesticide use to sustain yields. Atkins (1985) describes the terrible effects of this approach to agricultural management in the guise of heavily nitrate-polluted run-off on stream and river ecosystems.

4.2 *Mitigation strategies*

These two areas of strategic environmental development—irrigation and the use of fertilisers—can be seen to have directly contributed to the eventual failure of the agricultural system in the DPRK, which in turn led to the crisis period in the 1990s (Smith 1999). Both caused a lack of robustness within the agricultural environment that made the DPRK's system for food production incapable of responding positively to damaging or disruptive externalities. However the DPRK and its institutions have proved to be reflexive and reactive in response to such degradation in the realm of environmental management, perhaps as reflexive as they have been within the political arena. This developing institutional tendency towards mitigation revolves around two key elements. Firstly, the DPRK's political and theoretic approach seems to contain within itself an almost innate capacity for drawing on internal reflexive abilities supportive of the reconfiguration of both theory and popular expectation. One historical example of this is to be found in the period immediately after the incorporation of elements of Mao's Great Leap Forward into the Ch'ŏllima campaign. The widespread reorganisation of agricultural and industrial production during this campaign along completely collectivist lines was immensely difficult and disruptive within the heavy industrial sector as it generated significant labour shortages. Accordingly the sector missed its target within the Five Year Plan (1957–61) by quite some margin (Kuark 1963), and the economic planners of the DPRK designated a Special Absorption Period. This pause supported the reconfiguration of industrial systems at both a practical and an ideological level, taking into account the problems of pushing through such a radical change, as well as giving it breathing space necessary to develop its productive capacity. A more recent example, related to the collapse of the DPRK's productive abilities during the famine period of 1992 to 1997, was the ideological reclassification of this period. After the 1992 campaign

'Let's Eat Two Meals a Day' (recounted by Smith 2005: 66), instituted to conserve grains stocks during the initial period of disruption, Kim Jong Il declared that the years 1994 to 1996 would serve as an economic adjustment period. This transitional period was then defined as the 'arduous march', deliberately conflating the current stage of famine and environmental and institutional crisis within the DPRK with the period of guerrilla struggle against the Japanese of Kim Il Sung's United North East Anti-Japanese Army. Thus the DPRK's developmental approach attempted a re-orientation of state and personal survival strategies during the famine years into ones that served nationalist and ideological purposes.

This theoretical/practical reflexivity and mitigation-focused response of DPRK institutions has been matched by an increasing necessity, thanks to the famine and crisis years, for engagement with UN institutions, non-governmental organisations (NGOs) and other non-state bodies (Smith 1999). The DPRK was in need of financial, material and structural support on a long-term basis, and these would not be given by the world's institutions dedicated to aid and support unless Western standards of governance, audit and accountability were adopted. Thus since the famine period there have been many instances of institutional change within the DPRK and those of its organs dedicated to developing a framework of accountability and institutional response acceptable to Western external forces, such as revisions of the legal framework surrounding land tenure, land conservation, biodiversity and pollution (Williams, Von Hippel and Hayes 2000; Jo and Adler 2002). Although these developments in ability and practice are forced by circumstance, they are leading to a much more informed and responsive institutional structure within the DPRK.

This developing conventional approach to accountability and practice within the theory and institutions of the DPRK has been mirrored by the development of an environmental approach that is much more based on a recognisable paradigm of conservational approach and sustainable development. The DPRK has, for example, worked with UN organisations such as the United Nations Environment Programme and UNDP to develop development strategies of greater robustness, as well on projects with the FAO to determine and support the health of forests (FAO 2009) and develop more sustainable approaches to agricultural practice (FAO 2010). The DPRK has attempted to develop relationships with its near neighbours in support of greater environmental and agricultural sustainability across the region.

It has been a member of the Greater Tumen Initiative, a project shared between Russia, Mongolia, the PRC and the DPRK to reduce water pollution, habitat loss and reductions in biodiversity in the areas surrounding the Tumen (kor.: Tuman) river, as well as wider biodiversity issues (Koo, Lee and Yoo 2011). Such co-operation is reflected in pronouncements on biodiversity during the Kim Jong Il era:

> The state is pushing ahead with the protection of biodiversity through the institution of laws and regulations and the establishment of administrative and technical management systems. And it does not stint investment to the development of management technologies for analyzing, removing or minimizing the threat to the biodiversity. And the state is turning the protection of biodiversity into the work of popular masses through the education and propaganda (KCNA 2007).

The DPRK is also part of the North East Asian Forest Forum, which exists to promote and develop strategies for forest restoration in the region (Moon and Park 2004), and has followed a long-term strategy of afforestation since the floods of 1994 (Kim 2008). There have even been recent developments in the promotion of wind power within the DPRK (Hayes and Von Hippel 1997), and in 2010, KCNA reported Kim Jong Il pronouncements on the benefits of organic farming methods: 'The present trend...is to do organic farming without using chemical fertilizers and herbicide. It is necessary to actively apply organic and other new farming methods' (KCNAb 2010). Collectively these examples demonstrate that during the post- crisis era and subsequently the development of a mitigating approach towards the environmental consequences of agricultural and industrial productivity was developing within the institutional and ideological framework of the DPRK.

5 Conclusion

The contexualisation and analysis of the DPRK's approach and narratives towards matters environmental and developmental set out in the preceding sections of this paper is designed, at least in part, to undermine the conventional political, academic and media narrative which focuses on the 'opacity' of the DPRK, its ideology and institutional development. When it comes to the environmental realm, some element at least of the DPRK's ideological approach as expressed within texts such as the 'Theses' is knowable and accessible for analytical review. The DPRK's environmental approach is predicated on its belief that it is a place of utopian fulfilment, a 'paradise' indeed. In this essay I have shown that in those terms, the DPRK's environmental strategy has not at times led towards an environment that could conventionally be described as paradise. There have been instances of developmental failure and environmental destruction during the history of the DPRK, and at times the DPRK and its ideology acknowledge these failures and the destructive or negative outcomes of these episodes. If these periods are not accounted for within the narrative, the DPRK within both its presentation and its theoretical construction attempts instead a revision of strategic goals and practical policy, in order to at least move away from the most catastrophic of outcomes.

A significant degree of reflexivity also underlays the DPRK's environmental strategy and theorisation. I have identified the historical movement away from a monolithic Maoist reconstructive and transformative tendency in environmental approach towards a strategy based more upon small-scale technocratic and accumulative practice, from the Great Leap Forward to the Taean Work Team. However, more recently since 1992 and its period of crisis the DPRK appears to be in the midst of a new triangulating redevelopment of theoretical and strategic approach, inspired by the structural failings revealed during difficult and challenging times. Such reflexivity would include the incorporation of new environmental paradigms, strategies presented by the institutional actors it engaged with for the first time during the famine years of 1992 to 1997, such as NGOs and UN agencies, sourced from ultimately environmental or green movements. The DPRK has incorporated such theory, strategy and approach in its own way, one which we may not immediately recognise as environmentally focused at all. Just as it is difficult, if not almost impossible to assess the sincerity of any element of action, strategy or theory that derives from the DPRK, it is perhaps impossible to determine whether the DPRK has really undergone an ideological or policy transfer to a green or environmental paradigm. However, the fact of the incorporation of apparently green or environmental terminology and practice within the institutional management of some of the DPRK's priority areas such as energy production or industrial development and even beyond, perhaps suggests something that in DPRK terms is more important: that the environmental might be harnessed by the political and institutional framework of the DPRK and form part of and contribute to the wider realm of institutional practice and development.

REFERENCES

Atkins, P. (1985), 'The Dialectic of Environment and Culture: Kimilsungism and the North Korean Landscape', in: A. Mikherjee and V. Agnihotri (eds), *Environment and Development (Views from the East and West)*, New Delhi: Concept, pp. 309–31

Chay, P. (1976), 'The Analytical Model of the North Korean Politics and Administration', in: *Journal of East and West Studies: Perspectives on East Asian Economies and Industries*, 5 (1), pp. 99–132

Cumings, Bruce (2010), *The Korean War: A History*, New York: Modern Library

Eberstadt, Nicholas (1999), '"Self-Reliance" and Economic Decline: North Korea's International Trade, 1970-1995', in: *Problems of Post-Communism*, 46, (1), pp. 3–13

Eberstadt, Nicholas (1994), 'North Korea: Reform, Muddling Through, or Collapse', in: T. Henriksen, and K. Lho (eds), *One Korea? Challenges and Prospects for Reunification*, Washington DC: Hoover Institution Press

FAO (Food and Agriculture Organisation of the United Nations) (2010), *Global Forest Resources Assessment 2010*, Rome: FAO

FAO (2009), *Global Forest Resources Assessment 2009*, Rome: FAO

FAO (2005), *Global Forest Resources Assessment 2005*, Rome: FAO

Hayes, Peter and David Von Hippel (1997), DPRK: *Energy Sector Current Status and Scenarios for 2000 and 2005*, Berkeley CA: Nautilus Institute

Jo, J. and S. Adler (2002), 'North Korean Planning: Urban Changes and Regional Balance', in: *Cities*, 19 (3), pp. 205–15

KCNA (Korean Central News Agency) (2010a), *Great Advance Speed of Songun Korea*. Online: www.kcna.co.jp/item/2010/201002/news01/20 100201-16ee.html (accessed 27 January 2013)

KCNA (2010b), *Kim Jong Il inspects Mijok Cooperative Farm*. Online: www.kcna.co.jp/item/2010/201003/news13/20100313-13ee.html (accessed 27 January 2013)

KCNA (2007), *International Day of Biodiversity Observed in DPRK*. Online: www.kcna.co.jp/item/2007/200705/ news05/23.htm#11 (accessed 27 January 2013)

Kim Il Sung (1985), 'On Some Measures For The Reclamation of Tideland in a Well Defined Framework', in: *Works* 39, Pyongyang: FLPH, pp. 79–96

Kim Il Sung (1981), 'For the Implementation of the Rural Theses', in: *Works* 36, Pyongyang: FLPH, pp. 265–88

Kim Il Sung (1973), 'On Forcefully Accomplishing the Three Revoutions – Ideological, Technical and Culture in Industry', in: *Works* 28, Pyongyang : FLPH, pp.124–44

Kim Il Sung (1968), 'For the Large Scale Reclamation of Tidelands', in: *Works* 23, Pyongyang: FLPH, pp. 74–86

Kim Il Sung (1965), 'Rice is Immediately Socialism', in: *Works* 19, Pyongyang: FLPH, pp. 141–59

Kim Il Sung (1964a), 'Theses on the Socialist Rural Question in Our Country', in: *Works* 18, Pyongyang: FLPH, pp. 163–212

Kim Il Sung (1964b), 'Let us Make Effective Use of Mountains and Rivers', in: *Works* 18, Pyongyang: FLPH, pp. 255–66

Kim Il Sung (1961), 'On Planting Orchards Through an All-People Movement', in: *Works* 15, Pyongyang: FLPH, pp. 46–62

Kim Il Sung (1956), 'Rice is Immediately Socialism (Letter to the Chairmen of the South Pyongan Provincial Party Committee)', in: *Works* 10, Pyongyang: Foreign Languages Publishing House (FLPH), pp. 25–28

Kim, Woon-Keun (2008), 'Food Situation and Agricultural Reform in North Korea', in: *Journal of Rural Development*, 21 (1), pp.73–88

Koo, C., H. Lee, and D. Yoo (2011), *Northeast Asian Economic Cooperation: Assessment and Prospects of the Greater Tumen Initiative*, Kangwon University, Chuncheon: Asia-Pacific Cooperation Academy

Kormarov, B. (1980), *The Destruction of Nature in the Soviet Union*, London: Pluto Press

Kuark, Y (1963), 'North Korea's Agricultural Development during the Post-War Period', in: *China Quarterly*, 14 (2), pp. 82–93

Lu, Xin-An (2001), 'Dazhai: Imagistic Rhetoric as a Cultural Instrument', in: *American Communication Journal*, 5 (1), pp. 1–26

Medlicott, C. (2005), 'Symbol and Sovereignty in North Korea', in: *SAIS Review*, 25 (2), pp. 69–79

Ministry of Unification (1992), *Bukhan kyongje tong gae jip 1986*. Online: www.kinu.or.kr/servlet/Download?num=71&fno=170&bid=DB0102&callback =http://www.kinu.or.kr/info/info_04_01_01.jsp&ses= (accessed 14 May 2013)

Moon, K. and D. Park (2004), 'The role and Activities of NGOs in Reforestation in the Northeast Asian Region', in: *Forest Ecology and Management*, 201 (1), pp. 75–81

Myers, Brian (2006), 'The Watershed that Wasn't: Re-evaluating Kim Il Sung's "Juche speech" of 1955', in: *Acta Koreana*, 9 (1) (January 2006), pp. 89–115

Myers, Brian (2008), 'Ideology as Smokescreen: North Korea's Juche Thought', in: *Acta Koreana*, 11 (3) (December 2008), pp. 161–82

Myers, Brian (2010), *The Cleanest Race: How North Koreans See Themselves and Why it Matters*, New York: Melville House

Noland, Marcus (2004), *Korea After Kim Jong Il*, Washington DC: Institute for International Economics

Noumoff, S. (1979), 'The Struggle for Revolutionary Authenticity: The Experience of the DPRK', in: *Journal of Contemporary Asia*, 9 (1), pp. 27–52

Park, Han S. (2002), North Korea: The Politics of Unconventional Wisdom, Boulder CO: Lynne Rienner

Person, James F. (2007/2008), 'New Evidence on North Korea in 1956', in: *Cold War International History Project Bulletin*, 16 (Fall 2007/Winter 2008) pp. 447–54

Prybyla, J. (1964), 'Soviet and Chinese Economic Competition within the Communist World', in: *Soviet Studies*, 15 (4), pp. 464–73

Rhee, S. (1987), 'North Korea's Pragmatism: A Turning Point?', in: *Asian Survey*, 27 (8), pp. 885–902

Shapiro, J. (2001), *Mao's War Against Nature*, Cambridge: Cambridge University Press

Shimotomai, Nobuo (2007/2008), 'Pyeongyang in 1956', in: *Cold War International History Project Bulletin*, 16 (Fall 2007/Winter 2008) pp. 455–527

Shinn, R. (1987), 'North Korea in 1982: Continuing Revolution under Kim Jong Il', in: *Asian Survey*, 23 (1), pp.102–109

Smil, V. (1982), *China's Environmental Crisis*, Armonk NY: M.E. Sharpe

Smith, Hazel (1999), '"Opening up" by Default: North Korea, the Humanitarian Community and the Crisis', in: *The Pacific Review*, 12 (3), pp. 453–78

Smith, Hazel (2005), *Hungry for Peace: International Security, Humanitarian Assistance and Social Change in North Korea*, Washington DC: United States Institute for Peace

UNDP (United Nations Development Programme) (1998), *DPR Korea: Agricultural Recovery and Environmental Protection (AREP) Program: Identification of Investment Opportunities*, vol. 1–3, New York: UNDP

Williams, James H., David Von Hippel and Peter Hayes (2000), 'DPRK Briefing Book: Fuel and Famine: Rural Energy Crisis in the DPRK', Policy Paper, Institute on Global Conflict and Cooperation, University of California Multi-Campus Research Unit, Berkeley CA: Nautilus Institute

Yu, C. (2005), 'The Rise and Demise of Industrial Agriculture in North Korea', Paper No. 08-05, The Mario Einaudi Center for International Studies, Cornell University

BETWEEN AUTONOMY AND INFLUENCE? MULTILATERALISM AND NORTH KOREAN FOREIGN POLICY IN THE SIX PARTY TALKS

Eric J. Ballbach

ABSTRACT

The main thrust of this paper is an analysis of a generally ignored component of North Korean foreign policy—the realm of multilateralism. Theoretically informed by Neorealist Foreign Policy Theory and building on a conception of multilateralism as a strategic foreign policy phenomenon, this essay strives to discern the specific conditions and underlying motives that drive the DPRK's decision to refer to—or reject—multilateralism as a means of its foreign policy. Using North Korea's seemingly erratic foreign policy vis-à-vis the Six Party Talks as a case, the analysis suggests that whether the DPRK opts for cooperation or non-cooperation in a given situation depends heavily on the degree to which it considers itself threatened: when it perceives its security to be immediately threatened, it pursues an autonomy-seeking policy, whereas it will pursue an influence-seeking policy (within institutions) if its security is perceived to be less threatened. This suggests a highly instrumental understanding of multilateralism, which is either strategically adopted or rejected to achieve the DPRK's alterable foreign policy goals of influence and autonomy.

Key words: North Korea, multilateralism, foreign policy, Six Party Talks, Neorealist Foreign Policy Theory

1 INTRODUCTION: NORTH KOREA—THE MULTILATERALIST'S NIGHTMARE?

The third nuclear test carried out by the Democratic People's Republic of Korea (DPRK) on 12 February 2013 and the subsequent aggravation of the security situation on the Korean peninsula were only the latest reminders of the formidable challenge posed by the nuclear crisis. Among other developments, the recent escalation of this persistent conflict has led to a renewed debate on the possibility for a resumption of the stalled Six Party Talks (SPT). Established in 2003 and in abeyance since 2008, this multilateral format represents the latest diplomatic effort to date to engage the DPRK in a stable regional negotiation framework and thus to address what is widely considered to be one of the most pressing security challenges within Northeast Asia (NEA) in its present political existence. Yet, when the DPRK's regional post-Cold War foreign and security policy is analysed, the realm of multilateralism is largely ignored. At first glance, this seems hardly surprising given both the low level of institutionalisation in NEA—an area Paul Evans (2007) provokingly labelled an 'anti-region' with regard to multilateral security cooperation—and the sceptical stance of the DPRK vis-à-vis this form of cooperation. There is no doubt that, in common with other states in the region, the DPRK has traditionally been rather dismissive about the prospect of engaging in multilateral security structures in NEA. Uttering that the time is not (yet) ripe for the states in the region to adopt this form of cooperation and voicing concern that such initiatives might be directed against it, it time and again rejected proposals that called for the initiation of a multilateral security dialogue within NEA. For instance, it opposed the establishment of a CSCE-modelled consultation process that was repeatedly suggested by Gorbachev and Shevardnadze (Chung 2004) and rejected the proposals both of former South Korean President Roh Tae-woo, who called for a Consultative Conference for Peace in Northeast Asia (Mack and Kerr 1995), and of former US Secretary of State James Baker, who proposed a two-plus-four mechanism to deal with the tensions on the Korean peninsula (Baker 1991). Despite this doubting posture, however, the more recent post-Cold War reality saw increasing DPRK participation in regional multilateral security structures, from the Northeast Asian Cooperation Dialogue (NEACD) (from 1993/2002)[1] and the Council for Security Cooperation in the Asia Pacific (since 1994) on the Track-II level, to the Four Party Talks (1997–99) and the Six Party Talks (from 2003) on the Track-I level. This increasing participation notwithstanding, most scholars still seem to agree on the assumption that the DPRK holds a solely negative view of engaging in multilateral security structures in NEA. For example, George Friedman (2006) maintains that the DPRK raises serious questions about the 'limits of multilateralism', and Paul Evans

[1] North Korean representatives attended the founding meeting of the NEACD in 1993 and participated on a more regular basis from 2002.

(2007: 109–10) even describes North Korea as a 'multilateralist's nightmare' with regard to learning and socialisation as essential agents of multilateralism.[2] As the discussion in section 2 reveals, such assessments result from a very specific and narrow understanding of the multifaceted concept that is multilateralism. Yet this qualitative definition of multilateralism is highly problematic in the context of Northeast Asia and particularly in the case of North Korea, for it excludes the concept's crucial strategic dimension and its instrumental value as a distinct foreign policy tool.

Embedded in an examination of different scholarly perspectives on the concept, section 2 conceptualises multilateralism as a distinct foreign policy phenomenon and offers a broad definition of the concept that allows for analytically capturing its vital strategic dimension. Using North Korea's apparently erratic foreign policy vis-à-vis the SPT as a case, the empirical analysis in section three applies an approach that is theoretically informed by Neorealist Foreign Policy Theory (NFPT) as designed by Baumann, Rittberger and Wagner. The analysis draws specifically on the notions of autonomy-seeking and influence-seeking policy as the primary explanatory tools and strives to discern the specific conditions and underlying motives that drive North Korea's decision to refer to, or reject, multilateralism as a means of its foreign policy in the first place. The investigation period of the study is limited to the time span from the adoption of the 19 September 2005 Agreement to the adoption of the agreement reached at the end of the second session of the sixth round of the SPT in September 2007.[3]

2 Scholarly Perspectives on Multilateralism

While the first documented use of the term 'multilateral' dates back to the year 1858, the noun form of the word only came into use in the aftermath of World War I (see Powell 2003: 5). As James Caporaso (1992: 600–601) points out, the noun 'comes in the form of an "ism",

[2] For a notably different account, see Paik 2006.

[3] While an analysis of the entire Six Party process would go beyond the scope of this study, the particular investigation period chosen here is suggested by the theoretically deduced assumption that North Korea's influence-seeking and autonomy-seeking policies are linked to phases of cooperation and non-cooperation, both of which are apparent in the investigation period.

suggesting a belief or ideology rather than a straightforward state of affairs'. An understanding of multilateralism as it was debated in the United States (US) after 1945 seems to reinforce this rather normative perception of multilateralism, depicting it simply as the 'international governance of the "many"', while its central principle was said to be the 'opposition [of] bilateral and discriminatory arrangements that were believed to enhance the leverage of the powerful over the weak and to increase international conflict' (see Kahler 1992: 681). Despite such early efforts to approach the term, the disciplinary debate on multilateralism in the fields of International Relations and Foreign Policy Analysis is still comparatively young. For too long, to refer to a popular critique from Tom Keating (1993: 12), political science limited its research to the notions of 'institutions' and/or 'cooperation' without explicitly paying attention to the phenomenon of multilateralism. Although the term multilateralism is frequently used in various contexts—including the debate on the chances and limits of regionalisation in NEA and in the context of the nuclear issue—the concept still lacks analytical clarity and is 'seldom defined or even operationalized' (Dosch 2006: 2; see also Seol 2008).[4]

In the theoretical debate on multilateralism, two different perspectives can be distinguished, both of which refer to interrelating actors and therefore conceptualise multilateralism as a phenomenon of international politics rather than a foreign policy phenomenon. A first scholarly definition and a typical example of what was later labelled a quantitative (e.g. Baumann 2007: 443), formal (e.g. Diebold 1988: 1), or nominal (e.g. Ruggie 1993: 6) perspective was provided by Robert O. Keohane (1990: 731), who defined multilateralism as 'the practice of coordinating national policies in groups of three or more states, through ad hoc arrangements or by means of institutions'. While acknowledging its accuracy in principle, a number of scholars subsequently criticised this definition or, more precisely, its 'incomplete character'.[5] Arguably the most prominent critic was John G. Ruggie (1993: 6, 11), who notes that Keohane's nominal definition misses the

---

[4] For recent examples of scholarly works without a definition and/or operationalisation of the concept, see: Kang 2006 and Kwak 2006.

[5] For example, Jörn Dosch (2002: 25) states that multilateralism defined in a nominal way refers to nearly every form and type of cooperation which encompasses at least three actors. Similarly, Weiss and Rihackova (2010: 8, italics in original) note that 'according to this view, every interaction with more than two participants is multilateral, regardless of whether the coordination occurs only once or regularly, whether it is institutionalized or *ad hoc*.'

qualitative dimension of the phenomenon, thus overlooking those properties that differentiate it from other 'generic institutional forms', namely bilateralism and imperialism. Ruggie (1993: 11) defines multilateralism as

> an institutional form that coordinates relations among three or more states on the basis of generalized principles of conduct—that is, principles which specify appropriate conduct for a class of actions, without regard to particularistic interests of the parties or the strategic exigencies that may exist in any specific occurrence.

Although unquestionably insightful, for the study at hand, which strives to discern the key impetus and motives that drive North Korea's decision to refer to or reject multilateralism as a means of its foreign policy, this narrow qualitative defines definition is problematic for several interrelated reasons.

Firstly, Ruggie's definition conceptualises multilateralism solely as a phenomenon of international politics without paying attention to the motives of the respective states. As Baumann (2006: 23) correctly points out in this regard, the reference to the special quality of multilateralism does not relate to the motives of the interacting actors but rather to the form of their interactions. Baumann (2007: 445) subsequently defines multilateralism as the willingness of a single country to seek a type of cooperation with other countries, which is characterised by this institutional form. Hence, if the analytical focus is on the possible motives and motivations of a certain country (here: North Korea) to relate (or not to relate) to multilateralism in its foreign policy, the concept must be understood as a single-country foreign policy phenomenon, which in turn leads to an utterly different analytical focus.

Secondly, the qualitative definition brings with it a very narrow analytical focus that by and large excludes the vital strategic dimension of the concept. Ruggie (1993: 10, 12) himself characterises multilateralism as a 'highly demanding institutional form' and explicitly excludes particularistic interests or strategic exigencies from his definition. Baumann also emphasises the qualitative character of multilateralism when he maintains that to be characterised as 'multilateral', the relations between states should to a large degree be shaped by the principles of non-discrimination and indivisibility (Baumann 2007: 445–46). However, specifically in NEA, multilateralism is arguably best understood 'as an extension and intersection of national power and purpose rather than as an objective force in itself' (Green and Gill 2009: 3). Incorporating an instrumentalist perspective seems particularly relevant in the case of the DPRK, whose participation in multilateral structures is, according to the analysis below, first and foremost based on strategic calculations, not on specific values or norms and a high moral commitment. Against this background, a broader definition of multilateralism seems appropriate, one that allows for analytically capturing the strategic dimension and the instrumental value of multilateralism as a distinct foreign policy tool. Therefore, multilateralism is defined here as a specific type of foreign policy (behaviour) which is characterised by the willingness of a single country to coordinate its foreign policy on a specific issue and/or in a specific area with at least two other states within varyingly dense institutionalised structures to achieve its foreign policy objectives at hand—notwithstanding what this willingness is based upon. Using such a broad definition opens the possibility for distinguishing between various manifestations of multilateralism in the realm of foreign policy, ranging from reflective to highly instrumental (e.g. Anderson and Goodman 1993). Moreover, these different (ideal-type) manifestations can be analysed via different theoretical and methodological approaches: while the reflectivist position has been taken up primarily by social constructivists, the instrumentalist arguments can be associated with rationalist approaches to the study of multilateralism (see also Kratochwil 1993; Baumann 2006; Caporaso 1992; Fey 2000; Martin 1993). Ultimately, all approaches make assumptions about the basic motivations of state behaviour and can thus be drawn on to analytically address the motives of a specific country in referring to or rejecting multilateralism as a means of its foreign policy. In the following section, a neorealist approach is applied to help make sense of North Korea's seemingly inconsistent foreign policy vis-à-vis the SPT, characterised by both cooperation and non-cooperation.

3 Multilateralism and North Korea's foreign policy vis-à-vis the Six Party Talks: a test case for neorealism?

The multilateral format of the Six Party Talks, attended by North and South Korea, the US, China, Japan and Russia, was established in 2003 to defuse through diplomatic means the so-called second nuclear crisis on the Korean peninsula. The existing analyses on the talks may be cited as a particularly demonstrative example of the trend within international scholarship to approach multilateralism primarily as a phenomenon of international politics and to limit its theoretical portfolio mostly to the confines of neoliberal institutionalism and/or constructivism (Green and Gill 2009). As such, most analyses of the SPT have thus far been conducted either in the wider context of (multilateral) security cooperation in NEA (Park 2008) or have focused on specific issues such as the respective negotiation tactics and strategies of the involved states (e.g. Kim 2005; Park 2005; Snyder 2007c), the development and structure of the institution itself (e.g. Harnisch and Wagener 2010), particular negotiation instances such as specific agreements and/or negotiation rounds (Cheong 2004; Kim 2007), the chances for and limits of expanding the SPT to a regional security institution (Cerami 2005; Choo 2005), or on different identities and norms influencing the multilateral process (Shin and Koo 2008). As Green and Gill (2009: 3) rightly put it, the debate on multilateralism in (North-) East Asia has

> too often been trapped in the domain of liberal institutionalists who focus on the forums and institutions themselves (often in disappointment in comparative perspective to Europe) or of constructivists who are drawn to the region's seductive but misleading rhetoric about building an 'East Asian community'.

Using the DPRK's apparently erratic foreign policy vis-à-vis the SPT as a case, the following analysis draws on Neorealist Foreign Policy Theory as developed by Baumann, Rittberger and Wagner (1998; 2001) to discern the possible motives that drive the country's decision to use or reject multilateralism as a means of its foreign policy. The specific question asked is if and to what extent the notions of autonomy-seeking and influence-seeking policies are of analytical value to help expose these motives.

3.1 *The Six Party Talks as arena for North Korea's power politics?*

Starting from an assumption of rationality, which posits that states make their decisions in the context of cost-benefit calculations and which is seen as the link between the theory of international politics and foreign policy theory, NFPT acts on specific assumptions concerning a state's utility functions, that is, its fundamental interests (Baumann, Rittberger and Wagner 1998, 3-4).[6] While NFPT accepts the fact that states can pursue entirely different aims in their respective foreign policies, it is assumed that the anarchic international system leads all states to safeguard their own survival—their security—first, since the '[p]ursuit of manifold, issue-area specific aims is only possible on the basis of a sufficient degree of security' (Baumann, Rittberger and Wagner 1998: 4). Anarchy thus plays a crucial role in NFPT because it determines two fundamental interests in the foreign policies of all states: security and power. The latter is seen as directly related to a state's foreign policy (behaviour), in that autonomy and influence are regarded as two further fundamental aims of states (ibid.: 4–7). Accordingly, autonomy-seeking policy and influence-seeking policy are distinguished as two basic forms of power politics. Autonomy-seeking policy serves to preserve or reinforce a state's independence of other states, to prevent a new dependence on them, to reduce an existing dependence or to elude the influence of their environment. Influence-seeking policy, on the other hand, helps states themselves to exercise influence on their environment. However, autonomy and the maximisation of influence can occasionally conflict with each other. Especially within international institutions a policy to increase autonomy can result in a state's loss of influence, while a policy to increase influence can lead to a loss of autonomy (Baumann, Rittberger and Wagner 1998: 14).[7] In this context, these three authors (1998: 13–17) differentiate between a traditional and a modified neorealism: whereas the former approach argues in favour of autonomy gains, the latter can come to different pronouncements as to which form of power politics a state will primarily pursue. As Baumann, Rittberger and Wagner (2001: 55) point out:

> The higher the security pressures on a state, the greater its concern will be to preserve or even extend its autonomy. In contrast, the lower the security pressures on a state, the more it will be ready to accept autonomy losses for gains in influence.

---

[6] While critics of NFPT argue that neorealism is a theory of international politics, not a theory of foreign policy (e.g. Waltz 1996: 54–57), a number of authors have made the case that 'realist theories can substantially sharpen the analysis of foreign policy' (Wohlforth 2008: 32; see also Baumann, Rittberger and Wagner 1998; Elman 1996).

[7] In such cases NFPT must specify the importance a state attaches to gains or losses in autonomy and influence within their power-political possibilities.

Applied to the case under consideration, it is of concern if and to what extent the notions of autonomy-seeking and influence-seeking policy are of value in analytically capturing the DPRK's possible motives to resort to or reject multilateralism in its foreign policy vis-à-vis the SPT. As shown in Figure 1, two basic patterns of North Korea's foreign policy (behaviour) towards the SPT are distinguished, which are assumed to be directly linked to the notions of autonomy-seeking and influence-seeking policy: non-cooperative and cooperative foreign policy (behaviour).

Figure 1 The DPRK's main patterns of foreign policy behaviour vis-à-vis the Six Party Talks

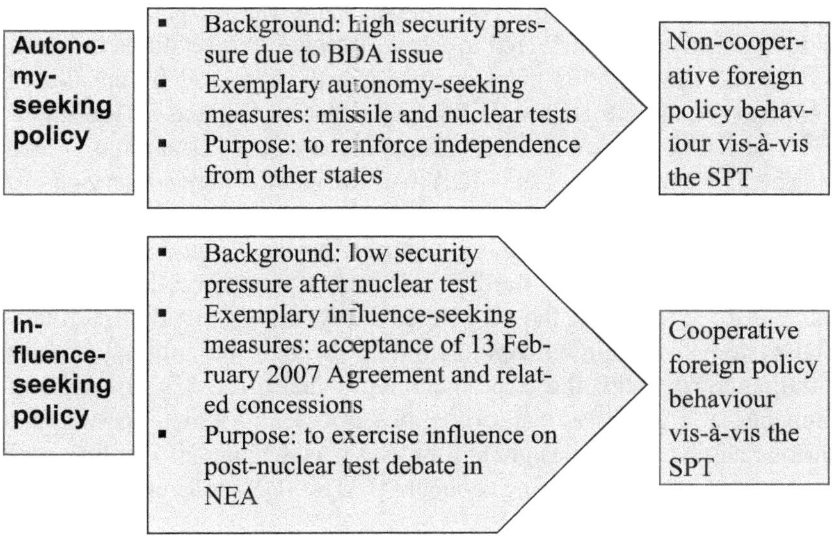

Source: Author.

Building on the logic of NFPT suggests that whether the DPRK opts for cooperation or non-cooperation in the SPT depends heavily on the degree to which it considers itself threatened: when the North perceives its security to be immediately threatened, it pursues an autonomy-seeking policy and thus rejects participation in the SP; whereas it will pursue an influence-seeking policy (within institutions) if its security is perceived to be less threatened.

3.1.1 *Autonomy-seeking foreign policy: the BDA issue and the DPRK's missile and nuclear tests*

The Six Party Talks were initiated in 2003 to facilitate a diplomatic solution to the nuclear crisis on the Korean peninsula. Yet in their initial stage the talks made little progress and the first three rounds were hardly considered as serious negotiations. It was only during the fourth round that discussions began in earnest. In September 2005, for the first time, the six parties were able to agree on a joint statement, the 19 September Agreement adopted at the end of the second session of the fourth negotiation round.[8] However, immediately after the adoption of what was hailed as the multilateral talks' first breakthrough, North Korea initiated a non-cooperative foreign policy in regard to the SPT. Above and beyond the vague wording of the agreement, which contributed to very different interpretations in North Korea and the US, this decision was mainly triggered by an altered definition of the DPRK's own security situation, created by the financial restrictions arising from the Banco Delta Asia (BDA) issue.

The US claimed that the BDA had provided financial services to the DPRK for more than 20 years and had facilitated many of its criminal activities, including money-laundering and counterfeiting US currency. Section 311 of the US Patriot Act authorised the use of financial force to isolate the designated entity and protect the US financial system from tainted capital running through the entity. Virtually simultaneously with the September Agreement, the US government launched a large-scale operation aimed at cracking down on such nefarious activities and designated the BDA as a financial institution of 'primary money-laundering concern'.[9] The US enforced financial

---

[8] In the Joint Statement of Principles the six parties agreed to the peaceful denuclearisation of the Korean peninsula. With the Agreement, the DPRK made several crucial commitments which seemed to break new ground. It agreed to abandon 'all nuclear weapons and existing nuclear programs', pledged to rejoin the Non-Proliferation Treaty (NPT), and furthermore promised to accept the International Atomic Energy Agency (IAEA) safeguards 'at an early date'. Moreover, North Korea also reaffirmed the 1992 denuclearisation agreement between North and South Korea and agreed to negotiations on a Korean peace regime. In return, the other five parties offered energy and humanitarian assistance. The US and the DPRK agreed to take steps toward normalisation of relations, which was considered the key element for the North Korean delegation. For a comprehensive analysis of the Joint Statement, see Niksch et. al. 2005.

[9] The US Treasury's decision to pursue, at the moment of agreement on the nuclear issue, other matters that had been on the table for years suggests that there is at least a debate here over spoiling tactics.

sanctions against the BDA, leading to the freezing of as many as 50 North Korean accounts and around US$25 million. The US announcement caused a run on the BDA and triggered a decision by the Macao Monetary Authorities to put the bank under its own supervisory authority and end its relations with the DPRK (see Kwak and Joo 2007; Gaylord 2008). The DPRK vehemently denied the US allegations and repeatedly stressed it would suspend its participation in the SPT unless the US agreed to lift its financial sanctions against the North. North Korea thus made the removal of the financial sanctions and of the US crackdown on its financial activities in general a direct precondition for its return to the SPT, thereby directly linking the BDA issue to its general participation in the talks.

Applying NFPT suggests that the DPRK's refusal to participate in the SPT was prompted by a perception of a heightened threat to its security following the BDA-related sanctions. Indeed, the BDA issue and the resulting steps by the US were interpreted by North Korea as directly threatening the security and prestige of its regime, as was made vividly clear by Kim Jong Il in January 2006. During a summit meeting with President Hu Jintao of China, Kim Jong Il reportedly stated that '[i]f U.S. financial sanctions continue, North Korea could collapse' (Chae 2007: 41; Kyodo News, 11 February 2006; *International Herald Tribune*, 18 January 2007). The increased security pressure that accompanied the BDA issue, defined by North Korea as significantly constraining its autonomy, led the DPRK to adopt an autonomy-maximising foreign policy, which, in line with the arguments of Baumann, Rittberger and Wagner (1998), first and foremost served to maintain or reinforce its independence from other states as well as to prevent any new dependence on others and reduce any existing dependence. Accordingly, any meaningful participation in the SPT was rejected by the North until the security pressure decreased and its autonomy was sufficiently ensured. It is therefore hardly surprising that the first session of the fifth round of the SPT, which took place on 9–11 November 2005, the initial goal of which was to agree on a roadmap for implementing the 19 September 2005 Agreement, ended without any tangible results. In fact, North Korea explicitly stated that it had participated in this session only to give voice to its demand for a complete settlement of the BDA issue before any further progress on the SPT could be made. After the November 2005 session failed to produce the desired result on this matter, the DPRK, again citing the BDA issue-related security pressures as the main reason, boycotted further participation in the talks for another 13 months. During this phase of non-cooperation, North Korea resorted to various types of behaviour which may be regarded as autonomy-seeking policies par excellence in the sense of NFPT, ranging from non-compliance with and the dissolution of existing obligations resulting from bilateral and multilateral agreements (e.g. by basically nullifying the Joint Declaration of South and North Korea on the Denuclearisation of the Korean Peninsula' of 1992 or disregarding the provisions of the NPT), to a refusal to accept any new obligations of this nature (e.g. by rejecting implementation of the Joint Statement from September 2005) (see Baumann, Rittberger and Wagner 1998: 9).

Arguably the most vivid example of North Korea's autonomy-maximising policy came in the form of the missile tests on 5 July 2006 and especially of its first-ever nuclear test on 9 October 2006. Viewing such policies as seeking autonomy indeed seems to give a better understanding of the underlying motives that drive such unilateral foreign policy acts. While it is true that these actions may have led to a further isolation of the DPRK (not least through the China-backed passage of UN Security Council resolutions 1695 and 1718), they were expedient as autonomy-maximising measures at a time when North Korea perceived its security as immediately threatened. As the DPRK Foreign Ministry announced on 11 October 2006, the nuclear test 'was inevitable to prove the North's nuclear capacity in order to protect its national sovereignty and existence' (KCNA, 11 October 2006). In fact, all three criteria presented by Baumann, Rittberger and Wagner (1998: 11) of what constitutes a state's striving for autonomy can be detected in the case of North Korea's nuclear test. Firstly, the test increased the country's freedom from positive obligations to display a certain foreign policy behaviour. Such obligations can relate both to procedural aspects, such as the requirement to consult or inform certain other actors (e.g. within the framework of the SPT) or the obligation to accept and implement the decisions of international organisations or bodies (e.g. the IAEA or the UN), and to material aspects, e.g. an obligation to comply with specific duties (such as those resulting from previous agreements). Secondly, the nuclear test was a specific autonomy-seeking move by the DPRK to maximise its freedom from negative obligations, i.e. from prohibitions of certain modes of foreign policy behaviour. As Baumann, Rittberger and Wagner point out (1998: 11), such prohibitions can relate to the acquisition of certain goods (e.g. nuclear weapons), the use of certain tools or resources (e.g. certain types of weapons), or modes of behaviour vis-à-vis other states (e.g. a ban on the proliferation of weapons of mass destruction). Thirdly, with the nuclear test North Korea increased its freedom from restrictions on its own liberty of action, which, according to NFPT, can be impaired by dependence in the sense of asymmetric interdependence to a state's disadvantage.

3.1.2 *Influence-seeking foreign policy: the 13 February 2007 Agreement and its aftermath*

Although North Korea's autonomy-seeking policy and the subsequent decision to refuse to participate in the SPT increased its autonomy, it simultaneously led to an inevitable loss in influence. Hence, while North Korea's search for survival and security must be regarded as the most central goal of its foreign policy according to NFPT (Baumann, Rittberger and Wagner 2001: 47), the country concentrated its attention increasingly on the possibility of (multilateral) influence-seeking as the external security pressure decreased, thereby relativising the (foreign policy) goal of autonomy. Accordingly, only after its security and autonomy were increased by proving its nuclear capability, North Korea

> became more amenable to a negotiated settlement, secure in the knowledge that it demanded respect as a nuclear power and possessed by a sense of safety from attack under its own nuclear umbrella (De Ceuster 2008: 31).

As the nuclear test apparently left the DPRK with a more positive outlook on its security and a sense of a diminution in immediate security pressures, the North's foreign policy (behaviour) shifted from one of non-cooperation to a foreign policy that was more cooperative towards the SPT (see also Snyder 2007a: 67). With North Korea converting its immediate policy goal from autonomy-maximisation to influence-maximisation, it attempted to influence in its own interest the decisive interaction processes with other states and the policies emerging from them—and tried to secure and extend the resources which allowed it to exercise this influence (Baumann, Rittberger and Wagner 1998: 9). To that end, North Korea used the Six Party Talks as an arena for converting capabilities into influence, and the multilateral process thus played a highly instrumental role for the DPRK. As such, North Korea's mere decision to participate in the SPT does not necessarily predict cooperative policies within the multilateral process per se, but rather suggests that it will pursue power politics as far as its power position will allow. Given that the nuclear test changed the security dynamics in NEA and was certain to become a matter of intense debate, North Korea was eager to influence this debate to gain advantages after the immediate security pressures were perceived as decreasing. As such, in the sense of NFPT at that time North Korea's motive for renewed participation in the SPT was to exert influence on the subsequent negotiations by instrumentalising the region's most important arena for influence-seeking policy (Rittberger, Mogler and Zangl 1997). In fact, various forms of influence-seeking policies as suggested by NFPT can be detected in the North's foreign policy behaviour vis-à-vis the SPT during this phase of cooperation. The mere decision by Pyongyang to renew its participation in the multilaterial talks (and to at least partially adhere to the 13 February 2007 Agreement) must be seen as a measure to secure its 'voice opportunities' (i.e. to make known its interests) by using the SPT as an 'arena' for its influence-seeking policies. North Korea's renewed participation in the multilateral SPT was judged necessary to achieve these policy goals. Hence, even though the nuclear test was certainly a crisis in that it caused international sanctions and pressure against the DPRK, the latter ironically also worked as a catalyst for renewed diplomatic activity (Snyder 2007b: 3). Moreover, North Korea's decision to return to the SPT also worked as an opportunity to get concessions by taking advantage of its increased bargaining power, thus enabling the country to capitalise on the situation created by the test (Chae 2007: 43).

Only ten days after the nuclear test, Tang Jiaxuan, a Chinese State Councillor and Hu Jintao's special envoy, met with Kim Jong Il in Pyongyang, conveying the message 'that China would do its utmost to support the North if it agreed to return to the six-party talks' (Yu 2007: 80). China was successful in bringing Christopher Hill and Kim Kye Gwan, the chief US and North Korean negotiators respectively, together for a trilateral meeting in Beijing on 31 October 2006, during which the US, North Korea, and China agreed to resume the SPT at the earliest possible date (Yu 2007: 77). While North Korea thus withdrew its insistence that the BDA issue had to be completely resolved before it would agree to come back to the negotiation table, it was granted the assurance 'that the issue would be addressed through a bilateral dialogue that would occur parallel to the six-party process' (Snyder 2007a: 68). Following another round of bilateral talks between Kim and Hill on 28–29 November 2006 in Beijing, the second session of the fifth round of the SPT was held on 18–22 December 2006, accompanied in parallel by bilateral talks between the US and North Korea on the BDA issue (*USA Today*, 31 January 2007).[10] On 16–18 January 2007, Christopher Hill and Kim Kye Gwan met in Berlin to discuss the key issues hampering the resumption of the SPT.[11] According to media reports, Kim said that he got a positive impression from Hill that the US would change its stance towards North Korea and that 'a deal had been struck' (Associated Press, 23 January 2007, Kwak 2007: 36). Diplomatic sources later revealed that Hill and Kim not only agreed to resume the next round of the SPT, but also concurred on the basic content of what later became the 13 February Agreement as well as on a general road map for its implementation (*International Herald Tribune*, 14 February 2007). Firstly, in return for 50,000 tons of heavy fuel oil the DPRK agreed to shut down its 5-megawatt nuclear reactor and its processing centre in Yŏngbyŏn within 60 days and to allow IAEA inspectors to monitor the plant (*International Herald Tribune*, 14 February 2007). Secondly, the US addressed the possibility of easing its BDA-related sanctions and reportedly considered the release of some legitimate funds from the total amount frozen in North Korean accounts (see Reuters, 16 January 2007). Hill promised to solve the BDA issue within 30 days (*Choson Sinbo*, 13 February 2007; Sigal 2007) and stated on 20 January 2007 that North Korea agreed to a bilateral working-level consultation between the DPRK and the US to settle the financial issue (Associated Press, 20 January 2007). Thirdly, the US promised to remove North Korea from the list of states sponsoring international terrorism and the Trading with Enemy States Act, a longstanding goal of the DPRK.

Against this background, the talks were resumed on 8 February 2007. At the end of the session the six nations reached an agreement

---

[10] North Korea has consistently requested bilateral dialogue and negotiations with the US, which it considers both its most important negotiation partner and the greatest threat to its security. The North has long stressed that the US should engage in direct dialogue to settle the problem of the dismantlement of North Korean nuclear weapons and the creation of diplomatic ties in North Korean–US relations, without the need for a third party.

[11] North Korea viewed these talks as the bilateral negotiations it had long wanted with the US. Accordingly, the *Choson Sinbo*, a pro-North Korean newspaper published in Japan, commented on 13 February 2007 that 'the U.S. approached bilateral discussions with North Korea in Berlin'. The bilateral talks between Kim and Hill were paralleled by a dialogue between the US and North Korea on solving the BDA issue (see *USA Today*, 31 January 2007).

officially labelled Initial Actions for the Implementation of the Joint Statement. Contained in the Agreement were specific arrangements that contributed to the North's re-definition of its security situation, such as the US assurance it would start bilateral normalisation talks with North Korea or would begin the processes of removing the DPRK from a list designating the North as a state sponsor of terrorism, and of ending US trade sanctions (Chae 2007; Kim 2007). Retrospectively it is evident that the bilateral understanding that was reached in Berlin was part and parcel of North Korea's re-definition of its security situation, which in turn had a profound influence on its decision to re-join the SPT. However, although 'the agreement triggered a fascinating sequence of developments over a broad diplomatic front' (Leurdijk 2008: 16–17), it nevertheless left a number of important questions unanswered and its implementation promised to be a complex endeavor for all the parties involved.

The six nations tried to tackle these pending issues during the first session of the sixth round of the SPT, which took place between 19 and 22 March 2007. As outlined above, while the US and the DPRK reached an agreement with regard to the BDA issue well before the resumption of the talks, the BDA had technical problems in transferring the sums of money agreed. This led to the situation where the six nations barely negotiated but rather waited for the money transfer. As it became known that North Korea would not receive the money for a while, the session broke down. Shortly afterwards, however, both the US and the DPRK took specific measures to implement the promises settled upon in the 13 February Agreement. On 10 April 2007, Sean McCormack, the US state department spokesman, said that 'a financial deadlock stalling North Korean disarmament efforts has been cleared' (quoted in *USA Today*, 11 April 2007) and the transfer of funds to the DPRK was finally completed on 14 June via a Russian bank (*Choson Ilbo*, 15 June 2007). Also in June 2007, Christopher Hill met Kim Kye Gwan for bilateral discussions in Pyongyang as part of the ongoing consultations among the six parties on the implementation of the Initial Actions Agreement. In July 2007, North Korea made good on its promise to shut down its 5-megawatt nuclear reactor at the Yŏngbyŏn nuclear facility as well as an uncompleted reactor at T'aech'ŏn. Moreover, IAEA personnel returned to the DPRK to monitor and verify the shut-down and to seal the facility. On 18 July, Mohamed ElBaradei confirmed that North Korea had closed down four other facilities at Yŏngbyŏn. North Korea received 6,200 tons (out of the agreed-upon 50,000 tons) of heavy fuel oil (HFO). This paved the way for the resumption of the second session of the sixth round of the SPT, which took place from 18 to 20 July 2007. In August and September, five working groups met in order to discuss detailed plans for the implementation of the next phase of the Initial Actions Agreement. On 1–2 September 2007, the working group between the US and the DPRK held a meeting in Geneva, during which North Korea promised to provide a full declaration of all of its nuclear programmes and to disable these programmes by the end of 2007. The six nations continued the second session of the sixth round of the SPT on 27–30 September 2007, which resulted in the Second-Phase Actions for the Implementation of the September 2005 Joint Statement. In this agreement, North Korea gave its assurance it would disable all nuclear facilities subject to the September 2005 and February 2007 agreements and would provide a complete and correct declaration of all its nuclear programmes in accordance with the 13 February 2007 Agreement by 31 December 2007. The US agreed to fulfil its commitments to the DPRK regarding the processes of removing its designation as a state sponsor of terrorism and terminating the application of the Trading with the Enemy Act to it. Moreover, economic, energy and humanitarian assistance up to the equivalent of one million tons of HFO (including the 100,000 tons of HFO already delivered in 2007 by South Korea and China) were to be provided to North Korea with specific modalities finalised through discussion by the Working Group on Economy and Energy Cooperation.

3.2 *Multilateralism and North Korean foreign policy: the limits of Neorealist Foreign Policy Theory*

The foregoing empirical analysis has revealed the analytical value of NFPT in helping to explain North Korea's seemingly erratic foreign policy (behaviour) over the multilateral SPT. Above all, the notions of autonomy-seeking and influence-seeking policy are valuable concepts with which to address analytically the DPRK's possible motives in either choosing or declining to participate in the multilateral SPT, and to scrutinise the conditions under which it made its choices. Nonetheless, applying NFPT to the North Korean case has also brought to the fore several limits to the explanatory power of this theoretical approach. While the basic disciplinary debate on the shortcomings of neorealism and the correlating discussion on the limits of positivist approaches have been dealt with at length elsewhere (e.g. Ashley 1984; Lapid 1989), the critique at this point is limited to the insufficient understanding of power inherent in the two approaches. NFPT directly links the possibility of pursuing power politics to the structural power position of the country in question. According to this assumption, the greater a state's power position, the more the foreign policy of that state will be characterised by autonomy-seeking and influence-seeking policy as two forms of power politics (Baumann, Rittberger and Wagner 1998: 10). Yet, in the traditional neorealist view, a 'small state' (as characterised primarily by its economic and military power) is simply regarded as too weak to pursue an autonomy- or influence-seeking policy with much success (Waltz 1979: 194). While its interest in autonomy and influence is by no means less than that of a great power, its opportunities for actually pursuing autonomy- and influence-seeking policy are considered far fewer (Baumann, Rittberger and Wagner 1998: 10). According to this perspective, the DPRK should hardly be able to induce any sort of influence on its main counterpart in the SPT—the US. While it is in fact disputable to what extent North Korea was and is able to exercise any direct influence on the US as suggested by NFPT (e.g. through obligations for action imposed on other states, by imposing prohibitions of certain modes of foreign policy behaviour on other states, and through restricting other states' freedom of action), the empirical analysis nevertheless shows that North Korea, despite its apparent 'weak state' status, has been fairly successful in pursuing autonomy- and influence-seeking policies to achieve its foreign policy goals. This explanatory shortcoming of NFPT can be attributed to the theory's narrow definition of power; this is limited to the (aggregate) structural power of a state, which is regarded as the decisive independent variable providing the main explanation for that state's behaviour. As such, NFPT is solely concerned with the overall capabilities and position of an actor in relation to the external environment as a whole, a position that only allows determining the relative power position of a state (resources, potential capabilities, etc.). While this is useful in providing an overall picture of the actor's position in the international or regional system, it disregards other forms and components of power that are of immediate relevancy, particularly in the analysis of North Korean foreign policy. As the empirical analysis suggests, the DPRK's power position in the context of the SPT mainly results from the power structure of its relationship with the other parties involved, primarily the US and China. This points to the importance of what Habeeb (1988: 19) describes as 'issue-specific power', which focuses on the power structure of a relationship and 'is concerned with an actor's capabilities and positions vis-à-vis another actor in terms of a specific mutual issue'—such as the nuclear question. While aggregate structural power indicates the totality of a state's capabilities and resources, it is mainly the interaction, through the use of tactics, of the actors' resources and capabilities that can be brought to bear on a specific issue that is crucial to bargaining outcomes. Through the use of appropriate tactics in the specific context of the SPT, the 'weak state' North Korea was able to achieve its desired outcomes at the expense of the strong, namely the US. Thus, while overall power (i.e. aggregate structural power) certainly cannot be ignored, it is not always possible for the strong state to bring all its resources to bear in its negotiations with the (apparent) weak state. Indeed, the weak may sometimes even have some advantages when confronting the strong, in that the former is usually prepared to focus comprehensively on and invest heavily in that one central foreign policy issue.

4 Conclusions

The main concern of this essay has been to address analytically a hitherto widely overlooked phenomenon of North Korean foreign policy: the realm of multilateralism. As the theoretical discussion has made clear, this necessitates a broader definition of multilateralism, one that allows for analytically capturing the strategic usage and instrumental value of the multifaceted phenomenon. Conceptualised as a foreign policy phenomenon, multilateralism is defined here as a specific type of foreign policy behaviour, characterised by the willingness of a single country to coordinate its foreign policy with at least two other states within varyingly dense institutionalised structures to achieve its foreign policy objectives at hand—notwithstanding the factors this willingness is based upon. This broad definition, so the argument goes, is essential for understanding multilateralism in the context of the DPRK's foreign policy, for it allows the incorporation of the phenomenon's strategic dimension.

Building on this definition of multilateralism, NFPT was introduced as the theoretical basis for the ensuing empirical analysis. Using

North Korea's foreign policy (behaviour) vis-à-vis the on-again-off-again Six Party process as a case, the analysis sought to discern the possible motives and specific conditions under which the DPRK resorted to (or rejected) multilateralism as a means of its foreign policy, drawing on the notions of autonomy-seeking and influence-seeking policy. The analysis suggests that the DPRK's decision to cooperate or not to cooperate in the SPT is heavily influenced by its definition of its security situation at a given moment. As such, if North Korea defined its security as being under acute threat it resorted to an autonomy-seeking policy, which led to the decision not to apply multilateralism as a means of its foreign policy and consequently to reject participation in the SPT (non-cooperative phase). On the other hand, if North Korea defined its security as being under no acute threat it resorted to an influence-seeking policy within institutions (cooperative phase). In this case, the DPRK used the SPT as an 'arena of influence-seeking policy' to convert capabilities into influence. To that end, the North's participation in the SPT does not necessarily predict a cooperative policy within the talks. Rather, the country pursues power politics as far as its power position allows, suggesting a highly instrumental use of multilateralism, strategically adopted or dismissed to allow the DPRK to achieve its alterable foreign policy goals of respectively influence and autonomy. While multilateralism has thus become increasingly important as a self-interested strategy, it certainly does not have a 'taken for granted' quality in the DPRK's overall foreign policy design. The North's approach to multilateralism is therefore not a reflective and indispensable one, as is not least made clear by its repeated rejection of further participation in the multilateral SPT if unilateral measures such as a nuclear test are deemed more successful in reaching its national interest. The DPRK's increasing multilateral participation in NEA has not led to an internalisation of the qualitative principles of multilateralism in the sense set out by Ruggie. Rather, the DPRK's multilateral foreign policy vis-à-vis the SPT has been strategically adopted with the prospect of specific advantages and/or rewards, not because of any normative commitment or responsibility. As such, its applicability seems altogether negotiable if the respective conditions (above all a perceived threat to the regime's security) should change. In such phases of non-cooperation, North Korea subordinates its influence-seeking policy to an autonomy-seeking policy. Multilateralism is therefore no substitute for bilateralism or unilateralism respectively, but rather a strategic and complementary element in the North's overall foreign policy design. As has been shown, multilateralism has in fact only emerged substantially if and when multilateral diplomacy has begun to play a complementary rather than a subsidiary role to bilateral diplomacy. Yet, although the DPRK clearly prefers to compartmentalise its international relations into 'sizable packages of bilateral relations' (De Ceuster 2008: 33), it has nevertheless discerned strategic value in multilateral negotiations as well, if and when those negotiations are deemed beneficial for their own foreign policy goal of influence-maximisation. For the present, however, multilateralism remains by and large non-existent in the official foreign policy ideology of the DPRK and it thus has to challenge the traditional principles that have for so long dominated the country's official foreign policy ideology.

References

Anderson, Jeffrey J. and John B. Goodman (1993), 'Mars or Minerva? A United Germany in a Post-Cold War Europe', in: Robert O. Keohane, Joseph S. Nye and Stanley Hoffmann (eds), *After the Cold War: International Institutions and State Strategies in Europe, 1989-1991*, Cambridge MA: Harvard University Press, pp. 23–62

Ashley, Richard K. (1984), 'The Poverty of Neorealism', in: *International Organization*, 38 (2), pp. 225–86

Associated Press, 23 January 2007, 'N. Korea Envoy Notes Movement in U.S. Stance on Nuclear Weapons'

Associated Press, 20 January 2007, 'U.S., N. Korea Agree to Hold Nuke Talks'

Baker, James A., III (1991), 'America in Asia: Emerging Architecture for a Pacific Community', in: *Foreign Affairs*, 70 (5), pp. 1–40

Baumann, Rainer (2007), 'Multilateralismus: Die Wandlung eines vermeintlichen Kontinuitätselements der deutschen Außenpolitik' [Multilateralism: the transformation of an alleged continuity element in German foreign policy], in: Thomas Jäger, Alexander Höse and Kai Oppermann (eds), *Deutsche Außenpolitik: Sicherheit, Wohlfahrt, Institutionen und Normen*, Wiesbaden: VS-Verlag für Sozialwissenschaften, pp. 442–61

Baumann, Rainer (2006), *Der Wandel des Deutschen Multilateralismus: Eine diskursanalytische Untersuchung deutscher Außenpolitik*, Baden-Baden: Nomos

Baumann, Rainer, Volker Rittberger and Wolfgang Wagner (2001), 'Neorealist Foreign Policy Theory', in: Volker Rittberger (ed.), *German Foreign Policy since Unification: Theories and Case Studies*, Manchester: Manchester University Press, pp. 37–67

Baumann, Rainer, Volker Rittberger and Wolfgang Wagner (1998), 'Power and Power Politics: Neorealist Foreign Policy Theory and Expectations about German Foreign Policy since Unification', Tübinger Arbeitspapiere zur Internationalen Politik und Friedensforschung, No. 30a. Online: www.uni-tuebingen.de/uni/spi/taps/tap30a.htm

Caporaso, James (1992), 'International Relations Theory and Multilateralism: The Search for Foundations', in: *International Organization*, 46 (3), pp. 599–632

Cerami, Joseph R. (2005), 'From the Six-Party Talks to a Northeast Asian Security Regime? Cooperative Threat Reduction Strategies and Institutional Development', paper presented at the International Studies Association Annual Convention, Honolulu, Hawaii, 3 March 2005. Online: http://bush.tamu.edu/research/wor kingpapers/jcerami/CeramiISA2005.pdf

Chae, Kyu-Chul (2007), 'Korea's Nuclear Strategy against the U.S.: With a Focus on Its Nuclear Test and the 2.13 Agreement', in: *East Asian Review*, 19 (3), pp. 32–50

Cheong, Seong-Hun (2004), 'Che2ch'a 6chahoedam punsŏkkwa chŏnmang' [The second round of the Six Party Talks: analysis and prospects], in: *T'ongiljŏngsebunsŏk* [Analysis of reunification affairs] 2004–06, Seoul: Korea Institute for National Unification

Choo, Jaewoo (2005), 'Is Institutionalization of the Six-Party Talks Possible?', in: *East Asia*, 22 (4), pp. 39–58

Choson Ilbo, 15 June 2007, 'N. Korea's Money Transferred Out of Macau', p. 1

Choson Sinbo, 13 February 2007, 'Establishment of Trust between North Korea and the U.S., "Action for Action"'. Online: www.koreanp.co.jp/news/ViewArt icle.aspx?ArticleID=25351 (accessed 13 November 2012)

Chung, Eunsook (2004), 'Cooperative Security Regimes: A Comparison of OSCE and ARF', paper prepared for the 5th Pan-European International Relations Conference, The Hague, 9–11 September 2004. Online: www.sejong.org/Pub_st/PUB_ST_DATA/kst001-06.pdf (accessed 18 November 2012)

De Ceuster, Koen (2008), 'Fear and Loathing in the D.P.R.K.: Beyond the Nuclear Crisis', in: Koen De Ceuster and Jan Melissen (eds), *Ending the North Korean Nuclear Crisis: Six Parties, Six Perspectives*, Clingendael Diplomacy Papers No. 18, The Hague: Netherlands Institute of International Relations, pp. 21–35

Diebold, William, Jr. (1988), 'The History and the Issue', in: William Diebold Jr. (ed.): *Bilateralism, Multilateralism and Canada in U.S. Trade Policy*, Cambridge MA: Cambridge University Press, pp. 1–36

Dosch, Jörn (2006), 'Does Multilateralism Work? European and American Approaches to Multilateral Peace-Building on the Korean Peninsula', paper prepared for the CSIS Conference on North Korea, Multilateralism, and the Future of the Peninsula, 20–21 November 2003, Seoul. Online: www.hjpeace.or.kr/word/0311_2_02.doc (accessed 12 November 2012)

Dosch, Jörn (2002), *Die Herausforderung des Multilateralismus: Amerikanische Asien-Pazifik Politik nach dem Kalten Krieg*, Baden-Baden: Nomos

Elman, Colin (1996), 'Horses for Courses: Why not Neorealist Theories of Foreign Policy?', in: *Security Studies*, 6 (1), pp. 7–53

Evans, Paul (2007), 'Constructing Multilateralism in an Anti-Region: From Six-Party Talks to a Regional Security Framework in Northeast Asia?', in: Gi-Wook Shin and Daniel C. Sneider (eds), *Cross Currents: Regionalism and Nationalism in Northeast Asia*, Washington DC: Brookings Institution Press, pp. 99–116

Fey, Jens (2000), *Multilateralismus als Strategie: Die Sicherheitspolitik Kanadas nach dem Ende des Ost-West-Konflikts*, Köln: SH-Verlag

Friedman, George (2006), 'North Korea and the Limits of Multilateralism'. Online: www.stratfor.com/memberships/36326/north_korea_and_limits_multilateralism (accessed 22 October 2012)

Gaylord, Mark S. (2008), 'The Banco Delta Asia Affair: The USA Patriot Act and Allegations of Money Laundering in Macau', in: *Crime, Law, and Social Change*, 50 (4-5), pp. 293–305

Green, Michael J. and Bates Gill (2009), 'Unbundling Asia's New Multilateralism', in: Michael J. Green and Bates Gill (eds), *Asia's New Multilateralism: Cooperation, Competition, and the Search for Community*, New York: Columbia University Press, pp.1–29

Habeeb, William Mark (1988), Power and Tactics in International Negotiation – How Weak Nations Bargain with Strong Nations, Baltimore and London: The Johns Hopkins University Press

Harnisch, Sebastian and Martin Wagener (2010), 'Die Sechsparteiengespräche auf der koreanischen Halbinsel: Hintergründe – Ergebnisse – Perspektiven' [The Six Party Talks on the Korean peninsula: backgrounds – results – perspectives], in: Dirk Nabers (ed.), *Multilaterale Institutionen in Ostasien-Pazifik: Genese-Strukturen-Substanz-Perspektiven*, Wiesbaden: VS-Verlag, pp. 133–80

International Herald Tribune, 14 February 2007, 'Seed of North Korean Nuclear Deal was Planted in Berlin: Bilateral Meeting Led North Korea Back to Negotiating Table'

International Herald Tribune, 18 January 2007, 'Squeeze on Banco Delta Asia Hit North Korea Where it Hurt: Disruption of Funds at Macao Bank Hits the Regime Hardest'

Kahler, Miles (1992), 'Multilateralism with Small and Large Numbers', in: *International Organization*, 46 (3), pp. 681–708

Kang, Choi (2006), 'The Six-Party Talks: A Platform for Regional Security Cooperation', in: *IFANS Review*, 14 (1), pp. 5–18

KCNA (Korea Central News Agency), 11 October 2006, Spokesman for DPRK Foreign Ministry. Online: www.kcna.co.jp/index-e.htm (accessed 22 July 2012)

Keating, Tom (1993), *Canada and World Order: The Multilateralist Tradition in Canadian Foreign Policy*, Toronto: Oxford University Press Canada

Keohane, Robert O. (1990), 'Multilateralism: An Agenda for Research', in: *International Journal*, 45 (4), pp. 731–64

Kim, Il-Hwan (2005), *2ch'a pukhaegwigiwa 6chahoedamŭi chŏn'gaewa chŏnmange kwanhan yŏn'gu*, [A study of the second North Korean nuclear crisis and the process and prospects of the Six Party Talks], Incheon: Incheon University Press

Kim, Yong-Hyeon (2007), '2.13 Habŭiwa tongbuga tajaanbo' [The February 13 agreement and multilateral security co-operation in Northeast Asia], in: *Bukhanhak yŏn'gu* [North Korea research], 3 (1), pp. 79–92

Kratochwil, Friedrich (1993), 'Norms versus Numbers: Multilateralism and the Rationalist and Reflectivist Approaches to Institutions – A Unilateral Plea for Communicative Rationality', in: John G. Ruggie (ed.), *Multilateralism Matters: The Theory and Praxis of an Institutional Form*, New York: Columbia University Press, pp. 443–72

Kwak, Tae-Hwan (2007), 'North Korea's Second Nuclear Crisis and the Six-Party Talks', in: Seung-Ho Joo and Tae-Hwan Kwak (eds), *North Korea's Second Nuclear Crisis and Northeast Asian Security*, Aldershot, Hampshire UK: Ashgate, pp. 15–44

Kwak, Tae-Hwan (2006), 'Resolving the North Korean Nuclear Issue through the Six-Party Process: A Creative Formula', paper presented at the annual meeting of the International Studies Association, 22 March 2006. Online: www.allacademic.com/meta/p_mla_apa_research_citation/1/0/0/3/4/p100344_index.html (accessed 1 November 2012)

Kwak, Tae-Hwan and Seung-Hoo Joo (2007), 'The U.S. Financial Sanctions against North Korea', in: *Pacific Focus*, 22 (1), pp. 73–109

Kyodo News, 11 February 2006, 'N. Korea could collapse if U.S. sanctions continue: sources'

Lapid, Yosef (1989), 'The Third Debate: On the Prospects of International Theory in a Post-Positivist Era', in: *International Studies Quarterly*, 33 (3), pp. 235–54

Leurdijk, Dick (2008), 'The Six-Party Talks, the UN and North Korea's Nuclear Programme', in: Koen De Ceuster and Jan Melissen (eds), *Ending the North Korean Nuclear Crisis: Six Parties, Six Perspectives*, Clingendael Diplomacy Papers No. 18, The Hague: Netherlands Institute of International Relations, pp. 9–19

Mack, Andrew and Pauline Kerr (1995), 'The Evolving Security Discourse in the Asia-Pacific', in: *Washington Quarterly*, 18 (1), pp. 123–40

Martin, Lisa M. (1993), 'The Rational State Choice of Multilateralism', in: John G. Ruggie (ed.), *Multilateralism Matters: The Theory and Praxis of an Institutional Form*, New York: Columbia University Press, pp. 91–121

Niksch, Larry A., Jong-Chul Park, Hak-Soon Paik, L. Gordon Flake Young-Ho Park, William M. Drennan and Young-Kyu Park (eds) (2005), *Implementing the Six-Party Joint Statement and the Korean Peninsula*, Seoul: Korea Institute for National Unification

Paik Haksoon (2006), 'Hanbando p'yŏnghwach'eje kuch'ukkwa tongbuga tajaanbohyŏmnyŏk: pukhanŭi ipchanggwa uriŭi taeŭng' [The establishment of a peace structure on the Korean peninsula and multilateral security co-operation in

Northeast Asia: North Korea's stance and our response], in: *Chŏngch'aekpogosŏ* [Policy report], 2006-05, Seongnam: Sejong Institute

Park, Hong-Do (2008), *Tongbuga tajaanbohyŏmnyŏgŭi kanŭngsŏng mit cheyagyoin: 6chahoedam saryerŭl chungsimŭro* [Possibilities and limitations of multilateral security co-operation in Northeast Asia: the case of the Six Party Talks], doctoral dissertation, Kyungnam University

Park, John S. (2005), 'Inside Multilateralism: The Six Party Talks', in: *The Washington Quarterly*, 28 (4), pp. 75–91

Powell, Lindsey (2003): 'In Defense of Multilateralism', paper prepared for the Conference on Global Environmental Governance: the Post-Johannesburg Agenda, 23–25 October 2003, Yale Center for Environmental Law and Policy, New Haven CT. Online: www.yale.edu/gegdialogue/docs/dialogue/oct03/papers/ Powell.pdf

Reuters, 16 January 2007, 'U.S. said considering release of some N. Korea funds'

Rittberger, Volker, Martin Mogler and Bernhard Zangl (1997), *Vereinte Nationen und Weltordnung: Zivilisierung der internationalen Politik?*, Opladen: Leske+Budrich

Ruggie, John G. (1993), 'Multilateralism: The Anatomy of an Institution', in: John G. Ruggie (ed.), *Multilateralism Matters: The Theory and Praxis of an Institutional Form*, New York: Columbia University Press, pp. 3–47

Seol, Gyoosang (2008), 'Tongbuga anbo tajajuŭiwa insikkongdongch'eŭi yŏkhal' [Northeast Asian security multilateralism and the role of epistemic communities], in: *Tongsŏyŏn'gu* [East-West studies], 20 (1), pp. 5–31

Shin, Soon-Ok, and Koo Kab-Woo (2008), 'Embedded Conflicting Identities in the Six-Party Talks: The Complexity of Regional Security in Northeast Asia', paper prepared for the International Studies Association Convention, San Francisco, 26–9 March 2008

Sigal, Leon V. (2007), 'Turnabout is Fair Play', in: *Foreign Service Journal*, July-August 2007, pp. 30–35

Snyder, Scott (2007a), 'The Second North Korean Nuclear Crisis: Assessing U.S. and D.P.R.K. Negotiation Strategies', in: *Pacific Focus*, 22 (1), pp. 47–72

Snyder, Scott (2007b), 'Political Fallout from North Korea's Nuclear Test', in: *Comparative Connections*, 8 (4). Online: http://csis.org/files/media/csis/pubs/0604q china_korea.pdf (accessed 15 August 2012)

Snyder, Scott (2007c), 'U.S-North Korean Negotiating Behavior and the Six-Party Talks', in: Seung-Ho Joo and Tae-Hwan Kwak (eds), *North Korea's Second Nuclear Crisis and Northeast Asian Security*, Burlington VT: Ashgate, pp. 151–66

USA Today, 11 April 2007, p. 7A

USA Today, 31 January 2007, 'Frozen Funds in Macau Could Thaw N. Korea Impasse', p. 8A

Waltz, Kenneth N. (1996), 'International Politics is not Foreign Policy', in: *Security Studies*, 6 (1), pp. 54–57

Waltz, Kenneth N. (1979), *Theory of International Politics*, New York: Random House

Weiss, Tomás and Vera Rihackova (2010), 'Promoting Multilateralism? Conceptualizing Multilateralism in the Czech Foreign Policy', in: *Perspectives*, 18 (1), pp. 5–22

Wohlforth, William C. (2008), 'Realism and Foreign Policy', in: Steve Smith, Amelia Hadfield and Tim Dunne (eds), *Foreign Policy: Theory, Actors, Cases*, New York: Oxford University Press, pp. 31–48

Yu, Suk-Ryul (2007), 'Assessment of North Korea's Return to the Six-Party Talks', in: *Korean Observations on Foreign Relations*, 9 (1), pp. 77–116

A PROPAGANDA MODEL CASE STUDY OF ABC PRIMETIME 'NORTH KOREA: INSIDE THE SHADOWS'

Sherri L. Ter Molen[1]

ABSTRACT

In 2006, Diane Sawyer became the first American journalist to broadcast live from inside North Korea. Her trip ended with an hour-long special programme scrutinising life in what she considers possibly 'the most dangerous flashpoint on Earth' (Sawyer 2006). The threat Sawyer actually presents, however, is not that of a nuclear-armed country but of a country whose regime, despite the will of the people, refuses to be a major market for US consumer goods. Applying Herman and Chomsky's propaganda model of media operations, I conduct a discourse analysis of the textual and visual symbols Sawyer uses in illustrating and evaluating the country's quality of life in *ABC Primetime 'North Korea: Inside the Shadows'*. I conclude that Sawyer is unable to overcome her ethnocentric worldview, and therefore, North Korea is unable to emerge from the shadows.

Key words: North Korea, propaganda model, propaganda analysis, Diane Sawyer, broadcast journalism, ABC Television Network

1 INTRODUCTION

In 2006, Diane Sawyer became the first American journalist to broadcast live from inside the Democratic People's Republic of Korea (DPRK).[2] Her historic trip ended with an hour-long special show scrutinising life in what she considers possibly 'the most dangerous flashpoint on Earth' (ABC News 2012; Sawyer 2006). Yet despite her deployment of fear (Klaehn 2009) in the first few minutes of the report

[1] The author would like to thank Barbara Speicher (DePaul University), Michelle Millard (Wayne State University), and Bekki Chapman (media professional) for their helpful feedback.

[2] I use DPRK and North Korea interchangeably. When referring to its southern neighbour, I use Republic of Korea (ROK) or South Korea.

regarding the country's military might and nuclear power, she spends much of the programme criticising the North Korean way of life and heralding evidence of a US cultural invasion in this supposed 'hermetically sealed nation' (Sawyer 2006).

Applying Herman and Chomsky's (2002) propaganda model of media operations (PM), I conduct a discourse analysis of the textual and visual symbols Sawyer uses in illustrating and evaluating the DPRK's quality of life in *ABC Primetime 'North Korea: Inside the Shadows'*. The US Department of State reports that the United States (US) exported only US$5.8 million[3] in goods to communist North Korea in 2005, the year before Sawyer's report (US Census Bureau n.d. a) compared to nearly US$27.6 billion in goods exported to its fellow capitalist country of South Korea during the same period (US Census Bureau n.d. b). Against this background, I specifically examine Sawyer's reliance on the capitalistic value of consumption as her primary measure of the standard of living and level of freedom in the DPRK to understand 'how ideological and communicative power connect with economic, political and social power' (Klaehn 2009: 43).

News frames are ways of organising information to allow journalists and the public to make sense of perceived realities (Lim and Seo 2009: 205); yet Sawyer, an employee of The Walt Disney Company, one of America's largest media conglomerates, does not take up an opportunity to provide an alternative to the axis of evil news frames that have painted the DPRK as a military threat, a human rights violator, and a nation at odds with the US since the state of the union address that the then president, George W. Bush, gave in January 2002 (Lim and Seo 2009). At one point, for example, Sawyer leads an English class at a foreign languages high school in a chorus of 'Do Re Mi' from the American film, *The Sound of Music*, as if this is evidence North Koreans crave the (market) freedoms they are denied. I challenge Sawyer's ethnocentric reinforcement of these negative news frames and question the power structures that prevent her from separating the people and their culture from the hostile political relationship between the DPRK and the US.

---

[3] All monetary amounts are presented in US dollars.

2 Review of the Literature

2.1 *Framing North Korea in the US media*

Cumings (2004: 15) contends that the media situate the US as a benevolent nation provoked by the DPRK's determination to acquire 'weapons of mass destruction'. From a framing perspective, the positions of these two adversaries in the media are created by arranging fragments of a 'perceived reality' to promote a narrative that supports a particular view (Entman 2007: 164). There is a large body of work on media framing to support this broad understanding, but there are relatively few studies that attempt to explain how North Korea specifically is constructed in the US media.

Generally, these few framing studies have contended that the DPRK is an enemy of the US, one that should be approached carefully. Lim and Seo (2009), for example, conducted a content analysis of US government policy statements in the *New York Times* from 29 January through to 31 May 2002 during the four-month period immediately following Bush's evocation of an 'axis of evil' in his state of the union address, and found that the US government's official hostile position on the DPRK was reinforced through the newspaper's framing. In contrast, the *New York Times* between December 2002 and February 2003 used framing to promote diplomatic rather than military engagement with North Korea, and US public opinion mirrored this framing (Khang 2004). In the two weeks immediately following the DPRK's first nuclear test in 2006, however, *USA Today* presented the option of military engagement with North Korea in addition to diplomacy and presented it with greater force than did peer publications in China, Japan, Russia or South Korea (Chung, Lessman and Fan 2008). The Associated Press also framed the DPRK as a threat in the larger context of the war on terror in October of that year (Dai and Hyun 2010). The evolution of these news frames from diplomacy to the possibility of armed conflict was reflected in public opinion polls, which indicated that between 2000 and 2007 the US public increasingly viewed North Korea as a threat (Kim et al. 2008), demonstrating that news frames do indeed shape public opinion. Yet despite the fact these studies have found that the US government, the media and the public identify the DPRK as an enemy state, the authors of these studies do not necessarily label the North Korea news frames as negative.

Choi (2006 and 2010), however, used framing analysis to examine newspaper articles that ran within a two-year window from January 2001 through to December 2002 in the *New York Times* and the *Washington Post*. He concluded that there were 20-times the number of negative North Korea news frames in the *New York Times* and 11-times the number of such news frames in the *Washington Post* as positive news frames about the country in either newspaper. He made his value judgment on the basis of his findings that the newspapers framed North Korea as an evil enemy and a terrorist state. It would certainly be difficult to argue that these news frames could be considered positive, and it is permissible to apply Choi's value judgment to the other news frames that have emerged in the North Korea framing research. It might even be permitted to go one step further and to identify these negative North Korea news frames as propaganda.

2.2 *Propaganda*

Giroux (2008: 126) states that 'propaganda is generally used to misrepresent information, promote biased knowledge, or produce a view of politics that appears beyond question or critical engagement.' Yet despite this definition, scholars have not generally labelled the framing of North Korea in US media as such. In contrast, however, Jang (2008) conducted a content analysis of editorials produced by the Korean Central News Agency (KCNA) in the DPRK from August 2003 to September 2007 in order to examine the news frames surrounding the Six Party Talks that took place during that four-year period. Not only did he conclude that the frames positioned the US as a 'diplomatic and economic concern', but he also connected this framing to the accusation 'that North Korea's media have historically been a propaganda tool of the ruling political party, the leader, and the government' (Jang 2008: 16).

It seems that there is a double standard here. One example may be found in an article that appeared in the *New York Times* in February 2013, which was keen to point out that a DPRK YouTube video showing New York engulfed in flames was 'North Korean propaganda' (Choe 2013). Yet, articles that also ran in the *New York Times* in 2004 failed to accuse the film, *Team America: World Police*, of being American propaganda despite the newspaper's reporting that 'Alec Baldwin…emerges as a villain almost as *evil* as Kim Jong Il' (emphasis added) (Waxman 2004: section 2, p.1) and despite its reporting that Kim Jung Il is portrayed as the mastermind behind 'a *diabolical* plot to arm global terrorists with weapons of mass destruction' (once again, emphasis added) (Scott 2004: E1).

Scholars and journalists might fail to recognise these double standards and biases as anti-North Korean propaganda because, as Herman and Chomsky (2002: 1) note, 'it is much more difficult to see a propaganda system at work where the media are private and formal censorship is absent.' However if Giroux (2008: 25) is correct that the media are largely tools of the elite who use them for targeted advertising, the promotion of anti-democratic ideologies that support corporate interests, and the goal of distracting the public from critical civic engagement with 'infortainment' such as celebrity scandals, it is exigent to consider the possibility that negative North Korea news frames in the US media are indeed propaganda and that those who present the view that the US is a righteous party to North Korea's aggressive provocations also benefit from it.

3 Method

The propaganda model offers a means for critiquing the mass media's power structures by focusing on the influence of economic power, which works to marginalise dissenting viewpoints in order to serve the interests of the dominant elite (Herman and Chomsky 2002: 2). The model is employed within the method of discourse analysis (Mullen 2009: 16), that is, the systematic inspection of the structures and functions of texts (van Dijk 1991: 108), and it assumes that when the media are under corporate rather than state control, programming and news coverage are influenced by a 'guided market system' (Herman and Chomsky 2002: lx; Mullen 2009: 13).

Within this framework, media in capitalist societies are constrained by five filters: (1) size, ownership, and profit orientation; (2) the advertising licence to do business; (3) sourcing mass media news; (4) flak and the enforcers; and (5) anti-communism as a control mechanism (Herman and Chomsky 2002: 5–31). These filters work together to 'mobilize and divert, promote and suppress, legitimize and endorse' media discourses to support the needs of those in power (Klaehn 2002: 152).

The PM is controversial, however, and critics argue that any accusation that thousands of journalists toe a single 'party line' assumes conspiracy (Herman 2000: 104). Proponents of the model repudiate this criticism and argue that the decisions made by journalists and other media producers to include some stories and viewpoints and to exclude others often constitute 'unconscious hegemony' (Klaehn 2002: 148–49), meaning that the tenets of domination are embedded deeply in 'a system so powerful as to be internalized largely without awareness' (Herman and Chomsky 2002: 302). They argue that this is possible because the mass media tend to hire like-minded individuals and because employees who do not initially share these ideologies adopt them through socialisation processes (Herman and Chomsky 2002: 304).

Other criticisms of the PM include the accusation that it is deterministic, but Herman and Chomsky counter that all models are. They argue further that if a model can make predictions or if it can lead to understanding, it proves its usefulness. Critics also dismiss the model on the grounds that it was designed during the Cold War and that communism is no longer relevant (Mullen 2009: 16–18). It is true that communism is perceived as less of a threat in today's world than when the PM was introduced. To take account of this change, the final filter has often been referred to in recent years as dominant ideology (Klaehn 2009: 45). Herman and Chomsky profess that the PM can be adapted for whatever threat to 'free market ideology' is salient at the time (Mullen 2009: 18), and Herman (2000: 111) believes it is actually more relevant in the post-Cold War era than when the PM was originally published in 1988.[4] Of course, in the case of North Korea, communism is still relevant but within a post-Cold War context.

Because the PM is controversial, it is often excluded from debates over media bias (Herman 2000: 101). In those rare studies where media critics employ the PM, they generally do so in two ways. The first method is to compare the media coverage of two disparate events that occurred during the same historical period. The second is to examine the framing of a single historical event across the media by investigating its sources and analysing its content (Klaehn 2002: 168). The analysis deployed in this paper closely resembles the second method, though I examine a single media artefact instead of the framing of an event across multiple media. Cumings (2004: 101) recalls that after

[4] For a discussion of further criticisms, see Mullen (2009).

George W. Bush identified North Korea as part of his axis of evil, 'a supine American media fell in line with the administration's caricature of the crisis in Korea, instead of doing serious investigative reporting.' The purpose of this case study of *ABC Primetime 'North Korea: Inside the Shadows'* is to investigate this claim. Sawyer may not always be accurate when describing North Korea, but times have changed. For instance, as of 2013, foreigners are allowed to carry their mobile phones into the country (*NK News* 2013), but in 2006, Sawyer's team were required to leave their mobile devices at the airport. The experiences Sawyer relays are thus not necessarily representative of what is happening in the DPRK in 2013. A case study is meant to be descriptive of a particular artefact, but it can lead to 'the development of more general, nomothetic theories' (Babbie 2007). Sawyer visited Pyongyang in October 2006, just days after the DPRK conducted its first nuclear test. Now, in 2013, the US media have been ablaze with reports on North Korea's third nuclear test, and this would seem a relevant time to revisit her report. I have chosen to apply the PM, despite the criticisms of the model, because I believe that it might be an appropriate device for examining the economic, political and social power at work in this particular report and because I believe this analysis might also be able to demonstrate some of the strengths of the controversial model.

ABC Primetime 'North Korea: Inside the Shadows' was a one-hour programme when it was originally shown on 8 December 2006. It was the culmination of Sawyer's live reports from Pyongyang that aired during ABC's news programmes in October of that year (ABC News 2012; IMDb n.d.; Sawyer 2006). I watched the original broadcasts of the live reports and the *ABC Primetime* special and subsequently reviewed a 41-minute commercial-free DVD of the programme 16 times for this analysis. In what follows, I apply each of Herman and Chomsky's filters (see above) to this video account of North Korean life, and deconstruct the visual and textual symbols presented by Sawyer as I ask the following research questions:

> RQ1: How do economic, political and social power work to reinforce negative North Korea news frames?
>
> RQ2: How do economic, political and social power work to obscure North Korean culture?

Cumings (2004: viii) describes North Korea as 'the country every American loves to hate'. Since previous studies have already found that the US media cultivate such views (e.g., Choi 2006 and 2010), it is important to decipher how these views are formed as well as to consider who benefits from their distribution.

4 Analysis

The first filter of the PM is size, ownership, and profit orientation. As Schiller (1989: 135) notes, the industries that manufacture culture and information 'have grown greatly in size, breadth, and productive capability in the years since World War II.' When Herman and Chomsky (2002) published their treatise on the influence of ownership on media content nearly 25 years ago, the broadcast industry in the US had only recently been deregulated, and two-thirds of the companies were still, in effect, family businesses, where originating family members still held high-level positions or retained a majority interest in stocks. By the mid-to-late 1980s, however, ABC had already been acquired by Capital Cities and was controlled by corporate officers and directors.

Today, ABC belongs to The Disney/ABC Television Group (Disney/ABC Television Group n.d.), a subsidiary that falls under the larger umbrella of The Walt Disney Company, which also includes Walt Disney Pictures, Pixar, ESPN, and a number of other brands. In 2011, the revenue of this media conglomerate topped US$40.1 billion (Free Press n.d.), and US$4.9 billion of this revenue was attributed to ABC alone (Steinberg 2012).

The consolidated corporate media set the agenda for the issues that are salient among the public (Giroux 2008: 24), and this makes the corporate voice 'the loudest in the land'. Because the purpose of corporations is to increase revenue (Schiller 1989: 4), this corporate voice primarily disseminates fiscally conservative ideologies including 'the breathless rhetoric of the global victory of free-market rationality' (Giroux 2008: 6). Corporations including media giants such as ABC employ free market activities to generate earnings and maximise profits.

The advertising licence to do business is the second PM filter, and ABC, like other commercial networks, is financially dependent on advertising. *ABC Primetime* earns the network 'millions of dollars in profits', and Sawyer, one of the highest-paid women in broadcast news, has been credited with the ratings and financial success of the programme (Lovdahl n.d.). Sawyer joined ABC in 1989 after working for one of the company's competitors, CBS, for nine years. Prior to her broadcasting career, she served on the Nixon-Ford transition team and assisted former President Nixon with the writing of his memoirs (ABC News 2012).

Observing this programme through the lens of the first and second filters uncloaks the power structures that colour Sawyer's judgment when she labels North Korean lives as 'Spartan' (Sawyer 2006).[5] Sawyer emphasises the 'sober clothes' that usually lack American brand names. At the same time, she is quick to point out US cultural products when she sees them, particularly those that represent her own company's brands, such as a small plush Minnie Mouse in the home of a famous former North Korean figure-skating champion. She says: 'But throughout the country, we keep seeing something puzzling. There! On that mirror! Isn't that Minnie Mouse?' A few minutes later, she reminds the viewers of her visit to the English class at the foreign languages high school, and she seems pleased to point out that, although the students claim they have never seen an American movie, their favourite films are *Toy Story*, a Walt Disney Pictures/Pixar collaboration (Guggenheim and Lasseter 1995), and *Shrek*. Sawyer clearly believes the enjoyment of these two Hollywood animated films signals a greater desire for American cultural products, while also noting the students had 'no idea that they came from the enemy camp' (Sawyer 2006). Perhaps this comes as no surprise, since Sawyer has been so long interwoven into the circles of the dominant elite in the US that her orientation is also economic, validating Herman and Chomsky's claim that the mass media hire like-minded individuals (Herman and Chomsky 2002: 304).

The model's third filter is sourcing mass media news. Sawyer's surprise that the refrigerator in the former champion figure-skater's home is 'a typical American refrigerator' (Sawyer 2006) suggests that she had pre-conceived notions about what she expected to find (and not to find) when she visited North Korea. It is likely that the same negative news frames that shaped US public opinion also shaped Sawyer's expectations. Lim and Seo (2009: 213–19) found that the American people relied on the news frames presented by the US government and the mass media, since other sources of information, such

[5] This and following paragraphs contain many quotations from Sawyer's programme *ABC Primetime 'North Korea: Inside the Shadows'* (2006). Where it is clear that the phrases and sentences quoted are taken from her reportage, they have not been further attributed.

as direct contact with the DPRK, were scarce. Yet the experts who supplied the information used to construct these news frames may not have had much more direct contact with North Korea than any other American citizen, since, as Sawyer notes, the North Korean government representatives who accompanied her team at all times—the team's 'minders'—told them that there were only 300 foreigners in North Korea, a country of 23 million, during the time of their visit.[6]

In addition to the possible lack of direct contact, Chomsky identifies another potential cause of misinformation generated by the experts: money. He accuses the 'liberal-intelligentsia' of participating in legitimising unconscious hegemony when they provide their expertise to the media, since their employers, usually universities, are often dependent on corporate donors (Klaehn 2009: 169–70). Objectivity was, at one time, the backbone of broadcast journalism in the US (Cushion 2012: 11), but since the Cold War, there has been a turn towards interpretive reporting, which emphasises causes and ideas rather than events (Applegate 2007: 5, 8). Even when the liberal intelligentsia do not feel constrained, journalists 'seem to govern both how the interview is conducted as well as how it is edited into the final news story' (Nylund 2003: 531), and these sound bites have been found to reinforce the status quo (Mason 2004).

Nevertheless, audiences expect the news media to be objective (Hackett 1984), and Sawyer does attempt to make her report appear balanced at times. She includes, for example, a sound bite offered by Donald P. Gregg, a former US ambassador to the ROK, who advocates greater dialogue between the DPRK and the US to increase understanding. Nonetheless, the majority of the academic and governmental sound bites Sawyer presents reinforce the pre-existing negative news frames, as when Dr Charles Armstrong, a professor of history at Columbia University, describes high-rise apartment buildings in Pyongyang that often do not have working elevators, running water, or consistent electricity. The positioning of the DPRK as a dialogue partner at odds with the US (Lim and Seo 2009) is reinforced with a carefully selected sound bite offered by Dr Meredith Jung-En Woo, who at the time was a professor of political science at the University of Michigan. She informs viewers that North Korea is 'run by a dead person'

[6] Americans were able to travel to North Korea in 2006, but Sawyer does not indicate whether the North Koreans specified the number of Americans among the 300 foreigners they declared were in the country at the time.

(Sawyer 2006). This is not quite accurate, but Kim Il Sung, the first leader of North Korea, who passed away in 1994, does retain the title of 'eternal president' (Sawyer 2006). Viewers experience this sound bite out of context and bookended with Sawyer's commentary, which shapes the overall narrative, and they are left to contemplate how the US, despite Donald Gregg's urgings, could possibly engage in increased dialogue with a ghost.

The reverence that North Koreans have for their leaders has traditionally elicited a response of mockery from US journalists. For example, a 2003 *New York Times* writer admitted he 'gleefully purchased a book with a stern photo of Kim Jung Il titled *The Great Teacher of Journalists* simply as a joke' (Kristof 2003: A27). Sawyer uses a copy of this same book in her report to illustrate the differences between North Korean journalism, which is controlled by the state, and American journalism, which she implies is free, but which Herman and Chomsky (2002) argue is controlled by the dominant elite. Yet Sawyer scoffs at North Korean propaganda without ever considering her views might also be shaped by America's own brand of propaganda. As a case in point, on her way to Pyongyang on 'an old Soviet jet' (Sawyer 2006), she dismisses an article in the North Korean airline magazine that accuses the US of committing atrocities during the Korean War, despite substantial evidence to support such accusations, including testimony gathered during the No Gun Ri massacre investigation (see Hanley, Choe and Mendoza 2001). In addition, she mocks the onboard announcement that heralds her 'arrival in a state, which is also a kind of state of mind' (Sawyer 2006). On all probability backed by the same governmental and media experts that inform the American public on the topic of North Korea, Sawyer's views had already been solidified before she arrived in the DPRK.

The fourth filter of the PM is flak and the enforcers. Flak can take on many forms including letters, telephone calls, or petitions that rebuke the media for something they have said or done. These communications can come from the public or from a powerful entity such as the White House (Herman and Chomsky 2002: 26), but there is no evidence to indicate that flak was ever a threat in the case of *ABC Primetime 'North Korea: Inside the Shadows'*. Blinded by the ideologies of the market system, Sawyer does not challenge the negative news frames that had preceded her visit. In fact, she reinforces them, which is fortunate for her, ABC, and *ABC Primetime*'s advertisers since, dating back to the McCarthy era, broadcasters judged as 'insufficiently anti-communist' have been chastised and subject to product boycotts by the public (Herman and Chomsky 2002: 26, 29).

In the case of this particular study, the fifth and final filter of the PM, anti-communism as a control mechanism, applies as the dominant ideology. Anti-communism and pro-capitalism may not be the only ideologies at play, but Sawyer's repeated emphasis on economic differences provides evidence to this claim. Time and again, Sawyer points out the disparity of wealth and material accumulation between the middle and elite classes of North Korea and America. Of the family of the former figure-skating champion, she says, 'They live in three rooms, small by Western standards, about 700 square feet [65 sq m]', yet Pyongyang is the largest city in the DPRK. In America's largest city, New York, the average size of a one-bedroom[7] apartment is a comparable 750 sq ft [69.6 sq m] (Apartments.com 2012; Nakedapartments n.d.). Sawyer does not live in one of these average New York City apartments, however. At the time she visited this North Korean home in 2006, she and her husband were living in a '12-room, full-floor apartment at 1030 Fifth Avenue' in New York City (Abelson 2008; Gaines 2005), and the couple also owned an estate on Martha's Vineyard in Massachusetts (CelebrityDetective n.d.). Sawyer's understandings of what constitutes the American standard might thus be slightly skewed. On another occasion, in a factory, Sawyer asks a young woman how much money she earns and explains: 'She confides she is paid 2,500 won a month, the equivalent of US$20.00, or, in the US, four lattes at Starbucks.' The young woman, however, says that US$20.00 a month 'is more than enough to live on' (Sawyer 2006), and perhaps in Pyongyang it is.

Sawyer, whose annual salary at the time was US$12 million, cannot fathom a society in which US$20.00 a month could be enough. Yet throughout the programme she implies that it is the North Korean people, rather than she, who have been brainwashed. When one woman on the street denounces the US while holding Sawyer's hand, Sawyer responds by boasting that the US is 'a very rich country, lots of food, lots of medicine, lots of opportunity for little children', implying that the DPRK does not possess any of these resources. However, this North Korean woman is not impressed with America's abundance and responds: 'I'm not concerned about how Americans live their lives. I just want Americans not to meddle in our Korean people's affairs'

[7] A one-bedroom apartment generally has one bathroom, a kitchen and a living area.

(Sawyer 2006). This woman's priorities diverge so far from Sawyer's that Sawyer does not appear to comprehend that her interlocutor may be just as personally invested in the ideology of the North Korean state as Sawyer is invested in the ideology of the market-driven economy and the profit-driven structure of The Walt Disney Company.

5 Discussion

As Giroux (2008: 7) expounds, '[m]oney, profits, and fear have become powerful ideological elements in arguing for opening up new markets and closing down the possibility of dissent at home', and *ABC Primetime 'North Korea: Inside the Shadows'* provides ample evidence to support this view. Looking at this report through the five filters of the PM, I have pointed to the power structures that induce Sawyer to rely on the capitalistic value of consumption as her primary measure of the standard of living and level of freedom in North Korea, and have interpreted the meanings of the textual and visual symbols embedded within the programme.

5.1 *Reinforcing negative North Korea news frames*

Turning to the two research questions I outlined above (Section 3), the first asks how economic, political and social power work to reinforce negative North Korea news frames. Sawyer invokes fear by depicting Kim Jong Il as 'a mysterious leader who has spread fear throughout the world by unleashing a nuclear explosion' (Sawyer 2006). She does not linger on the country's build-up of nuclear capabilities, however. What concerns her is how much longer North Korea can 'hold out against the barbarians at the gate', and she does not mean an invading US military force. What she actually means is a US cultural invasion, and she implies that 'bolting the door against a world of personal and political freedom, exuberant with PlayStations, paparazzi, and personal consumption' is a futile effort. She accompanies this indirect assertion with footage of a young, chubby South Korean man holding a giant soft serve ice cream cone as a reminder that US-led capitalism has already succeeded in the South.

Sawyer is preoccupied with the fact that the DPRK has a lavish military but that civilians are deprived of stockpiles of luxury goods.

After learning that a manager has barred the ABC crew from filming inside a department store, an irritated member of Sawyer's team proclaims: 'This is going to be part of our story. If that's what he wants America to see, that's what we'll show. Come on. Let's go' (Sawyer 2006). The crew is also barred from filming in a grocery store, and Sawyer is shown walking away frustrated. Together, these scenes imply the crew was forbidden to film because the North Koreans did not want Americans to see how little merchandise there was available to buy. Sawyer supports this deprivation narrative further while exploring the home of the former champion figure-skater. Looking at the small closet, she ponders, 'Imagine that for most American teens'; and is further astounded by the meagre inventory in the refrigerator. 'There were some eggs, some bottled water, but not the grocery excess you see a lot in the United States', she recalls. 'Of course, in the fridge I saw kimchi, the famous Korean pickled cabbage'.

Kimchi serves as a segue for her to relay yet another story about how North Koreans have so much less than Americans. The minders also forbid Sawyer and her team from taping a home preparation of this national dish, and irritated, she alleges, 'Perhaps they're concerned it will look like that's all there is to eat' (Sawyer 2006). Noting that the military gets fed first in North Korea, she reminds the audience of the famine that took place a decade earlier in the 1990s, during which, the US State Department estimates, a million North Koreans, primarily civilians, including children, died of starvation.[8] She notes the absence of overweight people on the streets and cites a statistic that North Koreans are four inches shorter than their South Korean counterparts, a figure evidently held to be accounted for by decades of food shortages. She boasts, 'At our hotel, the food is plentiful, but only foreigners can afford this. A single entrée would probably take the entire month's salary of a factory worker.' With their overflowing closets, full bellies, and hoards of money, Americans and their South Korean allies, Sawyer signals, are much better off than their communist rivals.

By equating 'consumption' with 'personal and political freedom' (Sawyer 2006), economic, political and social power converge to cre-

[8] Sawyer (2006) does not identify her State Department source, but one State Department report from 2003 estimated as many as one to two million North Koreans died as a result of the famine (Manyin and Jun 2003). Cumings (2004: 178) argues that the estimated number of North Korean famine victims ranges from 500,000 to two million.

ate a narrative that suggests the opening up of the North Korean market to US consumer products would free the people from oppression. Sawyer reinforces negative news frames by intermingling footage of North Korean tanks and starving children with images of an empty restaurant and commentary about the deficiency of brand-name clothes, revisiting here the old 'instrument of anticommunism' which, as Schiller (1989: 14) has argued, has proven in the past to be quite effective in drumming up fears of instability and a lack of prosperity. This 'culture of fear' (Giroux 2008: 53), which is perpetuated by the US media, summons up public support for any tactics the dominant elite may choose to employ as they hope to gain full access to the North Korean market.

5.2 *Obscuring North Korean culture*

The second research question asks how economic, political and social power work to obscure North Korean culture. Sawyer visits monuments to leaders of North Korea and meets a select number of military officials, but she spends much of her report interviewing Pyongyang residents in a park, visiting a bowling alley, and touring a film studio where she meets a North Korean film star, Pak Mi Hyang. Yet, instead of asking questions about the North Korean people and their way of life, most of her questions seem to seek testimony to support an assumption that North Koreans want to live like Americans.

She visits a beauty salon, for example, where she asks a young woman to look through the pages of a colourful American fashion magazine filled with flamboyant styles. The woman seems uninterested and tells her, 'We like to dress neatly in our own way' (Sawyer 2006). North Korean salons generally offer a range of 'recommended hair styles', and in 2005, the year before Sawyer's visit, the government had implemented a campaign aimed at men entitled 'Let us trim our hair in accordance with Socialist lifestyle' (*NK News* 2011). Whether Sawyer knows this or not, she does not accept the young woman's response as her own, and narrates that, after she and her crew had returned to New York, their translator, to use Sawyer's term, told them that another woman in the background actually instructed the young woman to say that she preferred North Korean styles. Sawyer also asks this same young woman if she would want blond hair. The woman responds, 'We prefer the traditional Asian black hair'

(Sawyer 2006). Once again, Sawyer, who has blond hair, cannot imagine that this woman would reject this hair colour of her own accord, and she dismisses the woman's preference as a sign that she has been brainwashed. 'And remember, it's not just style', Sawyer warns in regard to the North Korean woman's preference for her own hair colour. 'It's a kind of pride in racial purity.' In fact, each time a North Korean offers her or his perspective, Sawyer's words and/or tone suggest that she discounts their views and opinions. She does not seem to consider the possibility that her question might in itself be racist or that her perceptions of beauty might be steeped in her own culture or ethnocentrism.

Still in the beauty salon, Sawyer asks if a customer likes curly hair. The answer is somewhat obvious, since the woman has curly hair, but the interpreter responds, 'She doesn't like curly hair' (Sawyer 2006). Confused, Sawyer questions, 'She doesn't? Why is her hair curly?' Finally realising that the interpreter does not understand her question, she says, 'No, curly…curly', as she makes a curling gesture with her fingers while releasing an exasperated laugh. Although Sawyer is unapologetic that she does not speak Korean and awkwardly mispronounces the couple of Korean words she tries to say, she exhibits little patience for her North Korean interpreter when he does not understand. On the other hand, she takes the presence of the English phrase 'LOVE IS IN FAMILY' embroidered on a pillow in the home of the former figure-skater to mean that the North Korean people value the English language and desire American culture. After the students in the English class at the foreign languages high school reveal that although they were not aware the films were American, they had actually seen at least two Hollywood films, Sawyer narrates: 'So we decided to try one more test, a song almost every child can sing around the world'. She then leads the class in a rendition of 'Do Re Mi' from *The Sound of Music*, implying that the students' knowledge of the song proves that North Koreans crave American culture and its (market) freedoms (Sawyer 2006). If she had inquired how they knew these films and soundtracks, she might have learned that English language students in the DPRK are shown American and English films for language study (Lloyd-Roberts 2010).

Sawyer continuously notes that the government restricts knowledge of and contact with the outside world. She asks a 20-year-old university student studying to be a nuclear scientist if she knows about 'America's most common college tool, Google' (Sawyer 2006). In a country where she claims the 'Internet is forbidden', knowledge of Google would, of course, be useless. What Sawyer does not seem to know, though she shows a computer that rejects the abcnews.com address, is that an Intranet has operated within the DPRK since sometime around 2001 and that some North Koreans have access to the Internet, even though such access is 'severely restrained by politics' (Cumings 2004: 191). The university student does not know of Google, but she promises to study about it. Sawyer cites former Secretary of State Madeleine Albright's visit to the DPRK in 2000, during which Kim Jung Il asked for her email address, but is still amused when an 84-year-old Korean War hero offers her the Hotmail email addresses of his children who live in the US.

Sawyer is so convinced that the North Koreans actually want to look, speak and live like Americans that she never seriously considers that there may be some truth to the North Korean government's claim that 'its people wouldn't want consumerism if you gave it to them' (Sawyer 2006). The elderly Korean War hero, who had once lived in South Korea, criticises capitalism because, within this system, 'money comes first. It's survival of the fittest' (ibid.). Showing a map of the Korean peninsula at night with the northern half engulfed in darkness, Sawyer totes the bright lights of the southern portion as proof of capitalism's superiority, and she spends the majority of the report, at the expense of her journalistic objectivity, seeking evidence to support the notion that the North Korean people have consumerist desires. According to her assessment, the only thing standing between the North Korean people and the free market system is the government of the DPRK.

Examining *ABC Primetime 'North Korea: Inside the Shadows* through the five filters of the PM, reveals how economic, political and social power shape Sawyer's narrative in a way that advances the interests of US corporations such as her employer, The Walt Disney Company. The company would certainly like to line the shelves of the North Korean grocery and department stores with its products. Even when she witnesses what she considers to be an all-too-perfect performance by pre-schoolers, she compares the young musicians to 'a living version of Disney's "It's a Small World"' (Sawyer 2006). The ideological clash between North Korea and the US distracts Sawyer, and she squanders her opportunity to discover a different facet of North Korean culture to present to the American people.

5.3 *Evaluation of the propaganda model*

Like 'the deafening absence of any contrary argument' that presents a different view of North Korea (Cumings 2004: viii), studies that both argue for and demonstrate the usefulness of the PM are few and far between. Perhaps as Herman and Chomsky acknowledge, the controversial model is not applicable in every situation, but, in this case study of *ABC Primetime 'North Korea: Inside the Shadows'*, the PM, as predicted by Mullen (2009), has demonstrated its resilience and has led to understanding. Taking into consideration Giroux's definition of propaganda, which posits that biased or misrepresented information is disseminated to promote a particular view that 'appears beyond question of critical engagement' (Giroux 2008: 126), the five filters of the PM have revealed why Sawyer does not seem to question the pre-existing negative North Korea news frames and how she participates in their reproduction.

Sawyer is constrained because she works for a division of The Walt Disney Company, an extremely wealthy business. Herman and Chomsky (2002: xl) explain that

> the same underlying power sources that own the media and fund them as advertisers, that serve as primary definers of the news, and that produce flak and proper-thinking experts, also play a key role in fixing basic principles and the dominant ideologies.

It would not be in The Walt Disney Company's best interest, or in the best interests of their profit-driven advertisers who pay for ABC's programming, to challenge the pre-existing negative North Korea news frames. By viewing North Korea as a military threat, the US news media keep in line with NSC 68, a 1950 National Security Council report that guided US foreign policy during and after the Cold War. The document states that it is the US objective to 'foster a world environment in which the American system can survive and flourish' (Layne and Schwartz 1993: 5). As Cumings (1999: 289) points out, 'military power was of course important in constructing a liberal order', and positioning countries such as the DPRK as a military threat still keeps allies financially dependent on the US. Some companies such as 3M and The Dow Chemical Company may even also benefit from this impending threat, since they manufacture military products in addition to the consumer products they advertise on broadcast television networks such as ABC.

The negative news frame that presents the DPRK as a human rights violator also serves The Walt Disney Company and its advertisers because it juxtaposes 'the unipolar pre-eminence and comprehensive economic advantage that the United States now enjoys' (Cumings 1999: 271) with 'the vanguard of the anti-imperial, anti-American rejectionist front' (ibid.: 279). Sawyer recalls the food shortages of the 1990s and condemns the gulags, but she focuses much more of her attention on the lack of consumer goods available as well on as the modest possessions of the North Koreans she meets. In neoliberal societies such as the US, the free markets are equated with democracy (Harvey 2010: 7), and Sawyer pulls at the American public's heart-strings when she implies that the US could free the North Koreans from oppression simply by exporting its consumer goods into the country. In October 2006, the same month in which the DPRK conducted its first nuclear test and in which Diane Sawyer travelled to Pyongyang, a CNN poll found that 60 percent of Americans thought that the conflict with North Korea 'could be resolved economically and diplomatically' (Bowman and Rugg 2013). If and when North Korea opens its markets, it may benefit The Walt Disney Company, which will seek to flood the DPRK with its media products and branded merchandise, even if it may find that Chinese, Japanese and South Korean goods are in there ahead of it.

As Cuming (2004: xiii) states, '[i]n human rights circles, the easiest thing has always been to look one way and condemn the communists', and reinforcing the negative news frame that postures North Korea as a dialogue partner at odds with the US (see Lim and Seo 2009), rallies the public behind the belief that the US is the more righteous of the two parties. Sawyer suggests that the DPRK should reform to the American brand of neoliberal capitalism without ever presenting the idea that the US could meet North Korea part way, let alone reform to the North Korean brand of *chuch'e* socialism. Clearly, *chuch'e* socialism would be detrimental to The Walt Disney Company, and in the eyes of profit-driven media outlets and advertisers, capitalism cannot be negotiated. Yet despite North Korean markets generally being closed to US media and consumer goods, ABC may still be able to turn a profit with the help of the DPRK because, as the economic and military standoffs become routine, audiences may tune in, raising Nielsen ratings and revenues that could translate to millions of dollars (see Herman and Chomsky 2002: 16)

In short, this analysis indicates that *ABC Primetime 'North Korea: Inside the Shadows'* constitutes propaganda as defined by Giroux. The key now is to embrace this finding while considering its ramifications as well as alternative approaches for the future.

6 Implications and Recommendations

General Ri Chan Bok, who for more than four decades has been in charge of the Korean People's Army's troops stationed at the Demilitarised Zone, asks why the US president continuously insults his country. '[The United States] provoked us by calling us the Axis of Evil', he retorts. 'These kinds of malicious words all came from the United States…They all came from the lips of President Bush. Please tell him to stop telling these lies' (Sawyer 2006). By reinforcing the negative news frames that have saturated the US media since George W. Bush made his accusation, Sawyer adds insult to injury.

Cumings (2004: 47) blames the US media, which he maintains are 'almost bereft of good investigative reporters', of obscuring the nature of the conflict between the DPRK and the US, and he contends that North Korea not only wants diplomatic engagement but actually wants the US to remain involved in peninsular issues overall. He even imagines a time in which 'Americans will begin to enjoy touring this beautiful Hermit Kingdom and meeting its unknown but warm, proud, and dignified people' (ibid.: x). This is a very different story to the one Sawyer presents when she promises 'to look behind the mask, the giant army, the fierce isolation, the strange conformity' of a country she insists is 'repeatedly celebrating itself' (Sawyer 2006).

Instead of conducting in-depth investigative reporting, as predicted by the PM, Sawyer selects sound bites provided by the cheaper option of academic and governmental experts who support her preconceived notions. Sawyer explains, for example, that the Pyongyang subway tunnels double as bomb shelters to protect North Korean citizens during possible American attacks. She also describes the DPRK's demonstrations around the time of its first nuclear test in 2006. 'We saw the terrifying torch-lit processions,' she reminds, 'threatening banners…' This is followed by a sound bite supplied by Dr Roy Richard Grinker, a professor of anthropology at George Washington University. 'If we look at North Korea from our perspective, yeah, they can look pretty crazy', he remarks. 'But if we look at the world from their perspective, what they're doing makes sense.' Sawyer continues:

> What seems paranoid to the West, seems prudent to North Koreans. The Korean nation has fought back more than 900 invasions over the past two millennia. They see the US potentially as 901 (Sawyer 2006).

Grinker's sound bite reinforces Sawyer's general narrative that posits North Korean behaviour as absurd since she does not place it within the context of any possible wrongdoings committed by the US, which might have led to North Korea's justified fear of American attacks. These wrongdoings might include, for example, the occupation of the territory south of the 38th parallel for several years beginning in 1945 or the unloading of '866,914 gallons of napalm' on both soldiers and civilians across the Korean peninsula from June to late October in 1950 during the early stages of the Korean War (Cumings 2004: ix, 19). As previously noted, a former US ambassador, Donald P. Gregg, seems to recognise that the North Korean perspective is rooted in the past, and he offers a hopeful solution:

> They have been fed this diet of anti-Americanism, and so they have anti-American feelings. We need to change their diet. We need to talk to them more, so they will understand us better. And in the process, we will understand them better (Sawyer 2006).

Perhaps it is time to change the American people's diet as well with in-depth investigative reporting that allows academic and governmental experts as well as the North Korean people greater space in which to present alternative views that challenge the salient negative North Korea news frames. Now might be the time to dismantle anti-North Korean feelings and to promote real prolonged diplomatic engagement with this country through the US media so that both countries can understand and appreciate each other better.

7 Conclusion

The title *ABC Primetime 'North Korea: Inside the Shadows'* conveys fear since shadows contain the dangerous unknown. In this discourse analysis in which I have applied Herman and Chomsky's propaganda model, or PM, I have questioned how economic, political and social power work to reinforce negative North Korea news frames and to obscure North Korean culture. I have also illustrated that these powers converge to create media discourses that are bound to the interests of the dominant elite and 'shaped by market forces' (Klaehn 2009: 48, 52).

Interwoven into the power structures of her organisation, Sawyer is unable to overcome her ethnocentric worldview to present an alternative narrative that could have gone beyond the political positioning of the DPRK as a 'a major threat to the security of US citizens' (Lim and Seo 2009: 205). The threat Sawyer presents is not that of a country that possesses nuclear capabilities, rather a country where high-school students and women in beauty salons glance at American fashion magazines without interest. In other words, the threat she presents is of a North Korea that is not a major market for US consumer goods. Sawyer wastes the majority of her report expressing disbelief that the North Koreans could possibly be as happy and patriotic as they seem when they make so little money and have so few possessions. Certainly, ABC's advertisers as well as The Walt Disney Company would like to sell their wares in North Korea, and Sawyer provides anecdotal evidence, such as the appearance of Boston Red Sox and Nike logos on baseball caps worn by people going about their daily lives, to demonstrate that North Koreans actually have consumerist desires for American goods. Sawyer is so fixated on finding evidence that North Koreans would welcome a full-blown US cultural and economic invasion that she misses every opportunity to unpack the North Korean perspective or illuminate North Korean culture, despite the fact that she promises to show 'North Korea as you've never seen it before' (Sawyer 2006). As a consequence, despite the fact that ABC and Sawyer were given the unprecedented opportunity to spend 12 days among the North Korean people and to broadcast live from within their country, North Korea and its people were unable to emerge from the shadows.

Filmography

Guggenheim, Ralph, and John Lasseter (1995), *Toy Story*, motion picture, Walt Disney Pictures/Pixar, distributed by Walt Disney Pictures, USA

Sawyer, Diane (2006), ABC Primetime '*North Korea: Inside the Shadows*', 2006, DVD, ABC

REFERENCES

ABC News (2012), 'Diane Sawyer's Biography', in: *ABC World News with Diane Sawyer*, 6 February. Online: http://abcnews.go.com/WN/DianeSawyer/diane-sawyers-biography/story?id=9380180#.UW94D4KGsfE (accessed 18 April 2012)

Abelson, Max (2008), 'Are Eight Bedrooms Enough to Break a Record? 1030 Fifth Duplex Listed for $47.5 M', in: *New York Observer*, 1 July. Online: http://observer.com/2008/07/are-eight-bedrooms-enough-to-break-a-record-1030-fifth-duplex-listed-for-475-m/ (accessed 30 March 2013)

Apartments.com (2012), 'The Star Report: New York', in: *Apartments.com*. Online: www.apartments.com/starreport/reports/NewYork_DMA.pdf (accessed 30 March 2013)

Applegate, Edd (2007), 'The Concepts of "News Balance" and "Objectivity"', in: *Public Relations Quarterly*, 52 (4), pp. 5–8

Babbie, Earl (2007), 'Qualitative Field Research', in: *The Practice of Social Research*, international student edition, 11th edition, Belmont CA: Thompson Wadsworth, pp. 285–317

Bowman, Karlyn and Andrew Rugg (2013), 'Public Opinion on the North Korean Threat: What You May Have Missed in the Polls', in: *AEI Ideas*, 12 April. Online: www.aei-ideas.org/2013/04/public-opinion-on-the-north-korean-threat/ (accessed 14 April 2013)

CelebrityDetective (n.d.), 'Diane Sawyer's House Profile Martha's Vineyard—Home Pictures, Rare Facts and Information', in: *CelebrityDetective.com*. Online: www.celebritydetective.com/CelebrityHomesDiane-Sawyer-house-Marthas-Vineyard.html (accessed 30 March 2013)

Choe, Sang-hun (2013), 'In Korea Clip, Only North Sleeps Easy', in: *New York Times*, 6 February, late edition, p. A4

Choi, Jinbong (2010), 'The Representation of North Korean National Image in National Newspapers in the United States', in: *Public Relations Review*, 36, pp. 392–94

Choi, Jinbong (2006), 'Framing the National Image of North Korea in the U.S. News Media', paper presented to the meeting of the International Communication Association, Dresden, 19–23 June

Chung, Mun-young, Justin Lessman and Meijing Fan (2008), 'Framing the Nuke: How News Media in Six-Party-Talk Countries Framed North Korea's Nuclear Test', paper presented to the meeting of the International Communication Association, Montreal, 22–26 May

Cumings, Bruce (2004), *North Korea: Another Country*, New York: The New Press

Cumings, Bruce (1999), 'Still the American Century', in: *Review of International Studies*, 25 (5), pp. 271–99

Cushion, Stephen (2012). 'Introduction', in: *Television Journalism*, London: Sage, pp. 1-12

Dai, Jia and Kideuk Hyun (2010), 'Global Risk, Domestic Framing: Coverage of the North Korean Nuclear Test by US, Chinese, and South Korean News Agencies', in: *Asian Journal of Communication*, 20 (3), 299–317

Disney/ABC Television Group (n.d.), 'Corporate and Press Information', in: *Disney/ABC Television Group*. Online: www.disneyabctv.com/web/in dex.aspx (accessed 16 June 2012)

Entman, Robert M. (2007), 'Framing Bias: Media in the Distribution of Power', in: *Journal of Communication*, 57, pp. 163–73

Free Press (n.d.), 'Who Owns the Media?', in: *Free Press*. Online: www.freepress.net/ownership/chart#charts_tv-radio (accessed 16 June 2012)

Gaines, Steven (2005), 'One Apartment, 75 Years', in: *New York Real Estate*, 7 November. Online: http://nymag.com/nymetro/realestate/vu/14943/ (accessed 30 March 2013)

Giroux, Henry A. (2008), *Against the Terror of Neoliberalism: Politics Beyond the Age of Greed*, Boulder CO: Paradigm Publishers

Hackett, Robert A. (1984), 'Decline of a Paradigm? Bias and Objectivity in New Media Studies', in: *Critical Studies in Mass Communication*, 1 (3), pp. 229–59

Hanley, Charles J., Sang-Hun Choe and Martha Mendoza (2001), *The Bridge at No Gun Ri,* New York: Henry Holt and Company

Harvey, David (2010), *A Brief History of Neoliberalism*, New York: Oxford University Press

Herman, Edward S. (2000), 'The Propaganda Model: A Retrospective', in: *Journalism Studies*, 1 (1), pp. 101–12

Herman, Edward S. and Noam Chomsky (2002), *Manufacturing Consent: The Political Economy of the Mass Media*, revised edition, New York: Pantheon Books

IMDb (n.d.). 'North Korea: Inside the Shadows', in: *Internet Movie Database (IMDb)*. Online: www.imdb.com/title/tt1350312/ (accessed 16 June 2012)

Jang, Won Yong (2008), 'News as Propaganda in North Korea: An Analysis of News Editorials of the Six-Party Talks, 2003–2007', paper presented to the meeting of the International Communication Association, Montreal, 22–26 May

Khang, Hyoungkoo (2004), 'Framing "Axis of Evil"', paper presented to the meeting of the International Communication Association, New Orleans, 27–31 May

Kim, Jibum, Carl Gershenson, Jaeki Jeong and Tom W. Smith, (2008), 'How Americans Think About North Korea: 2000–2007', in: *Public Opinion Quarterly*, 72 (4), 804–21

Klaehn, Jeffery (2002), 'A Critical Review and Assessment of Herman and Chomsky's "Propaganda Model"', in: *European Journal of Communication*, 17 (2), pp. 147–82

Klaehn, Jeffery (2009), 'The Propaganda Model: Theoretical and Methodological Considerations', in: *Westminster Papers in Communication and Culture*, 6 (2), pp. 43–58

Kristof, Nicholas D. (2003), 'North Korea's Secret,' in: *New York Times,* 14 January, p. A27

Layne, Christopher and Benjamin Schwartz (1993), 'American Hegemony: Without an Enemy', in: *Foreign Policy*, 92, pp. 5–23

Lim, Jeongsub and Hyunjin Seo (2009), 'Frame Flow Between Government and the News Media and Its Effects on the Public: Framing of North Korea', in: *International Journal of Public Opinion Research*, 21 (2), pp. 204–23

Lloyd-Roberts, Sue (2010), 'Life Inside the North Korean Bubble', in: *BBC News*, 1 June. Online: http://news.bbc.co.uk/2/hi/programmes/newsnight/8701959.stm (accessed 14 April 2013)

Lovdahl, Lynn T. (n.d.), 'Sawyer, Diane: U.S. Broadcast Journalist', in: *The Museum of Broadcast Communications*. Online: www.museum.tv/eotvsection.php?entrycode=sawyerdiane (accessed 16 June 2012)

Manyin, Mark E. and Ryun Jun (2003), 'U.S. Assistance to North Korea', report to Congress, 17 March (Order Code RL31785). Washington DC: US State Department. Online: http://fpc.state.gov/documents/organiza tion/27532.pdf

Mason, Anthony (2004), 'Elite Sources, Journalistic Practice, and the Status Quo , in: *Pacific Journalism Review*, 13 (1), 107–123

Mullen, Andrew (2009), 'The Propaganda Model After 20 Years: Interview with Edward S. Herman and Noam Chomsky', in: *Westminster Papers in Communication and Culture*, 6 (2), pp. 12–22

Nakedapartments (n.d.), 'One Bedroom Apartments in NYC', in: *Nakedapartments.com*. Online: www.nakedapartments.com/nyc/one-bedroom-apartments-nyc (accessed 30 March 2013)

NK News (2013), 'Exclusive: Foreigners Now Permitted to Carry Mobile Phones in North Korea', in: *NK News*, 19 January. Online: www.nknew s.org/2013/01/ exclusive-foreigners-now-permitted-to-carry-mobile-phones-in-north-korea/ (accessed 13 April 2013)

NK News (2011), 'Select your hairstyle!', in: *NK News*, 30 October. Online: www.nknews.org/2011/10/select-your-hairstyle/ (accessed 13 April 2013)

Nylund, Mats (2003), 'Asking Questions, Making Sound-Bites: Research Reports, Interviews and Television News Stories', in: *Discourse Studies,* (5) 4, pp. 517–33

Schiller, Herbert I. (1989), *Culture Inc.: The Corporate Takeover of Public Expression*, New York: Oxford University Press

Scott, Anthony Oliver (2004), 'Moral Guidance from Class Clowns', in: *New York Times*, 15 October, late edition, p. E1

Steinberg, Brian (2012). 'After 2010 Rebound, Broadcast Networks See 2011 Ad Revenue Fall', in: *Adage*. Online: http://adage.com/article/media/ 2010-rebound-broadcast-tv-sees-2011-ad-revenue-fall/233345/ (accessed 16 June 2012)

US Census Bureau (n.d. a), 'Trade in Goods Korea, North', in: *U.S. Census Bureau Foreign Trade.* Online www.census.gov/foreign-trade/balance/c5790.html (accessed 17 June 2012)

US Census Bureau (n.d. b), 'Trade in Goods Korea, South,' in: *U.S. Census Bureau Foreign Trade*. Online: www.census.gov/foreign-trade/balance/ c5800.html (accessed 17 June 2012)

van Dijk, Teun A. (1991), 'The Interdisciplinary Study of News as Discourse', in: Klaus Bruhn-Jensen and Nicholas Jankowksi (eds), *Handbook of Qualitative Methodologies for Mass Communication Research*, London: Routledge, pp. 108–120

Waxman, Sharon (2004), 'The Boys from "South Park" Go to War', in: *New York Times*, 22 August, late edition, section 2, p.1

ABOUT THE AUTHORS AND EDITORS

Eric J. Ballbach
is a research fellow and lecturer at the Institute of Korean Studies at Freie Universität Berlin. He received his M.A. in Political Science at the University of Trier and is about to finish his Ph.D. thesis on 'Identity and North Korean Foreign Policy'. His main research interests concern North and South Korean foreign policy, inter-Korean relations, processes of regionalisation in Northeast Asia and critical theories of International Relations.
Email: eric.ballbach@fu-berlin.de

Sabine Burghart
is PhD candidate and lecturer at the Chair of East Asian Economy and Society of the Department of East Asian Studies, University of Vienna. She holds a M.A. in political science from the University of Leiden. Between 2004 and 2007, she served as project coordinator at the Korea office of the German Friedrich Naumann Foundation for Freedom in Seoul. She was in charge of the foundation's training programmes and capacity building projects in the DPR Korea. In 2011-2012, she temporarily returned to the voluntary sector to facilitate cooperation projects with the DPRK.
Email: sabine.burghart@univie.ac.at

Judith Cherry
is lecturer in Korean Business and Management at the School of East Asian Studies, University of Sheffield. Dr Cherry is the author of *Foreign Direct Investment in Post-crisis Korea: European Investors and 'Mismatched Globalization'* (2007); her research interests include EU–Korea trade and investment relations and South Korea's soft power.
Email: j.a.cherry@shef.ac.uk

Rüdiger Frank
is Chair and Professor of East Asian Economy and Society at the University of Vienna and Head of its Department of East Asian Studies. He is also an adjunct professor at Korea University and the University

of North Korean Studies (Kyungnam University) in Seoul. He holds an M.A. in Korean Studies, Economics and International Relations and a Ph.D. in Economics. In 1991/1992, he spent one semester as a language student at Kim Il Sung University in Pyongyang and has been researching North Korea ever since. Visiting professorships have included Columbia University New York and Korea University, Seoul. In addition to memberships and associations with a number of Korea and East Asia related societies, he is a Council member and for the 2011-2013 period the Secretary of the Association for Korean Studies in Europe. He is also an Executive Board Member of the European research network 'EastAsiaNet'. In 2012, he became Vice President of the U.S. and Hong Kong-based Asia Pacific History Association. Prof. Frank is, among others, Deputy Chief Editor of the A-ranked *European Journal of East Asian Studies*, Member of the Editorial Board for the book series *Brill's Korean Studies Library*, an Associate at *The Asia Pacific Journal*, Member of the Editorial Board of *Korea Review of International Studies*, Co-Founder and Member of the Editorial Board, *Vienna Graduate Journal of East Asian Studies* and *Vienna Studies on East Asia*. He is also the founding editor of a new book series at Brill titled *Security and International Relations in East Asia*. His major research fields are socialist transformation in East Asia and Europe (with a focus on North Korea), state-business relations in East Asia, and regional integration in East Asia. His most recent books are: (with S. Burghart, eds., 2010): *Driving Forces of Socialist Transformation: North Korea and the Experience of Europe and East Asia*, Vienna: Praesens, (ed., 2011): *Exploring North Korean Arts*, Nuremberg: Verlag fuer Moderne Kunst, (with Heung Chong Kim and Sung-Hoon Park, eds., 2012): *Korea and East Asia in a Changing Regional and Global Environment*, Seoul: KIEP and (with John Swenson-Wright, eds., 2013): *Korea and East Asia: The Stony Road to Collective Security*, Leiden and Boston: Brill.. Professor Frank is regularly consulted by governments, media and businesses on North Korea and East Asia. This included consultancy work and a background policy paper for the visit by former presidents Martti Ahtisaari, Jimmy Carter and Mary Robinson and former prime Minister Gro Brundtland to the Korean peninsula and China. In 2011, he joined the World Economic Forum, Global Agenda Council on Korea. For more information, see http://wirtschaft.ostasien.univie.ac.at

For publications, see http://univie.academia.edu/RuedigerFrank
Email: ruediger.frank@univie.ac.at

James E. Hoare
retired from the British Diplomatic Service in 2003. His last appointment was as British Chargé d'Affaires and Consul General in Pyongyang. He now writes and broadcasts about East Asia. Among his recent publications are *Historical Dictionary of the Democratic People's Republic of Korea* (2012), and *Culture Smart! Korea* (2nd revised edition 2012). He also edited *Critical Readings on North and South Korea* (3 vols., 2013). He is an Honorary Research Associate and Senior Teaching Fellow at the School of Oriental and African Studies, London, where he teaches a course on North Korea. He lives in London.
Email: jim@jhoare10.fsnet.co.uk

Stephanie K. Kim
is a doctoral candidate in Education at the University of California, Los Angeles, where she specialises in Comparative Education. She was a Fulbright Scholar in South Korea from 2011 to 2012, where she conducted fieldwork for her dissertation on the integration of American pedagogical practices into Korean higher education. She holds an M.S. in Global Affairs from New York University, and a B.A. in English Language and Literature from the University of Michigan.
Email: stephaniekim@ucla.edu

Patrick Köllner
is director of the Institute of Asian Studies, GIGA German Institute of Global and Area Studies, and professor of political science, with a focus on political systems in East Asia, at the University of Hamburg. He holds a Ph.D. and a *venia legendi* in political science. Between 1996 and 2006 he was sole editor of the German-language predecessor of the *Korea Yearbook*. His research focuses on Japanese and Korean politics and political regimes, parties and other organisations more generally. He has published in journals such as *Japan Forum*, *Japanese Journal of Political Science*, *Journal of East Asian Studies*, *Politische Vierteljahresschrift*, and *Social Science Japan Journal*.
Email: koellner@giga-hamburg.de

Susan Pares
has worked in Research Department of the Foreign and Commonwealth Office and, since 1987, as an editor and writer in East Asian subjects. She edited *Asian Affairs*, 1997–2001, and between 2000 and 2007 the *Papers of the British Association for Korean Studies*. She served in the British Embassy in Beijing, 1975–76 and accompanied her husband, James Hoare, on postings to Seoul (1981–85), Beijing (1988–91) and Pyongyang (2001–02). They are co-authors of several books dealing with East Asian and specifically Korean affairs. The most recent is *North Korea in the 21st Century: An Interpretative Guide* (2005).
Email: spares@myway.com

Lukas Pokorny
is Bruce Lecturer in East Asian Religions and deputy head of the School of Divinity, History and Philosophy at the University of Aberdeen. He holds an M.A. in Religious Studies, History, Philosophy, and Korean Studies, and a Ph.D. in Philosophy. His current research focuses on Korean Neo-Confucianism and millenarian beliefs in new religious movements (East Asia and beyond). He has conducted extensive field research in China, Japan, Korea and Vietnam as well as study and research stays at Beijing Language and Culture University, Peking University, Kyoto University, Tokai University and Yonsei University. Dr Pokorny has taught at several universities, including the University of Vienna, Georg-August University in Göttingen, Charles University in Prague, Masaryk University in Brno, Comenius University in Bratislava, and Babeş-Bolyai University in Cluj-Napoca.
Email: l.pokorny@abdn.ac.uk

Sherri L. Ter Molen
is a doctoral candidate in the Department of Communication at Wayne State University in Detroit, Michigan, where she studies the complicated mediated relationships between the divided Koreas and the United States. Her work has previously been published in *Media Asia*, and her dissertation project explores the ways in which non-Koreans participate in the proliferation of Korean culture in America through their participation in Korean affinity groups.
Email: commresearch@me.com

Robert Winstanley-Chesters
holds a B.A. degree in divinity from the University of Edinburgh and an M.A. degree from the School of Geography, Leeds University. He received his Ph.D. at the School of Geography, Leeds University, in April 2013 with a thesis entitled 'Ideology and the Production of Landscape in the Democratic People's Republic of Korea', and is hoping for new fieldwork opportunities in Kangwon province, DPRK. He also serves as environmental analyst to the online journal *SI-NO:NK: China, North Korea Borderlands, Relations, History*, for which he has published extensively.
Email: gy07r3m@leeds.ac.uk

MAP OF THE KOREAN PENINSULA

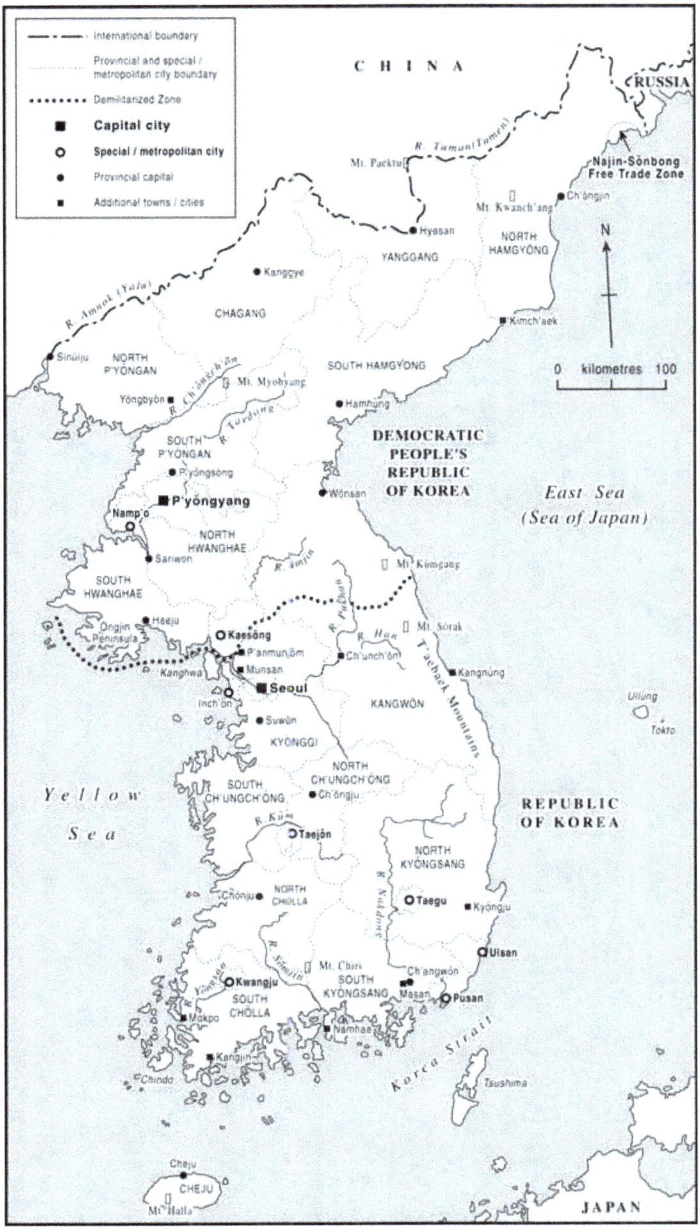

Design and Imaging Unit, Durham University.

www.ingramcontent.com/pod-product-compliance
Lightning Source LLC
LaVergne TN
LVHW011118300926
849160LV00008B/435
9789004261136